GREAT MYSTERIES
OF THE 20th CENTURY

GREAT MYSTERIES OF THE 20th CENTURY

FOREWORD

As the millennium draws to a close, **THE EVENTFUL CENTURY** series presents the vast panorama of the last hundred years — a century that has witnessed the transition from horse-drawn transport to space travel, and from the first telephones to the information superhighway.

THE EVENTFUL CENTURY chronicles epoch-making events like the outbreak of the two world wars, the Russian Revolution and the rise and fall of communism. But major events are only part of the glittering kaleidoscope. It also describes the everyday background—the way people lived, how they worked, what they ate and drank, how much they earned, the way they spent their leisure time, the books they read, and the crimes, scandals and unsolved mysteries that set them talking. Here are fads and crazes like the hula hoop and Rubik's cube . . . fashions like the New Look and the miniskirt . . . breakthroughs in entertainment, like the birth of the movies . . . medical milestones like the discovery of penicillin . . . and marvels of modern architecture and engineering.

GREAT MYSTERIES OF THE 20th CENTURY presents the most profound puzzles of the century. Deaths in mysterious circumstances, like that of the Italian banker Roberto Calvi . . . unexplained evidence at the heart of historic events, such as the assassination of President Kennedy . . . strange disappearances, like that of Agatha Christie, a story worthy of one of her own novels . . . paranormal phenomena, like the heavenly vision that appeared to three Portuguese children at Fatima . . . and mysteries of modern science. It might be possible to dismiss all paranormal reports as products of the fallible human mind, were it not that modern science itself challenges every commonsense belief about space and time. Black holes, it appears, may act as conduits into another dimension. Time, it seems, does not run in a ruler-straight line; past, present and future may exist simultaneously. The great mysteries of the 20th century warn at every turn against the closed mind; the best we can do is to sift the evidence and acknowledge all realms of possibility.

GREAT MYSTERIES
OF THE 20th CENTURY

The Reader's Digest Association, Inc.
Pleasantville, New York/Montreal

GREAT MYSTERIES OF THE 20th CENTURY
Edited and designed by Toucan Books Limited
Written by Tim Healey
Edited by Mandie Rickaby, Robert Sackville West
and Jo Wells
Designed by Bradbury and Williams
Picture research by Vickie Walters and
Christine Vincent

AMERICAN EDITION
Edited and produced by The Reference Works
Harold Rabinowitz, Executive Editor
Ross Mandel, Managing Editor
Doug Heyman, Research
Bob Antler, Antler Designworks, Production

FOR THE READER'S DIGEST, US
Group Editorial Director Fred DuBose
Senior Designer Judith Carmel

READER'S DIGEST GENERAL BOOKS
Editor-in-Chief Christopher Cavanaugh
Art Director Joan Mazzeo

Copyright © 1999
The Reader's Digest Association
Reader's Digest Road
Pleasantville, NY 10570

Copyright © 1997
Reader's Digest Association Far East Limited
Philippines copyright © 1997
Reader's Digest Association Far East Limited
All rights reserved

First English edition copyright © 1996
The Reader's Digest Association Limited,
Berkeley Square House, Berkeley Square,
London W1X 6AB

Copyright © 1996
Reader's Digest Association Far East Limited
Philippines copyright © 1996
Reader's Digest Association Far East Limited
All rights reserved

Printed in the United States of America, 1999.

Library of Congress Cataloging in Publication Data

Great mysteries of the 20th century.
        p. cm. — (The eventful 20th century)
    Includes index.
    ISBN 0-7621-0267-5
    1. Curiosities and wonders.
    2. Twentieth century — Miscellanea.
    I. Reader's Digest Association. II. Series.
AG243.G737 1999
031 . 02 — dc21
                          99-16600

FRONT COVER
From Top: UFO abduction, 1960s; Marilyn Monroe;
Hindenburg, 1930s.

BACK COVER
From Top: Amelia Earhart; JonBenet Ramsey
gravesite 1990s; John F. Kennedy, 1960s.

Page 3 (from left to right): Sir Harry Oakes, the
millionaire who was murdered in the Bahamas in
1943; a 1939 propaganda poster for Stalin's rule; the
remains of an unknown animal, thought
by some to be those of a yeti; Our Lady of the
Rosary appears before three shepherd children
at Fatima, 1917.

Background pictures:
Page 13: A fingerprint.
Page 51: Crowds await news of survivors of the
Titanic, April 1912.
Page 89: Water.
Page 113: An aerial view of a crop formation near
Hungerford, Berkshire, England in the 1980s.
Page 141: A Kirlian photograph of a human hand.

CONTENTS

MYSTERY IN MODERN TIMES

THE MYSTERIES OF THE 20TH CENTURY TEACH US TO KEEP AN OPEN MIND AND TO ACKNOWLEDGE ALL REALMS OF POSSIBILITY

FIRST FAMILY John Kennedy (center) and his brother Robert (center right), photographed in 1960, were both alleged to have had affairs with Marilyn Monroe.

The tremendous advances of scientific understanding in the 20th century sometimes lead us to believe that we have answers to all the questions, and yet there is much that continues to baffle the modern mind, whether in the annals of statecraft or crime, the records of the natural world or of the cosmos. Bizarre phenomena, strange deaths, inexplicable disappearances and miraculous cures…all in their different ways open windows into the unknown, challenging orthodox assumptions about the world and the recent past.

At the time of Marilyn Monroe's death in 1962, few doubted that the Hollywood superstar died of a self-administered drug overdose in her mock-adobe hacienda at Fifth Helena Drive in the Los Angeles suburb of Brentwood. Today, more than 30 years later, stories of her affair with President Kennedy—and discrepancies in the official reports concerning her death—prompt widespread rumor and speculation. The circumstances of Kennedy's own sensational death have long provoked debate and disquiet. Was the president really shot from behind by a lone gunman in the Texas School Book Depository? What of the witnesses who reported that the shots came from an area known as the "grassy knoll," in front of the president's car?

Elements of mystery surround a wealth of historic events, and in some cases the fates of nations have hung on their outcomes. Other less portentous enigmas are no less intriguing for the human dramas which they

THE MISFIT The actress Marilyn Monroe appears on location in 1960 during the making of *The Misfits*, a film written by her third husband, Arthur Miller. The marriage came to an end not long afterwards.

MISSING Embroiled in Teamster politics and amid allegations of Mob associations, Union leader Jimmy Hoffa vanished in 1975.

evoke. Who killed the vicar and choirmistress in the New Jersey lovers' lane killings of 1922? What happened to the pioneer woman aviator Amelia Earhart, whose plane vanished in 1937 over the Pacific? And where is Jimmy Hoffa, the teamster's leader who disappeared one day in July 1975?

Hi-tech investigation

Mystery hunters have acquired a wealth of hi-tech aids to investigation in recent years. Undersea search equipment has located the remains of the ill-fated luxury liner *Titanic*, and genetic fingerprinting has identified the remains of the last Russian Tsar's family. Push-button electronic indexing allows detectives to computer-match fingerprints at rates of tens of thousands per second, while

THE FATE OF THE FAMILY Tsar Nicholas II and his family enjoy a holiday in Sweden in 1909. Did any of them survive the brutal massacre nine years later?

spectrographic analysis permits police laboratories to identify a culprit by a single hair from his or her head.

Yet for every puzzle that is solved by science it seems that a new one emerges. In 1988 newspapers reported that the Turin Shroud, a relic that was said to bear the imprint of Christ, had been exposed through radio-carbon analysis as a medieval fake. But how did a 14th-century forger achieve such astonishing photo-like results? In 1996 a computer for the first time beat a world champion at two games of chess. Does that mean that electronic brains are attaining levels of true consciousness? Can machines really think?

How did life begin?

The biggest enigmas surround the origins and destiny of life and the cosmos. In centuries past, creation myths from around the world told how gods with very human attributes shaped our planet and caused living things to flourish upon it. Modern scientists have challenged scriptural accounts of the Creation, proposing alternative models that are harder for the layman to grasp. Many scientists believe that life on Earth began in what is called a "cosmic soup" of chance chemical reactions in the gases surrounding the primeval planet. Lightning, meteorites and cosmic radiation bombarded the fog and produced amino acids, which make up the proteins on which all life is based. This theory is supported by some experimental evidence. Since the 1950s scientists have found it possible to manufac-

ture amino acids in the laboratory by passing heat or electricity through mixtures of methane, hydrogen, ammonia and water vapor. They have also created amino acids by bombarding a mixture of carbon monoxide, water and nitrogen with high-energy atomic particles, to simulate the radiation that issues from solar flares. One way or another, it

MARVELS OF MODERN SCIENCE Gary Kasparov, the world chess champion, eventually defeated IBM's Deep Blue computer 4-2 (top). Thanks to hi-tech underwater cameras, thousands of artifacts from the wreck of the Titanic (above) have been identified and salvaged.

appears, intense energy acting on the Earth's ancient fog could have created the organic molecules necessary to form primitive life forms. And from primeval seas of bacteria and blue-green algae, evolutionary forces are

CREATIVE CHEMISTRY Scientists probe into the origins of life by producing amino acids in a flask containing water, hydrogen, methane and ammonia (left). Sir Fred Hoyle (below) argued that amino acids may be distributed throughout the Universe.

gravity, impacting in a Big Crunch. Such a collision could cause another Big Bang—and trigger a new Universe.

The inner mysteries

If an aura of mystery surrounds the gigantic issues of life and the cosmos, it clings no less to the minutiae of everyday life. Doctors who can now transplant human hearts and perform eye surgery with lasers are still no closer to finding a cure for that unglamorous, familiar infection—the common cold.

And if the galaxies seem infinite in their grandeur and complexities, so too are the mysteries of the human brain. In the bundle of nervous tissue lying within the skull is a cosmos composed of 100 billion nerve cells, each of which has 10,000 connections. Here is the control center for all our bodily movements, a communications headquarters to process information from the senses, and a storehouse for all our memories. Today, the PET (positron emission tomography) scan provides us with images of the brain at work, while the EEG (electroencephalograph) traces fluctuations in its electrical activity.

thought to have shaped the Earth's flora and fauna: octopus, eagle, primrose—and man.

That, at least, is the theory most widely accepted among scientists. But an alternative model has been proposed by the British astronomer Sir Fred Hoyle, following the discovery that organic molecules do exist—albeit thinly distributed—in interstellar space. Hoyle has theorized that life-carrying amino acids travel through space aboard comets and meteorites. According to Hoyle, the seeds of life were sown on the Earth, and may also be sown when they reach any planet with a suitably hospitable atmosphere. In 1996 examination of meteorites from Mars suggested that primitive single-celled life forms have existed there.

The Big Bang

How did the Universe itself begin? Hoyle was among a group of cosmologists who in 1948 advanced a "Steady State" theory, which holds that the Universe is eternal and has always existed. More widely held, though, is the so-called "Big Bang" theory. This suggests that, about 15,000 million years ago, there was a gigantic explosion whose outrush of gases formed the galaxies, stars and planets of today. This belief is derived from the discoveries of the American astronomer Edwin Hubble. Working in the 1920s, he discovered that the galaxies are moving away from one another and that the more distant galaxies are rushing away faster than those nearer at hand. By dividing the galaxies' distance by their speeds, Hubble could work out when the great cosmic explosion took place. The answer (by the best available calculations) is somewhere between 10 and 20 billion years ago.

But although many astronomers agree about how the universe was born, there is much debate on how it will end. Some believe that the momentum from the Big Bang will keep the galaxies flying apart for many millions of years, when the stars will at last burn out and collapse to become black holes or dark, solid objects known as black dwarfs. So the universe will die. Another theory proposes that the exploding galaxies will eventually start to come together again under the force of their mutual

HUBBLE'S LAW Edwin Hubble, shown in front of the telescope at Mount Wilson Observatory in California, provided the first direct evidence for an expanding Universe.

The brain functions with astonishing clarity and efficiency to order our daily lives. It governs the craftsman's eye, the hands of the concert pianist and the limbs of the gymnast. Yet its control collapses every night as each of us plunges into the mysterious otherworld of dreams—and no one knows quite why.

In our dreams we fly through the air, meet alligators in the street, or have lunch with Lincoln. Forested with strangely connected ideas and images, dreams are experienced by everyone. Research shows that they occur particularly in what is called "paradoxical sleep," when the EEG apparatus records bursts of brain activity and the eyeballs can be seen darting about behind the lids. In REM (Rapid Eye Movement) sleep,

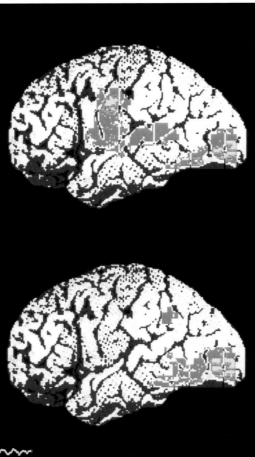

BRAIN SCAN A PET scan of the human brain (right) shows a person reading aloud (top) and silently (bottom), while an EEG print-out (below) reveals electrical activity in the brain.

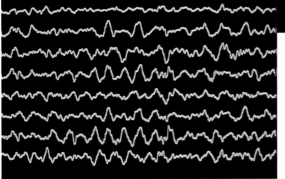

as it is also known, the dreamer is evidently responding to particularly vivid visual events. Most people experience REM sleep four or five times a night, in 20-minute episodes. Whether or not the dreams are remembered depends on how quickly after the episode the sleeper wakes up.

Dream symbols

In societies of past times, dreams were always regarded as intensely significant phenomena, loaded with omens and prophecies. Entire nations might be guided by the dreams of their leaders, as interpreted by diviners such as Joseph in the Old Testament. In the 20th century there is no scientific consensus on the relevance of dreams to waking life. The Austrian psychiatrist Sigmund Freud analyzed dream contents in terms of unconscious erotic desires and suppressed memories of sexual experiences, often dating from childhood. However, Freud's one-time pupil, the Swiss psychologist Carl Jung, came to believe that the master had placed far too much emphasis on the sexual urges buried in the subconscious. Jung thought that dreams had a more profound religious and magical significance, both to the lives of the individual and to his or her social group.

Neither Freud's nor Jung's ideas are accepted wholesale today. Many modern scientists have come to doubt whether dreams have any profound meaning; according to one school of thought, they reflect little more than the random processing of sights and sounds from the dreamer's waking life.

EXPLORING THE MIND Carl Jung was one of the founding fathers of modern psychology.

Whatever theory they adhere to, all investigators agree that there are different types of dreams. Some seem to be compensatory; people deprived of food, for example, are often tormented by dreams of luscious meals. Other dreams clearly recall stressful real-life experiences. For example, soldiers who have just gone through intense battle ordeals may relive their combat terrors in nightmare dreams. And there are dreams which very clearly reflect facets of the dreamer's own culture. In Western society, for example, a common dream is of appearing naked and embarrassed among strangers.

In other respects, however, dreams are so private, disjointed and transient that they resist scientific analysis. All that can be said with certainty is that we need these nightly mysterious excursions for our own good health. Studies have shown that if subjects are repeatedly deprived of the opportunity to dream (by being woken when REM begins) they become irritable and inefficient, and eventually succumb to hallucinations.

Just as the 20th-century citizen still needs to dream, so 20th-century society seems still to need the supernatural. In a scientific age, we have not lost our fascination with ghosts, premonitions and miracles.

In fact, throughout the century there have been numerous reports that the United

States' most famous building—the White House—is haunted. The shimmering spirit of Abigail Adams, wife of the nation's second president, has been seen hanging laundry in the East Room, passing through closed doors with her arms outstretched. The mournful specter of Anne Surratt, the daughter of a woman executed for her part in Lincoln's assassination, is thought to appear on the White House steps on the anniversary of her mother's execution, banging angrily on the doors of the North Portico. But it is the spirit of Lincoln himself, a devoted believer in the afterlife, which seems to spook the place most vigorously. Grace Coolidge, Winston Churchill, Margaret Truman, Jackie Kennedy, and Ladybird Johnson all admitted sensing Honest Abe's ghostly presence. Presidents were by no means immune to these sightings. Harry Truman wrote in a letter to his wife, "I sit here in this old house, all the while listening to the ghosts walk up and down the hallway. At 4 o'clock I was awakened by three distinct knocks on my bedroom door. No one there. Damned place is haunted, sure as shootin'!"

Science and superstition

This haunting has its counterpart in newspaper stories of apparitions and miracles which continue to be reported all around the computer-age world. In 1994 the American media proclaimed an epidemic of visions of the Blessed Virgin Mary. For a brief period in 1995, India was brought to a standstill as 800 million Hindus were seized by devotional frenzies following reports that statues of the gods were drinking milk in the temples.

An interest in the supernatural is not necessarily a hangover from the pre-scientific

MIND BENDER Uri Geller surveys a collection of spoons that have been bent by force of mind.

GHOST STORY The Duke of Norfolk attends a ceremony of exorcism at Corpus Christi Church in London.

age. Many 20th-century thinkers, including Carl Jung, have sought to marry their scientific interests with a belief in other realities. Even the most hardened skeptic may, at some time in his or her life, experience a perfectly extraordinary coincidence which prompts him or her to wonder whether life is not, after all, governed by unseen powers.

Jung coined the word "synchronicity" to describe significant, coincidental events which seem to violate the laws of cause and effect. Indeed, 20th-century physics, at the subatomic level, challenges the very idea of simple causal connections; the idea of scientific predictability has given way to the notion of statistical probability.

There are other respects in which 20th-century science hints at realities that defy common sense. Einstein proposed that journeys at very high speeds ought to make time

travel possible. Scientists have suggested that black holes in space may lead to other dimensions. And they have postulated a Multiverse principle, by which ours may be just one of an infinite number of parallel universes. It could be that uncanny happenings sometimes leak into our everyday existence from an alternative reality.

Smart, modern aficionados of the paranormal do not fear the claims of science; in fact, they have embraced scientific findings. Hi-tech astrologers, casting horoscopes, use the latest results of space research to determine the supposed influence of the heavenly bodies on their human clients. In 1996 the Israeli superstar Uri Geller announced a thoroughly up-to-date challenge to the world's psychics: to bend a spoon over the Internet and win $1 million. The challenge involved trying to bend an Internet video image of a spoon which was placed inside a see-through safe in Geller's home. If the piece of cutlery suddenly bent, anyone who was logged on at the time would be invited to repeat the feat in front of a panel of judges.

Prophet of the unexplained

Among 20th-century students of bizarre phenomena, none has been more assiduous than the wealthy New York eccentric, Charles Hoy Fort. From 1916, he accumulated newspaper reports on all kinds of remarkable occurrences, such as frogs falling from the sky, mysterious disappearances, wild children and weird coincidences. It was Fort who coined the word "teleportation" to describe cases where people or objects had reportedly been transported through space and time. Dubbed by cynics "the patron saint of cranks," Fort was fascinated by the fact that although newspapers and scientific journals often reported strange phenomena, they generally failed to provide any kind of explanation. In *The Book of the Damned* (1919) and three further volumes, he collected thousands of unexplained occurrences and, despite a quirky, hard-to-read style, he

established himself as a notable prophet of the unexplained.

The classic Fortean phenomenon is the fall of strange objects from the skies. Remarkable showers of living creatures from above have often been reported by newspapers

WEIRD AND WONDERFUL Charles Hoy Fort (above) inspired massive public interest in strange phenomena, such as frogs falling from the sky— featured on the cover of a magazine in 1958 (right).

with little attempt at explanation; fish, worms and frogs are typical subjects. Skeptics often propose in such cases that the creatures do not fall from above but emerge from dormancy in the earth with the sudden rainfall. But this theory can hardly be used to explain a case, in June 1954, when witnesses in Birmingham, England, saw hundreds of little frogs bouncing off people's heads. Nor could it satisfy a South Carolina doctor who reported seeing eight baby alligators fall from the sky one evening.

Fort heard the dark laughter of the gods in such events. Falling objects, he suggested, might come from "a region somewhere above the earth's surface in which gravitation is inoperative." Into this mysterious zone, he theorized, objects were sucked from the ground to be shaken down later by storms. The more prosaic scientific explanations suggest freak whirl-winds, although it has also been proposed that dew, sea or lake water rising through evaporation on hot days may carry lightweight fish or frogspawn up into the clouds, which then fall when different atmospheric conditions prevail.

Fort preferred mystery zones and extraterrestrial forces. After his death in 1932, his achievements were neglected by all but a handful of admirers who formed a Fortean Society to carry on his work. But his reputation gained ground with the worldwide UFO mania which spread after Kenneth Arnold's Flying Saucer sighting of 1947. Fort had been among the first to suggest that mysterious

lights seen in the sky might be craft from outer-space. He had also speculated on alien landings. Above all, he criticized scientists' doctrinaire hostility to life's marvellous possibilities, noting how often scientists themselves argued according to their own narrow beliefs, tending to suppress or discredit any data that challenged cold materialism. Colin Wilson, a modern writer on

FACT OR FANTASY? So-called UFOs hover in the sky above a Yorkshire town in a photo of 1966 (above). Are they any more real than the artist's reconstruction on a magazine cover of 1939 (top right)?

the paranormal, has explained Fort's fundamental principle thus: it may well be that some people have a psychological need to believe in marvels, but it is also true that the orthodox scientist has a psychological need not to believe in marvels.

Marvels in the modern age

Suppose that supernatural powers—even alien landings and abductions—were a reality and that the authorities were aware of the fact. Might they not suppress the evidence in the interests of public tranquillity? *Project Blue Book*, the U.S. Air Force's official investigation of UFOs, provoked strong criticism that it censored the truth about flying saucers in order to reassure an already alarmed population.

Suspicion of government and big business has been a feature of Western thought in the late 20th century. It has recently been revealed that, during the early 1970s, the CIA contracted the Stanford Research Institute to begin a study of controlled clairvoyance—known as *Project Scanate*. The context was the Cold War, and the aim was to discover whether the apparent psychic ability of some people to visualize hidden objects could be employed in espionage against Soviet installations.

Renamed Operation Stargate, the project was for nearly 20 years based at Fort Meade, Maryland, headquarters of the National Security Agency

LIFT-OFF Worshippers at a temple in the north of England appear to levitate.

(NSA). The "Mystics of Fort Meade" were alleged to have identified a major Soviet submarine project in 1979 and a suspected Libyan training facility for PLO terrorists some ten years later. However, in 1996 the CIA recommended to Congress that it discontinue funding for Operation Stargate.

For all the money that has been spent on research into ESP, no evidence has ever been accepted by the scientific community as a whole. Investigators have never caged a ghost; Loch Ness refuses to yield a Monster; no one has levitated in a laboratory—not, at least, to the satisfaction of watching scientists. Skeptics argue that research into the supernatural is doomed to disappoint. Yet the urge to dream mad dreams that possesses us in our sleep, also animates society in its waking life. It appears that people of the 20th-century need mysteries as much as our ancestors who drew their magic on cave walls.

DEATHS IN MYSTERIOUS CIRCUMSTANCES

ACCORDING TO THE 17TH-CENTURY ENGLISH DRAMATIST PHILIP MASSINGER, "DEATH HAS A THOUSAND DOORS TO LET OUT LIFE." WHEN A BODY IS FOUND OVERDOSED WITH SLEEPING PILLS OR FLOATING IN THE SEA, IT IS NOT ALWAYS EASY TO DETERMINE WHETHER THE CAUSE OF DEATH WAS SUICIDE, ACCIDENT OR MURDER. AND EVEN WHERE EVIDENCE OF FOUL PLAY IS COMPELLING, THE QUESTION REMAINS—WHODUNNIT?

DEATH OF A CARD PLAYER

THE BAFFLING MURDER OF A FAMOUS BRIDGE EXPERT AND PLAYBOY AT HIS NEW YORK HOME

The discovery of the body of Joseph Bowne Elwell in his elegant Manhattan home on the morning of June 11, 1920, made front page news at home and abroad. Elwell was acknowledged as a world expert on bridge, and his books *Elwell on Bridge* and *Elwell's Advanced Bridge* were both international best-sellers.

Profits from the card table, lessons to the rich and famous, royalties from book sales, and wise investments had made Elwell—a former insurance salesman who learned to play cards at a church youth club—a wealthy man. By 1920, at the age of 47, he owned a luxurious New York home, three country retreats, a yacht, an art collection and a partnership in a stud farm.

An irresistible man

Elwell's reputation as a womanizer was enhanced after his death and probably considerably embellished by the press. Newspaper reports claimed that his address book contained the names of between 53 and 400 women, many of whom were reputedly his mistresses. His New York residence included a luxury boudoir, and the female guests whom he regularly entertained there ranged from show girls to chic divorcées and titled ladies. All became names of interest to the police after 8:10 on the morning of June 11, when Elwell's housekeeper found her employer dying, slumped in a chair and bleeding from a single fatal shot, exactly between his eyes.

It was a puzzling murder. Joseph Elwell had been shot sometime between the delivery of the morning mail at 7:10 a.m. and his discovery an hour later. There was a letter in his lap, and several others lay unopened at his feet. Blood had stained the carpet and his pajamas, and was spattered on the wall behind the chair where he still sat.

What baffled detectives was the fact that all the doors were locked and all the windows fastened from the inside except Elwell's own bedroom window high up on the third floor. There was no evidence of a break-in or struggle, and a search of the house ruled out burglary as a motive, since none of the many valuables or any

MAN ABOUT TOWN **This picture of Joseph B. Elwell (right) was taken at Palm Beach, Florida, where he had a luxury home. Income from books on bridge (far right) helped to finance his lifestyle .**

cash had been touched. Suicide was also ruled out early in the investigation as the gun had been fired on an upward trajectory —virtually from the hip—from a distance of 3–4 feet. No, the evidence pointed to mur-

der by someone well known to the victim. Either he or she had been in the house with Elwell all night, or the victim had let him or her in early in the morning. Elwell must have felt perfectly relaxed if he continued to leaf through the morning mail, barefoot, in pajamas, and without the toupé or false teeth he was accustomed to wear in company.

The combination of money, sex and fame proved irresistible to the press and speculation was rife. Had he been killed by a female friend who had stayed overnight?

On his last evening Elwell had dined at the Ritz-Carlton and watched a show with his recently divorced lover Viola Kraus and a

| 1900 Joseph Elwell marries Helen Derby Hanford | 1915 Helen and Joseph begin to live apart | 1920 Elwell found shot | 1925 *Great Gatsby* published. May have been partly based on Elwell's life |

SPORTING LIFE Joseph Elwell (on horseback) with a group of jockeys and trainers at his Kentucky stud farm.

couple named Lewisohn. Elwell took a cab home alone at about 2 a.m. after a tiff with Viola. Despite the discovery of a pink silk kimono found hanging in his wardrobe, it did not, in reality, look as if he had enjoyed a torrid last night of love. His bed had been only lightly slept in and the telephone company records reinforced the impression that he was awake and alone for much of that night. Shortly after his arrival, he took a phone call from Viola. At 4:39 a.m. he rang William H. Pendleton, his partner in a stud farm in Kentucky, but got no reply. At 6:09 am he rang a Long Island number, the owner of which is not known.

A crime of passion?

The postman delivered the mail at 7:10 a.m. According to the likeliest scenario, Elwell admitted the killer himself, then returned to his mail. After what must have been a brief conversation, the murderer fired the fatal shot.

It is not hard to picture a love quarrel as the motive. But the shot that killed Elwell was fired from a .45 calibre army revolver, a heavy weapon that was scarcely a natural choice for a woman. A male assailant was just as likely: perhaps the jealous husband or lover, or outraged relative, of one of Elwell's mistresses.

The pink silk kimono in the wardrobe belonged to Viola Kraus, but the Lewisohns confirmed that she had spent the night with them. Neither William H. Pendleton nor any other business associate stood to profit from Elwell's demise. Elwell's ex-wife Helen came under some suspicion, for he had recently cut her out of his will. But she stood to lose an allowance of $2,400 a year if Elwell died, and she had a strong alibi.

There remained the names in the notorious "love file": a well-known lady of fashion, a Polish countess, an Egyptian princess . . . the police had no shortage of leads, but they were as short of evidence as suspects were well stocked with alibis. A cigarette butt found at the scene that was believed to have belonged to the killer yielded no fingerprints.

No one ever stood trial for the card player's murder—the killer took the trick.

SCENE OF THE CRIME The house at 244 West 70th Street, New York, where Elwell was shot dead in the front room.

TURFMAN On his last night Elwell tried to contact William H. Pendleton, his associate and partner in a stud farm.

1958 World Bridge
Federation formed

1987 Publication of *The Slaying of Joseph Bowne Elwell* by J. Goodman

THE VICAR AND THE CHOIRMISTRESS

A LOVERS' LANE KILLING THAT SCANDALIZED NEW YORK'S COMMUTER BELT

On Saturday, September 16, 1922 a couple taking a stroll down a lovers' lane in New Brunswick, New Jersey, came upon evidence of a savage double killing. Sprawled on their backs under a crab-apple tree were the bodies of a man and a woman strewn with their own torn-up love letters. When the identity of the victims became known it created a sensation. The man was the Reverend Edward Wheeler Hall, rector of St. John's Episcopal Church. The woman was Mrs. Eleanor Mills, the sexton's wife and a choir singer at St. John's.

Both victims had been shot, and whoever murdered them had also arranged their bodies side by side in an awkward embrace. A single bullet through the head had dispatched the minister, but the attack on the choir-singing Eleanor Mills was more ferocious. She had been shot three times in the

SLAIN LOVERS The Reverend E.W. Hall and Mrs. Eleanor Mills, the sexton's wife. When their torrid correspondence appeared in the newspapers, the readers were shocked.

UNEASY ACQUAINTANCES Eleanor Mills, the murdered choir singer, with an unsmiling Mrs. Frances Hall, the rector's wife.

head and, for good measure, had her throat slashed and tongue and vocal chords cut out.

The love letters found at the scene of the crime and others which came to light later bore witness to a passionate illicit liaison. "I want you—your arms to hold me close," wrote the 34-year-old Mrs. Mills. "When my arrow enters your haven I am transported to ecstasy," replied the balding pastor. He was her "Babykins". She was his "Gay Gypsy." They wrote to each other of deep, true and eternal love, of crushing embraces and of the pain of separation.

When published in the newspapers, the torrid correspondence helped to spread the scandal far beyond the local area. But the tormenting question remained: who killed the lovers?

The motive for double murder

Although someone had gone through the pastor's pockets and stolen his gold watch, robbery could hardly have motivated this grisly crime. Slain at their secret rendezvous, with their love letters strewn all around them, the couple seemed the obvious victims of retribution. The police naturally questioned the two spouses of the deceased. Frances Hall, the wife of the dead minister,

was a dignified, gray-haired woman who claimed to know nothing of her husband's affair with his choirmistress. She could say no more than that, on the evening of Thursday, September 14, her husband had received a telephone call and left the house, never to return.

James Mills, husband of the murdered Eleanor, told a similar tale. He knew nothing of any affair. His wife had simply gone out on the Thursday evening and not come back.

Wronged spouses become suspects

Doubt was to be cast on James Mills's version of events when he later sold a cache of love letters to the newspapers. Did the sexton really know nothing of his wife's affair?

Further doubts about both spouses were aroused when it became known that neither Mrs. Hall nor James Mills had called the police to report husband or wife missing when they failed to come home on Thursday night. But as the investigation proceeded, a plausible explanation for their apparent lack of concern emerged. Rumors of the illicit liaison had, it appeared, been rife for some

1900   1950

1922 The secret lovers are found dead   1927 Mrs. Hall and her brother are acquitted   1942 The chief suspect Mrs. Hall dies a recluse

WRONGED COUPLE James Mills and Mrs. Frances Hall, both injured spouses, appeared to have a motive for murder.

did, the prosecution case was directed against Mrs. Hall, together with two of her brothers, William and Henry Stevens. The star witness for the prosecution was a 58-year-old widow, Mrs. Gibson, who raised hogs on a small farm and became celebrated in the case as the "Pig Woman." She testified that on the Thursday evening, the night of the murder, she had heard noises in the lane and had gone out on her mule to investigate. In the shadows of the crab-apple tree, she saw two men and two women arguing. One was a white-haired lady and the other a man with bushy hair (these the Pig Woman later identified as Mrs. Hall and her brother Willy Stevens). "Explain these letters," the white-haired woman had cried. The name Henry was mentioned and someone shouted "Don't, don't, don't . . . " Then four shots cracked the night air and the Pig Woman fled the scene.

It was a powerful testimony—made all the more convincing by the fact that the Pig

Woman was brought into court on a stretcher because she was dying of cancer. Why would she falsely accuse Mrs. Hall? Unhappily for the prosecution, the Pig Woman's mother had an answer. This vociferous old lady, tracked down by the defense counsel, turned up at the trial and caused

SICK EVIDENCE By 1927 Mrs. Gibson, a key witness, was dying of cancer and had to give her testimony from a bed in the courtroom.

much consternation by interjecting "She's a liar, a liar, a liar! That's what she is, and what she's always been." The defense also forced James Mills to admit under questioning that he had known all along about his wife's affair with Mr. Hall. Was he beyond suspicion? Was it even permissible to speculate (the defense counsel went so far as to argue) that the Pig Woman did it—mistaking the lovers for thieves?

After a five-hour deliberation at the end of the long and much publicized trial, the jury brought in a verdict of not guilty. Mrs. Hall and her brothers were acquitted, and Mrs. Hall subsequently went into seclusion, to die in 1942.

The case continued to intrigue long after that, however; in a 1964 study, author William Kunstler proposed that the Ku Klux Klan, which had active branches in New Jersey, might have committed the murders as a warning against such a flagrant breach of Biblical teaching on adultery. True or not, the lovers' lane killer or killers were never brought to justice. The case remains one of the most intriguing in America's annals of crime.

time in the pastor's congregation. It was possible that Mrs. Hall and James Mills both knew of the affair, but failed to call the police because they suspected an elopement.

It was four years before the case came to trial, at Somerville, New Jersey. And when it

THE PIG WOMAN Mrs. Gibson, who was a key witness in the trial, shown here at her pig farm near the scene of the crime.

1964 Kunstler publishes his book which points the finger of blame at the Ku Klux Klan

THE UNTIMELY DEATH OF STARR FAITHFULL

THE UNSOLVED MYSTERY OF HOW THE JAZZ-AGE PARTY GIRL MET HER WATERY END

The body of a young woman was found at dawn on June 8, 1931, on the wet sand of Long Beach only 20 miles from the heart of New York. Dark bedraggled hair framed a beautiful face which was marked with small cuts and bruises. An expensive, brightly colored silk dress and silk stockings —her only garments—clung to her body.

Before long, millions of newsprint words would be expended on what one reporter called "this mystery with the wonderful name."

The corpse was identified as that of Starr Faithfull, the 25-year-old stepdaughter of a Mr. Stanley E. Faithfull. High-spirited and good-looking, Starr was a typical product of America's young Jazz Age generation. She loved to dance and to drink, even though these were Prohibition days. She frequented illegal speakeasies and late-night parties on the luxury liners which glittered with lights at the docks of New York harbor.

Starr's stepfather was adamant that she had been murdered and pointed the finger

TROUBLED BEAUTY Good looks concealed a disturbed psyche. Starr had needed psychiatric help on several occasions.

PEACE AT LAST? The post-mortem recorded more than 100 injuries on the body.

BODY ON THE BEACH Police cluster around a beachcomber's grisly early-morning find on the Long Island shore—Starr Faithfull's body.

1900					1950
	1906 Born Starr Wyman	1924 Starr's parents are divorced	1931 Starr found dead on the beach		1949 Stanley Faithfull dies

HANDWRITING ANALYSIS

The case of Starr Faithfull in 1931 exposed some of the problems still associated with handwriting analysis. Letters stating that she intended to end her life were declared forgeries by her family, and the case remains controversial to this day. Handwriting comparisons are problematic because the same hand may change considerably according to the writer's circumstances and state of mind. For example, in an optimistic mood an individual may write with a vigorous right slant which is absent when he or she is feeling more cautious.

Nonetheless, when a letter flops onto the doormat, it is often easy enough to spot at a glance that it is from a particular friend or relative. Experts become skilled at recognizing the multitude of distinguishing features: the size of capitals in relation to smaller letters; pen pressure; letter connections and the spacing of words; and quirks of spelling and punctuation. Disguised writing can often be spotted through a lack of fluidity in the script: little tremors, for example, and evidence that the pen has stopped and started as the forger copied a model.

Handwriting evidence can be crucial. For example, evidence from ransom notes was vital in the conviction of Bruno Hauptmann (left), in 1934, for the kidnap and murder of the baby of the aviator Charles Lindbergh.

EVIDENCE An expert displays similarities between Bruno Hauptmann's signature and handwriting on the ransom notes sent to Lindbergh.

of blame firmly at a one-time family friend of considerable social standing: Andrew J. Peters, former Congressman and former Mayor of Boston. Faithfull claimed that Peters had seduced Starr when she was only 11 years old, and that the relationship had persisted over the years. One entry in Starr's diary ran: "Spent night A.J.P. Providence. Oh, Horror, Horror, Horror!!!" The investigation revealed that Peters had paid the Faithfull family a "considerable sum of money." Mr. Peters denied having had improper relations with Starr Faithfull, and refused to comment about payments to her parents. His alibi was strong and he was dismissed from police enquiries.

For the young Starr Faithfull, good-time living put pressure on a damaged personality. Her party-going highs were matched by desperate lows. Her love-life was complex; only four days before her death, she was found in a hotel with a man named Joseph Collins, naked, drunk and so badly beaten that she had to be hospitalized. She also nursed a violent, unrequited love for a ship's surgeon called Jameson-Carr.

Dr. Jameson-Carr returned from England about a fortnight after Starr's body was found, bearing three letters that she had written to him shortly before her death. In them she said that she was going to end her "worthless, disorderly bore of an existence," and that she had promised herself one last delicious meal. Examination showed that Starr had eaten a large meal shortly before dying and that she had also taken enough of the barbiturate veronal to cause unconsciousness. The coroner's verdict was that Starr had drugged herself and walked into the sea—suicide.

Officially the matter was closed, but many people were dissatisfied with the verdict. After all, the body bore many marks of violence; was she killed by thugs employed by her childhood seducer? A respected investigator from the *New Yorker* magazine proposed that she was effectively "murdered on her suicide

THE FAITHFULL FAMILY Starr's sister (left), stepfather and mother refused to accept that Starr had written the suicide notes.

night" by a casual pick-up. Another theory suggested that Starr was abducted and killed by a notorious Brooklyn bootlegger and racketeer in an attempt to obtain blackmail material against "A.J.P." The truth may never be known, but the legend lived on. The tragic heroine of John O'Hara's bestselling novel *Butterfield 8* was based on Starr Faithfull.

OLDER MEN A.J. Peters (left) was a suspect in the Faithfull case. Starr was infatuated with Dr. G. Jameson-Carr (far left).

1960 Elizabeth Taylor wins an Oscar for her part, based on Starr Faithfull, in the film of *Butterfield 8*.

DID DILLINGER REALLY DIE?

PUZZLES STILL SURROUND THE SHOOTING OF A MIDWESTERN OUTLAW HERO

On July 22, 1934, federal agents lay in wait outside Chicago's Biograph Cinema and ambushed and shot dead Public Enemy Number One—the infamous outlaw John Dillinger. But was the man who was shot that night really John Dillinger, as the government agents claimed?

The "Dillinger Gang" robbed banks in the Midwestern states between 1933 and 1934. John Dillinger's own ability to evade capture and to escape from even the tightest security had made him something of a living legend. To many Midwestern farmers struggling through the depression, the banks which foreclosed on their loans were enemies and Dillinger was a folk hero.

Despite a spree of over a dozen robberies and several murders in three different states, local police forces alone were left to try to contain the trail of destruction. The national Bureau of Investigation (which would later become the FBI) could not act until a federal law was broken. Then, while escaping from prison, Dillinger drove a sheriff's car over a state boundary, thereby committing a

CASH INCENTIVE The Bureau of Investigation and individual states offered rewards for the capture of Dillinger in a major campaign.

DEADLY DESPERADO The infamous and much-photographed John Dillinger poses with a Colt .38 and submachine gun, shortly before his supposed death.

federal offense, and the government men were on his trail at last.

According to the official story, Anna Sage, a landlady and madam in Chicago, tipped off the Bureau that one of her tenants was dating a man calling himself Jimmie Lawrence, whom she believed to be John Dillinger. She told the Bureau agents that "Jimmie Lawrence" had admitted to her that he was the infamous bank robber. Mrs. Sage arranged to accompany "Jimmie Lawrence" to the cinema, where federal agents could arrest him, on Sunday, July 22. At 10:30p.m. as the suspect emerged, he spotted the danger and sprinted for an alleyway, drawing out

1903 John Dillinger born

1924 Dillinger jailed for assault

1933 Dillinger robs his first bank
1934 Dillinger shot dead by the FBI

A JOB WELL DONE? Director of the Bureau of Investigation, J. Edgar Hoover (above). Headlines proclaim Dillinger's demise (below).

noted as having brown eyes—Dillinger's were recorded as gray on police files. None of Dillinger's identifying scars was mentioned: one on his upper lip and another on his left hand. The body was too short and too stocky, and the heart showed signs of childhood illnesses which Dillinger had never had.

If it was a case of mistaken identity, it would not have been the first. Dozens of men had been arrested during the search for Dillinger. Had the Bureau of Investigation covered up a mistake, or had the ambush been a stage-managed fraud? And if so, by whom? Why did the Bureau keep Chicago's "Dillinger Squad" in ignorance of their plans? Was it to avoid a leak, or to keep all the glory?

One theory is that the shooting was a charade organized by Dillinger and Lewis Piquett, his mob-connected lawyer. Perhaps the "leaping bandit" had lost his taste for crime once many of his accomplices and lovers were dead or behind bars. For years rumors that he was alive were fuelled by reported sightings. In 1969

FATEFUL SPOT Dillinger was reportedly shot outside the Biograph Cinema, which was showing *Manhattan Melodrama* that night.

the *Indianapolis Star* received a letter from "John Dillinger," enclosing a photograph of a man resembling a much-aged John Dillinger. There was no return address.

a gun. Before he could pull the trigger, he was shot dead.

The Bureau of Investigation could hardly have asked for a more newsworthy outcome. Previously the department had been dismissed as an ineffectual organization of "College Cops."

A dubious trophy

Doubts exist, however, as to the identity of the Bureau's prize catch. Sensational rumors surrounded Dillinger's death, as they had his life: allegedly the fingerprints didn't match, and people who knew him didn't recognize the body. When the autopsy report was uncovered 35 years later, it contained controversial information. The corpse was

PRYING EYES The public file past the supposed body of the outlaw as it lies in a Chicago morgue. But was the corpse really Dillinger's?

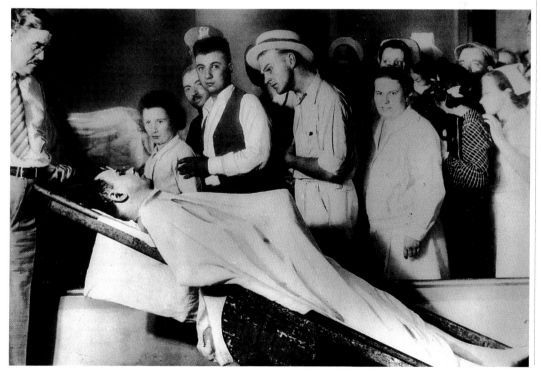

THE SHARK ARM AFFAIR

MACABRE AQUARIUM DISCOVERY PROVOKES A MURDER INVESTIGATION WITHOUT A BODY

For bizarre detail, nothing could match the mystery of Australia's Shark Arm Affair, which hit the headlines on April 25, 1935. The identification of a tattooed arm, disgorged by a captive shark in Coogee Aquarium, led to one of the most grotesque murder cases of the 20th century.

The affair began in the seas off Sydney, where a fisherman hauled in a 14-foot tiger shark. Rather than kill the saw-toothed giant, he towed it ashore and offered the live specimen to his brother, who managed an aquarium at Coogee.

Some days later, while the shark was swimming around in front of spectators at the aquarium, the creature suddenly went into a spasm and expelled its stomach contents which included a human arm. The limb trailed a piece of rope from the wrist and was found to bear the tattoo of a pair of boxers. At first, this grisly relic was assumed to have resulted from the shark biting a swimmer. But no one had reported an attack in the area, nor had any swimmer gone missing.

Police puzzlement deepened when further examination revealed that the arm had been severed with a knife.

Fingerprints identified the owner of the arm as James Smith, a 40-year-old ex-boxer with a police record. Smith had once been arrested for illegal bookmaking. Inquiries revealed that he had been missing for over

SHADY CHARACTERS Left: Reginald Holmes, the prosecution's star witness, was murdered. Right: Prime suspect Patrick Brady.

LONELY LIMB The tattooed arm disgorged by a captive tiger shark. Below left: James Smith, the arm's owner, who is believed to have been murdered.

two weeks. His wife, Gladys, believed that he had gone on a fishing trip. The police assumed that Smith was dead and began a major investigation.

Police make an arrest

When detectives arrested 42-year-old Patrick Brady, a criminal associate of Smith's who was wanted on forgery charges, he admitted that he had recently spent a holiday on the coast with Smith, but denied any involvement with his death. Brady did, however, implicate Smith's employer, a boatbuilder called Reg Holmes, in forgery dealings. The relationship between Holmes and Brady now became of central importance to the police investigation. Reg Holmes denied even knowing Brady, but he clearly had something to hide. After he tried to shoot himself aboard his speedboat in Sydney Harbor, he was apprehended and placed under police guard in a hospital for four days while surgeons removed a bullet from his forehead. Holmes then changed his story and accused Brady of killing James Smith.

On May 17, Brady was charged with the murder of James Smith, but on the day before the Coroner's Inquest there was a sensational development. Reg Holmes, the key police witness, was found shot dead in his car near Sydney Harbor Bridge.

Another dramatic twist followed the next day. The coroner ruled that he could not hold an inquest without a body. And he did not have a body—he only had an arm.

Despite the coroner's objections Brady was tried for murder, but after a trial lasting just two days the judge directed the jury to bring a verdict of not guilty; the main prosecution witness was gone, and there was no proof that Smith was dead. Two men later charged with Reg Holmes's murder were also acquitted, and the whole police case collapsed. The case remains unsolved.

The police theory is that Smith and Brady were involved in an insurance fraud involving a yacht, which resulted in a quarrel. Brady murdered Smith and dismembered the body which he crammed into a tin trunk for disposal at sea. The arm would not fit in so it was lashed to the outside (hence the piece of rope trailing from the wrist). It worked loose and was swallowed by the shark, which then revealed its ghastly secret to pleasure seekers at Coogee Aquarium.

A SHOOTING IN KENYA'S "HAPPY VALLEY"

THE GUNSHOT WHICH SHATTERED A COLONIAL HAVEN OF PARTIES AND FUN FAR FROM THE WAR

TROUBLED HOME The house at Karen that was leased by Jock Broughton to share with his young and beautiful new wife Diana.

When Josslyn Hay, 22nd Earl of Erroll, was found shot dead with a bullet through his head just outside Nairobi in January 1941, the scandal rocked the upper classes throughout the English-speaking world. It was wartime, and the Blitz was still raging in London where rationing had been introduced and austerity styles held sway. Amid the white colonial community of Kenya, however, decadent pleasure-seeking and misbehavior were rife.

Handsome 36-year-old Lord Erroll, the Military Secretary in Nairobi, was a notorious member of the "Happy Valley Set"—a permissive elite whose homes lay along the Wanjohi river in Kenya's "White Highlands." There were rumors of orgies, drug-taking, wild drinking and wife-swapping.

Lord Erroll was a voracious womanizer who had been named as a "very bad blackguard" by one shocked judge in an English divorce court. "To hell with husbands" was the motto of this old Etonian, who seems particularly to have relished seducing the wives and girlfriends of his own upper-class friends and acquaintances. No one doubted the motive for the killing; "Passionate Peer Gets His" read one headline, when news of the murder broke.

The chief suspect was quickly identified as 57-year-old Sir Henry "Jock" Delves Broughton—the latest in a trail of wronged husbands. It was well known in Happy Valley that Jock Broughton's wife Diana had been having an affair with Erroll. At a party in the exclusive Muthaiga Country Club on December 22, 1940, the lovers had been seen dancing together locked in a passionate embrace. In the first week of January the following year they had shared a weekend together at a friend's home.

Early in January Broughton received the first of several spiteful anonymous notes: "You seemed like a cat on hot bricks at the club last night. What about the eternal triangle? What are you going to do about it?" It would hardly be surprising if the injured husband did take violent action.

ONE OF THE GANG Lord Erroll sports a bow tie in the back row of this picture taken in 1928 at the wedding of two of the "Happy Valley Set"—Nina Layman and Jack Soames.

But he had never seemed greatly troubled by his wife's illicit liaison with the murdered peer. When he brought her from England to Kenya, a friend asked if he realized that every man in Nairobi was going to fall madly in love with her. Jock said, "Oh, that's all right. I'm not the least bit jealous."

Jock Broughton had been born into a great English landowning and horse-racing family. He had recently been divorced from his first wife and married Diana. Six weeks before they were married in a register office in Durban, Jock and Diana made a remarkable contract that if she should fall in love

with a younger man, he would not stand in the way of a divorce. Indeed, he would supply her with an income of about $20,000 a year for at least seven years. It was a peculiarly generous arrangement, which seemed to acknowledge Jock Broughton's low expectations of enduring loyalty or affection from his beautiful young wife.

When Diana's affair with Erroll became common knowledge Jock saw his lawyer about a divorce. In a letter to a friend he said: "They say they are in love with each other and mean to get married. It is a hopeless position and I'm going to cut my losses. I think I'll go to Ceylon. There's nothing for me to live in Kenya for."

The matter seemed to have been resolved amicably when on January 23, at a dinner at the Muthaiga Club, Jock Broughton toasted the lovers: "I wish them every happiness, and may their union be blessed with an heir. To Diana and Joss."

A "blackguard" is murdered

At about 2 a.m. the next day Broughton was driven home, reportedly rather drunk. Later Lord Erroll dropped Diana back at the Broughtons' house. Just 45 minutes later at around 3 a.m. he was found dead in his Buick a couple of miles from the house. Erroll's body was found by two African dairy workers. The peer lay on the floor of his Buick that was plunged, with its headlights still blazing, at a steep angle into the sloping grass shoulder near a road junction.

At first the police could not identify the body in the Buick because it was crammed down into the space under the dashboard. When the police examined the corpse it was found to be Lord Erroll, who had been shot at point blank range with a .32 calibre revolver. Two shots had been fired in the car, and the fatal bullet had penetrated just behind the peer's left ear. The position of the wound, which was scorched with black powder, suggested that Lord Erroll had been

AN IMPERFECT MATCH The second Lady Broughton (above) was blonde with striking good looks, but she did not have a faithful heart. Months after marrying Jock Broughton (left) she fell for another man.

shot either by someone sitting in the front passenger seat, or through the open window from the running board. The precise manner in which the murder was accomplished still remains a puzzle.

When the police arrived at the Broughton's house to take statements that morning they made no reference to murder, but said that Lord Erroll had broken his neck in a motor accident. Diana became too hysterical to face questioning, and Broughton's reaction was to ask "Is he all right? Is he all right?"

Broughton made no attempt to hide the affair between his wife and the deceased. In fact Diana asked Jock to take something personal of hers to lay on Erroll's body, so he visited the mortuary and gave one of her handkerchiefs to one of the officers to leave on the body of his rival, with the words "My wife was very much in love with Lord

1900 ━━━ 1950

1918 Hay "asked to leave" Eton

1924 Hay moved to Kenya

1935 Jock meets Diana

1940 Jock marries Diana
1941 Erroll shot
1942 Jock commits suicide

Erroll." However, the police were suspicious of Broughton's actions when he got home that afternoon; he built a large bonfire in the grounds of his home, and had it dowsed with gas by a servant. Later the charred remnant of a bloodstained golf sock was recovered from the ash.

The investigation began to focus more and more on the injured husband who had both motive and opportunity for the killing. Broughton could well have entered the Buick before Erroll drove away—whether secretly, forcibly, or quite openly, claiming that he had things to discuss with the murder victim. He could even have gone ahead to the intersection and flagged Erroll down on the road so as to murder his rival out of earshot of the house.

Suspicious behavior

Broughton had come to the room of a houseguest, Mrs. Carberry, at 3:30 am. to ask if she needed anything and to say goodnight. This appeared to give him an alibi. But, had he hurried back after shooting Erroll and knocked on her door for just that reason?

—and Erroll had been shot with a .32 calibre revolver. Was it possible that Broughton had faked the burglary in his house so that there should be no evidence of the murder weapon? This hints at a premeditation untypical of love triangle shootings. Was the

STICKY END Lord Erroll and his second wife, Molly, in London in 1937. She was one of many rich older women he courted. She died in 1939 from drink and drug abuse. He was shot dead in 1941 (left).

urbane 57-year-old Jock Broughton capable of such deviousness? The police case implied that he was.

Sir Henry Delves Broughton was arrested and charged with murder. He was tried in May 1941 at Nairobi's Central Court, and the public galleries overflowed with smartly dressed members of Kenya's elite. Diana, the grieving adulteress, came to court day after day in a succession of spectacularly elegant outfits; it was said that she never wore the same one twice. The world's

Other suspicions were raised by the fact that only days before the murder, Broughton had reported a burglary to the police. He claimed that two revolvers, a cigarette case and a small sum of money had been stolen from the living room. One of the missing guns was a .32 calibre weapon

press watched too, as the prosecution witnesses locked horns in cross-examination with Broughton's brilliant South African defense counsel H.H. Morris.

In the end, the defense won the day. The police case rested strongly on ballistics evidence connecting the two murder bullets with Broughton's "stolen" .32 calibre revolver. Experts testified that the bullets came from a gun which had scored them with five grooves and a right-hand twist. But the defense was able to prove that Broughton's two stolen guns were Colts—all Colts had six grooves and a twist to the left. Erroll had not then been shot with either of Broughton's guns.

When the verdict of "not guilty" was announced in the packed courtroom there was an audible sigh of relief from the audience, and some clapping. But questions lingered long afterwards. If Broughton was innocent, who was the killer? Another outraged husband? A scorned woman of the Happy Valley set? Or did Broughton hire an assassin to do the job?

After the trial Broughton took Diana on a cruise to Ceylon, but during the trip he sustained a paralyzing back injury. In December 1942 he died in Liverpool, having taken a massive overdose of Medinal to combat the pain. Two suicide notes referred to his suffering, and the strain of the recent trial, but he did not admit to the murder. It has been reported that Broughton privately confessed his guilt to various acquaintances, but the stories do not entirely tally. In one version, Broughton planned the murder with an accomplice who had his own reasons for wanting Erroll dead, and they employed an African killer who hid in the back of the car. In another, Broughton shot Erroll himself and threw the gun into the Thika Falls.

A recent book by Leda Farrant, a Kenyan writer, suggests that it was not Jock but Diana who committed the murder, after being spurned by Erroll. In this scenario, Jock built the bonfire to burn his wife's—rather than his own—blood-stained clothes.

WHO KILLED SIR HARRY OAKES?

A BRUTAL MURDER IN A TROPICAL BRITISH COLONY THAT WAS DUBBED THE "CRIME OF THE CENTURY"

THE MURDERED MILLIONAIRE Machete in hand, Sir Harry Oakes poses for a photograph. Below, the murder bedroom, with Sir Harry's body still on the bed.

W hite sands, turquoise seas and sparkling sunshine have made the Bahamas a paradise for millionaire tourists for many years. On the night of July 7, 1943, the thunder of a tropical storm rocked the capital Nassau, lashing the city with high winds and pelting rain. And next morning, dawn light played upon the burned and battered corpse of Sir Harry Oakes—one of the islands' most prominent citizens.

Sir Harry's body was found in bed at his palatial home in Nassau. His skull had been fractured by four blows from a heavy object with one or more sharp points. The body had also been partially burned, so that charred remnants of his flimsy pajamas clung to his flesh. He was still alive—barely—when he was set on fire, or the flesh would not have blistered as it did. Unaccountably, feathers from a pillow had been scattered over the corpse.

Set as it was in a millionaires' playground, the case was to become even more colorful through association with British royalty, Mafia interests, an aristocratic French playboy, black magic ritual, and a suspected Nazi spy ... small wonder that the Oakes Case was billed in its day as the Crime of the Century.

SHUTTERED ROOM Sir Harry was killed in the room behind these shuttered windows.

Oakes was aged 69 at the time of his death. This American-born businessman had made his fortune as a gold prospector in Canada. To strengthen his connection with the country which had furnished his riches, Oakes renounced his U.S. citizenship and became a Canadian.

The "uncrowned king" of the Bahamas

He moved to the Bahamas, at that time a British colony, because of the tax advantages. Subsequently he poured millions of dollars into the islands, through both tourist development and charitable works.

He was regarded by many as the uncrowned king of the Bahamas, and when, in August 1940, the Duke of Windsor was appointed Governor-General of the islands, Sir Harry Oakes was among the first to welcome him. The duke, who was the former King Edward VIII of England, had provoked a constitutional crisis within the Empire when he abdicated his throne to marry the American divorcée Wallis Simpson. He had been appointed Governor-General of the Bahamas to isolate him from the intrigues

1939 Harry Oakes made a Baronet

1943 Sir Harry Oakes found murdered

GOOD FRIENDS Harry Oakes at a polo match with the Duke of Windsor (far left). The Duke called in U.S. detectives Barker, Conway and Melchen (left) to investigate Oakes's death.

and perils of wartime Europe. Sir Harry, the self-made millionaire, became good friends with the outcast duke, and they often played golf together.

On the morning that the tycoon's battered and burnt corpse was discovered, the Duke of Windsor was roused immediately from his sleep by an attendant.

The duke's actions on that fateful day were decidedly odd. He first invoked his authority under the Emergency War Powers Act to impose press censorship and try to hush the case up. In this he was frustrated, for the news had already been cabled out of the Bahamas and was making headlines around the world. Some hours afterwards—notably late in the day—he opened inquiries, not by handing the case over to the Bahamas police or to Scotland Yard, but by calling in a personal contact, Captain Edward Melchen from the Miami police. The duke's request was puzzling: "I think one of our leading citizens has committed

BAHAMAS QUARTET
Clockwise from top left: the accused playboy Alfred de Marigny; the Duke of Windsor; Swedish industrialist and mystery man Axel Wenner-Gren; Harold Christie, who found the body.

suicide. Can you come and confirm this?"

By no stretch of the imagination had Sir Harry killed himself. When Melchen arrived with a colleague named Barker to investigate the case he came quickly to the point. "Face up to it," Melchen told the duke. "This is no suicide."

Harry Oakes had made many enemies on his road to riches, but the two American investigators settled very quickly on one man as prime suspect: Sir Harry's son-in-law, Alfred ("Freddie") de Marigny. This tall and dashing native of Mauritius had a reputation as a shiftless womanizer, and it was widely believed that he had married Sir Harry's eldest daughter only for her money. The murdered tycoon had quarrelled vigorously with the playboy on more than one occasion.

"Freddie" had been near Oakes's house late on the fateful night, while driving two dinner guests home. He had the opportunity for murder. Moreover, the American detectives discovered singed hairs on the suspect's arms, which they took to result from the fire that had burnt Sir Harry. The detectives' most damning accusation was that de Marigny's fingerprints were found on a Chinese screen in the murder bedroom.

But in the course of the ensuing much-publicized trial it became clear that the detectives had bungled badly or, more sinisterly, fabricated evidence to frame de Marigny. The significance of the singed hairs on the playboy's arms was quickly dismissed by the defense counsel with a witness's testimony that de Marigny had scorched himself while trying to light a candle inside a lantern at the dinner party he had hosted that night. The defense

1952 Captain Barker dies

1959 Scotland Yard refuses to re-open the case

1983 Meyer Lansky dies of cancer

demonstrated that the supposedly damning fingerprints could not have been taken from the Chinese screen as claimed, but must have come from a smooth, clean surface, probably a glass or cigarette packet which the detectives handed to de Marigny during questioning.

Other disquieting features of the investigation emerged. For example, it transpired that the Commissioner of the Police in the Bahamas had not believed in the case against de Marigny and had been transferred to Trinidad, with the result that he could not testify at the trial. Vital fingerprint evidence had been destroyed or ignored, including a bloody handprint on the wall; camera film of the handprint was mysteriously exposed to the light and ruined. Two watchmen who might have shed light on the murder—one in the grounds of the Oakes house and another in the adjacent Nassau Country

MAFIA MAN Meyer Lansky, a key figure in organized crime, has been connected with the Oakes murder case.

Club—had vanished without trace since the fatal event. It took the jury only two hours to reach their verdict—not guilty.

Many theories but no conclusions

No one else was ever charged with the crime. But many theories have been proposed to explain the case, and they often point to a Mafia connection through a tough, intelligent gangster named Meyer Lansky, who ran the syndicate's operations in Florida and Cuba. Lansky badly wanted to open a gambling casino in Nassau, a city close to Miami and already well known to the mob's powerboat skippers, who had once used it as a base for running bootleg alcohol into the United States. Gambling was illegal in the

Bahamas, but perhaps that could be changed through the influence of Sir Harry Oakes and the Duke of Windsor? According to one theory, Sir Harry was killed because he refused to be pushed around by the mob. In this version, the ritualistic elements of the murder—the fire and feathers—were seen as trademarks of a Mafia contract killing. It is interesting that Captain James Barker, one of the two Miami policemen brought into the case, was to die in 1952, corrupt and drug-addicted, on Meyer Lansky's payroll.

Suspicion has also fallen on Harold Christie, a Bahamian property developer who was Sir Harry Oakes's best friend. Christie had dined with Oakes on the fateful night and slept in a bedroom just down the corridor from the murder room; in fact it was he who discovered the body and raised the alarm. He and Oakes were the only two people in the house that night, and Christie swore an oath that he never left the building after going to bed at 11 p.m. However, a local traffic policeman, Captain Edward Sears, testified that he saw Christie in George Street, Nassau, at 1 a.m. on the day of the murder, travelling in a car speeding away from Nassau harbor.

Sears had known Christie all his life and had no apparent motive to lie. Although Christie was widely thought of as a public-spirited, kindly man, he may have had some

FINGERPRINTING TO SOLVE MYSTERIES

A century of scientific crime detection opened in 1901 when a man named Edward Henry was put in charge of the Criminal Investigation Department at Scotland Yard. He had pioneered the classification of fingerprints as a means of identifying criminals while inspector-general of the Indian Police. Everyone, it had been discovered, had their own unique pattern of skin ridges. Henry's particular contribution was to discern, amid the infinite variety of loops, whorls, deltas and arches, five basic patterns which he then broke down into subdivisions.

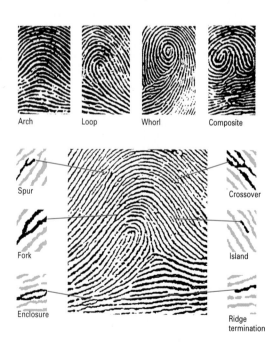

Arch   Loop   Whorl   Composite

Spur   Crossover
Fork   Island
Enclosure   Ridge termination

POINTING THE FINGER In court an expert must show at least sixteen points of similarity between the prints from the scene of a crime and those of a suspect.

The first great test for Edward Henry's system of analyzing fingerprints came in a case in 1905 when an elderly couple living above their shop in southeast London were murdered. Police managed to obtain a clear thumbprint from a cash box emptied out by the intruders. Suspicion fell on two young criminals—the Strattons—who were arrested. Their fingerprints were used as evidence in an historic trial. The prosecution pointed out eleven points of similarity between the thumb print of Alfred Stratton and that found on the cash box. The Strattons were found guilty and sent to the gallows.

Police forces worldwide soon began to build up card index files of fingerprints; these have been replaced since the 1980s with push-button electronic indexing, and computer systems that can match prints at a rate of 60,000 comparisons a second.

The traditional method for obtaining prints at the scene of a crime is to dust surfaces with a substance such as powdered aluminum, then place sticky tape over the mark to lift away an impression.

New technology has brought improvements. Since 1988 the FBI has been using laser and other devices to pick up fingerprints from such unpromising surfaces as Styrofoam cups. It has also now become possible to take a fingerprint from the body of a murder victim.

ACQUITTED De Marigny with his wife Nancy Oakes, pictured after he was found not guilty of murdering her father.

involvement with rum-running to Florida during Prohibition. He may well have known more about the Harry Oakes case than ever emerged at the trial. One version of events proposes that he and Oakes both went to Nassau harbor on the fateful night, to meet emissaries from Meyer Lansky on a powerboat. The obdurate Oakes was beaten up there before being driven back to his home, with Christie shivering in the passenger seat.

TRAFFIC COP Captain Edward Sears, Bahamas chief of traffic police, gave important evidence at the de Marigny trial.

That could explain the mud tracks found on the stairs, and the evidence that suggested that, after being beaten, Sir Harry had been turned over or repositioned on the bed in some way. (Although the corpse was lying on its back, blood from a wound at the back of the head had run across the face, indicating that the corpse must have been face down at some time.)

Another more forthright accusation proposes that Christie killed Sir Harry because Oakes was about to ruin him financially. Some newly declassified FBI documents have been invoked to show that the Nassau police believed Christie guilty at the time.

But there have been many other theories. One centers on the wealthy Swedish industrialist Axel Wenner-Gren, who had a house in the Bahamas and was well acquainted with Sir Harry Oakes and the Duke of Windsor. The Swede was also friendly with Hermann Goering and Mussolini, and was widely rumored to be a Nazi spy. Wenner-Gren had set up a bank in Mexico, and some researchers believe that he was helping his Bahamian friends to evade wartime currency restrictions through its facilities. The big money, combined with a pro-fascist government in Mexico, would have made Sir Harry a figure of key interest

to both Allied and Axis intelligence. He could have fallen foul of either.

Other speculation focuses on the ritualistic elements of the murder. Some suggest that the fire and the feathers were linked with the Bahamian magical practice called Obeah, which is comparable in some ways to Haitian voodoo. Was Sir Harry Oakes killed by a witch-doctor hitman brought in from southern Florida? Some argue that the Duke of Windsor tried to hush up the case because the notion of such a prominent white citizen being victim of a black cult murder would inflame racial tensions on an island which had seen recent riots.

Whatever the truth, when in 1944 the Duke of Windsor was asked to reopen the case, he refused. Not long after the end of the Second World War, the duke returned to Europe. He never again discussed the Oakes murder.

DID THE DETECTIVES LIE?

In the trial of Alfred de Marigny for the murder of his father-in-law Sir Harry Oakes, a fingerprint, which was allegedly found on a Chinese screen next to Sir Harry's bed, turned out to be a key piece of the prosecution evidence.

During a brilliant cross-examination of Captain Barker, one of the investigating detectives on the case, the defense counsel, Godfrey Higgs, pulled no punches:

Q. I suggest that you and Captain Melchen deliberately planned to get the accused alone in order to get his fingerprints.
A. We did not.
Q. I suggest that Exhibit J did not come from that screen.
A. It did come from that screen, from the number five panel.
Q. You can show none of that scrollwork from the screen on Exhibit J, can you?
A. I cannot.
Q. This is the most outstanding case in which your expert assistance has ever been requested, is it not?
A. It has developed into that.
Q. May I suggest that your desire for personal gain and notoriety has caused you to sweep aside truth. I put it to you, sir, you have fabricated evidence!

1983 Meyer Lansky
dies of cancer

HOW DID MARILYN DIE?

THE TRAGIC END OF A HOLLYWOOD SUPERSTAR SPARKS YEARS OF CONTROVERSY

At 4:25 on the morning of August 5, 1962, the West Los Angeles police station received a telephone call: "Marilyn Monroe is dead; she committed suicide." About ten minutes later, on arrival at the film star's house on Fifth Helena Drive, Sergeant Jack Clemmons was led into Marilyn's bedroom where he found America's ultimate sex symbol lying naked, face downwards in bed with a sheet pulled over her body. On her bedside table, among various vials of drugs and medications, was an empty bottle of Nembutal sleeping pills.

The housekeeper, Mrs. Eunice Murray, who had discovered the body, Marilyn's psychiatrist, Ralph Greenson, and her doctor, Hyman Engelberg, were present when the police arrived. The conclusion seemed clear

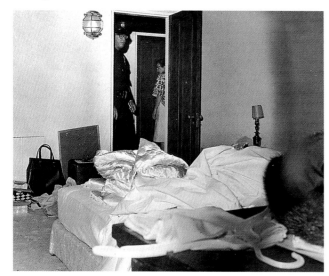

A FINAL SCENE The bedroom where Marilyn Monroe was found dead. The housekeeper, Eunice Murray, and a policeman are just visible through the doorway.

enough: the depressed actress, who had been fired by 20th Century-Fox from the filming of *Something's Got to Give*, had swallowed an overdose of sleeping pills, either in a deliberate attempt to take her own life or in a dangerous gamble with death. Marilyn had long been reliant on a psychiatrist to help her to cope with the pressures of superstardom, and was in the habit of taking drugs

THE HOUSEKEEPER'S TALE Mrs. Eunice Murray made strangely evasive, inconsistent statements about the time when she found Marilyn's body.

to cope with her insomnia and nerves. Her work was suffering; the studio had fired her for persistent lateness. In *Life* magazine, the actress had spoken of her difficulties. "Everybody is always tugging at you. They would all like sort of a chunk of you."

The autopsy revealed that Marilyn's blood contained 8 mg. of chloral hydrate (a relatively mild sedative which the film star was taking) and 4.5 mg. of the stronger sleeping pill, Nembutal. Moreover, there was a much higher concentration of Nembutal—13 mg.—in the liver. These quantities greatly exceeded normal therapeutic doses, and in combination had proved lethal. There were no external signs of violence, and so the coroner's verdict was one of "probable suicide." On August 8, following a quiet service for relatives and friends at the Westwood Village Mortuary, the body adored by millions was laid to rest.

Only after the mourners had left were the crowds of journalists, photographers, celebrities and Hollywood hangers-on admitted to the cemetery garden. In the judgment of some close to Marilyn, the superstar had been killed by the monstrous pressures of her public legend.

The questions begin

But had quite different forces connived at her death? There were discrepancies in the official verdict. For example, no residue of pills had been found in Marilyn's stomach during the autopsy. If the actress had recently swallowed a handful of Nembutal capsules, they should have left the yellow colored dye of their gelatine jackets in her stomach; but no such residue was present. Had she been injected with the fatal dose? If so, by whom?

Further inconsistencies surrounded the precise timing of Marilyn's death. The housekeeper, Eunice Murray, at first told the police that she had found the body "about midnight" but later changed the time of discovery to "about three o'clock." Detective Sergeant Robert E. Byron, in control of the

the case, found Mrs. Murray particularly vague and evasive in answering questions about this critical period. In fact, from early the night before, friends of the actress had become aware that something was very wrong with her. Between 7 and 7:15 p.m. Marilyn had been chatting cheerfully on the phone to the son of Joe DiMaggio, the baseball star who had been her former husband.

LAST EXIT The film star's blanketed body is wheeled out on a stretcher from her home at Fifth Helena Drive.

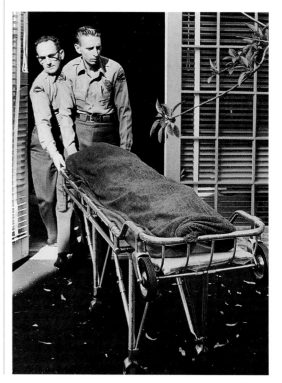

1926 Marilyn born Norma Jean Baker

1942 Marilyn marries James Dougherty

1946 Marilyn gets her first film contract

ON STARDOM Marilyn mistrusted her own legend. "A sex symbol becomes a thing," she said. "I hate being a thing."

But only half-an-hour later she was called by the British actor Peter Lawford (married to President Kennedy's sister Pat) and was speaking in thick, slurred, almost inaudible tones. At the end of their conversation, with great effort, Marilyn managed to say: "Say goodbye to Pat, say goodbye to the president, and say goodbye to yourself, because you're a nice guy."

Lawford was seriously alarmed and telephoned various friends trying to persuade them to go over to her house. It now appears that well before midnight, information had reached Milton Rudin, Marilyn's attorney, and Arthur Jacobs, her publicist, that Marilyn was dead.

What happened at Fifth Helena Drive in the four-and-a-half hours before the police were called to the scene?

Extraordinary comings and goings at Marilyn's house have been alleged, with tales of plain-clothes men who burnt tapes and

ON THE LINKS President J.F. Kennedy (third from left) golfing in Florida with his brother-in-law Peter Lawford (far right).

documents in the fireplace, and of missing phone records. Soon after her death sensational claims charged the family of President Kennedy with a politically motivated murder. Marilyn, it has been suggested, had been having an affair with the president's younger brother, Attorney-General Bobby Kennedy; Bobby made promises of marriage, and when he tried to ditch her she threatened to go public with the story so the Kennedys had Marilyn murdered. Afterwards the house on Fifth Helena

1926 Marilyn born
Norma Jean Baker

1942 Marilyn
marries James
Dougherty

1946 Marilyn
gets her first
film contract

THE BROTHERS The names of John F. Kennedy (right) and Bobby Kennedy (far right) have both been linked with Marilyn Monroe's death.

Drive was thoroughly sanitized to dispose of incriminating evidence before the police arrived.

Taking another look

The story hit the headlines again in 1973 with the publication of a biography, *Marilyn*, by Norman Mailer. In his book, Mailer speculated that Robert Kennedy might have been involved in Marilyn's death; or that she might have been killed by government agents in an attempt to frame the attorney-general. The book sparked a flurry of sensational books,

ated in an attempt to overthrow the communist regime in Cuba, and "Boss of Bosses" Sam Giancana allegedly feared that in damaging the Kennedys, Marilyn might damage a valuable relationship with the government.

In a meticulously researched biography published in 1993, author Donald Spoto dis-

ILL-FATED MOVIE Both Monroe and her co-star Clark Gable died shortly after making *The Misfits* in the Nevada desert.

TV investigations, dramatizations, memoirs and magazine articles all compounding the sense of mystery with new allegations; it was said that Marilyn's home had been wire-tapped by men acting on orders from Robert Kennedy's arch enemy, union boss Jimmy Hoffa. A Mafia connection was also alleged; the CIA and the Mafia had cooper-

OFF THE SET Marilyn between scenes during the filming of *The Misfits*—written by her third husband, Arthur Miller.

missed such stories as fantasies which originated in smears by right-wing factions hostile to the Kennedys. He said that there was no evidence of any affair with Robert Kennedy, and that Marilyn was not especially depressed at the time of her death; on the contrary, Fox intended to reinstate her in *Something's Got to Give*, and she was plan-

1950   2000
1954 Marries and divorces Joe DiMaggio
1956 Marries Arthur Miller
1962 Found dead

"SAY GOODBYE TO THE PRESIDENT"

It has often been alleged that Robert Kennedy was involved in Marilyn's life and her death. Equally sensational claims have also been made that the actress once had an affair with Bobby's

BIRTHDAY GREETINGS A sexy "happy birthday" song, in front of a crowd of 20,000, was Marilyn's gift to the president.

elder brother, President John F. Kennedy. These stories have more substance, for while Bobby was a devoted husband, the president had a reputation as a womanizer. It is known that Monroe and JFK met at least four times between October 1961 and May 1962, and that on Saturday, March

LOVERS' TRYST? Marilyn's last meeting with JFK was at his birthday party at Madison Square Garden in New York.

24, 1962, Marilyn and the president spent a night together while they were house guests of Bing Crosby at Palm Springs. They even phoned one of Marilyn's friends, Ralph Roberts, from a bedroom there. A passionate, long-term liaison has been reported by some but, according to Roberts, "Marilyn gave me the impression that it was not a major event for either of them; it happened once, that weekend, and that was that."

The last known occasion on which the two supposed lovers met was at a celebrated birthday gala for the president, held at Madison Square Garden in May 1962.

THE PSYCHIATRIST Dr. Ralph Greenson with his wife. The couple were among the mourners at the movie star's funeral.

ning to marry Joe DiMaggio for a second time. She was taking control of her own life with new confidence.

How, then, to explain the mysterious time lapse between death and police discovery? And how to explain the lack of capsule residue in Marilyn's stomach? Spoto's attention focused on three characters hitherto regarded as very minor actors in the drama: the housekeeper, Eunice Murray, the psychiatrist, Ralph Greenson and the doctor, Hyman Engelberg. Greenson had stopped prescribing Nembutal for the actress and was weaning her onto chloral hydrate. Unknown to him, however, Engelberg had continued to prescribe Nembutal. It was a

LAST RESTING PLACE Marilyn's funeral casket stands in front of the curtain-covered crypt where she was finally laid to rest.

combination of these drugs that killed Marilyn. The actress had taken a powerful dose of Engelberg's prescription earlier in the day, but not all of it had been metabolized by the evening when, it is alleged, Greenson arranged for Marilyn to take the sedative chloral hydrate. There was no injection (when the district attorney reviewed the case in 1982 he rejected the possibility of a lethal needle shot, which would have caused

instant death, a much higher level of barbiturate in the blood and a conspicuous bruise on the body). Instead, Greenson recommended an enema, a powerful and quite fashionable method of administering the drug.

The fatal enema was, it is alleged, administered by the housekeeper Eunice Murray—untrained as a nurse—after Greenson left. The slow absorption of the drug gave Marilyn time to take Lawford's phone call and deliver her last, slurred utterances.

If this was indeed how Marilyn died, the housekeeper—who had recently quit—would have had to face some awkward questions from the police, and Greenson's professional reputation would have been ruined. Perhaps they combined efforts to remove any trace of their involvement in the death of the woman who was in their care.

When Marilyn slipped into a drug-induced coma, she would have expelled the enema, soiling bed clothes and any nightwear. Here, perhaps, lies the explanation of the time lapse between Marilyn's death and discovery and the call to the police. When police arrived at the house, Eunice Murray was washing linen and garments. "Why, under these circumstances," the deputy district attorney asked, "would a housekeeper be doing the laundry at such an hour?"

THE FATE OF DORA BLOCH

WHAT HAPPENED TO THE GRAY-HAIRED GRANDMOTHER WHO VANISHED AT ENTEBBE?

For sheer drama, few news stories of modern times could match the Entebbe Raid. On the night of July 3, 1976, Air France flight 139 sat on the tarmac of Entebbe airport. It had been hijacked a week earlier by Palestinian terrorists, and Uganda's pro-Palestinian government had given the aircraft sanctuary. Then out of the darkness appeared three Hercules transport planes filled with Israeli commandos on a daring mission to rescue the 105 hostages.

After a furious gun battle, involving commandos, terrorists and Ugandan soldiers, the freed hostages were in the transporter planes and heading home to Israel. The swoop was justly celebrated as a triumph for the Israelis, and for counter-terrorism worldwide.

SADLY MISSED Mrs. Dora Bloch, photographed here with her granddaughter, missed the escape from Entebbe.

UNDER ESCORT "Major" Bob Astles, Amin's adviser, in the custody of Ugandan soldiers. Did he order the death of Dora Bloch?

However, after the raid on Entebbe one of the passengers from the hijacked plane was missing—a 75-year-old grandmother named Dora Bloch, who had been on her way to her son's wedding in New York.

The Ugandan authorities revealed that Mrs. Bloch had been "released" on the day before the air raid and admitted to Mulago General Hospital in Kampala. The day after the raid, a British Embassy official visited her there. She was guarded by two plainclothes men who indicated that she would soon be taken to the Imperial Hotel in Kampala. But just one hour later, when the official returned with some food for the patient, he was denied entry. No one at the hospital could say what had happened to her, and the Ugandan authorities said only that Mrs. Bloch was missing and was being searched for. They added that, from the time of the Israeli raid, Uganda had ceased to be responsible for Mrs. Bloch.

On July 7 the Ugandan Ministry of Health further muddied the waters by asserting that Mrs. Bloch had in fact been returned to the hijacked aircraft before the raid, a story which was obviously untrue.

Where had Dora Bloch gone? Eyewitnesses reported that the gray-haired old lady had been dragged screaming from her bed. Although it was accepted fairly quickly that she was dead, no one could say for certain until 1979, when Amin's regime was overthrown. With a new government in Kampala, investigators were at last able to piece together her fate. They discovered that four Ugandan secret policemen had come to the hospital, dragged her from her bed and bundled her screaming into a waiting Mercedes. "I saw armed men carrying machine guns pulling her down the stairs. They were firing to frighten people out of the way," recalled a doctor.

She was then taken to a forest and shot. In 1979, Dora Bloch's remains were recovered from an unmarked grave at a place called Nakapinyi and brought to Israel for burial.

But who was responsible for Mrs. Bloch's murder? Did Amin order the killing in

NOTORIOUS AFRICAN DICTATOR The whereabouts of former Ugandan president Idi Amin are currently unknown.

revenge for the humiliation of Entebbe? According to Amin's British aide, "Major" Bob Astles, the secret police had acted of its own accord: "I think, in all honesty, that he was ashamed that his State Research Bureau had killed her." One man who knows the answer is Amin himself, whose whereabouts have themselves provided an enduring mystery since his overthrow and exile.

1900

1902 Dora
Bloch born

1971 Coup brings Amin to power
1976 Air raid on Entebbe
1979 Amin overthrown

2000

THE DEADLY UMBRELLA

THE FURTIVE JAB THAT ENDED THE LIFE OF BULGARIAN DISSIDENT GEORGI MARKOV

One September evening in 1978 a Bulgarian author and broadcaster working for the BBC World Service was killed on a busy street in London by a poisoned umbrella point. Georgi Markov had just finished work at the BBC and was waiting for a bus on Waterloo Bridge. Suddenly, something jabbed him sharply in the thigh from behind. As he looked around, he saw a thick-set man pick up an umbrella that had fallen to the ground. The man muttered an apology in a voice with a heavy foreign accent, jumped into a taxi and disappeared.

Back home in Clapham, in southwest London after dinner, Markov began to feel

WORRIED MAN Markov feared for his life. He believed that his defection and his criticism of Bulgaria's communist regime made him a target for assassination.

FRONT PAGE NEWS Headlines in Britain announced that the examination of Georgi Markov's corpse had led to the discovery of a minuscule metal projectile in his leg.

sick. When he was no better the next day he mentioned the umbrella episode to his wife, Annabel. "I have a horrible feeling that this may be connected with something that happened yesterday," he told her, and showed her the small puncture mark on his thigh. With his temperature soaring to a feverish level, Markov was rushed off to St. James's Hospital in Balham. The doctors there at first took his symptoms for those of septicaemia, a blood infection, but he did not respond to treatment with antibiotics, and fell into a coma. Four days after being admitted to the south London hospital Georgi Markov died of a heart attack.

An enemy of the state

The incident might have been taken for a natural death but for Markov's own insistence that the umbrella incident had caused his fever. His past had made him suspicious.

In 1961 he had published two volumes of short stories, the success of which had resulted in his joining an elite corps of Bulgarian writers. He was a regular visitor to Mount Vitosha, where many leaders of the Zhivkov regime had villas. But Markov's skill for satire made him unpopular in the corridors of power, and in 1969 he defected to Britain. There he began working for the World Service and Radio Free Europe. In his broadcasts and writing the defector did not shrink from criticizing the Bulgarian authorities.

Unlike many defectors from the East, Markov had not been assigned an "uncle" from the British secret service to look after him, but he was a potential target for assassination. So when he died suddenly, protesting that he had been attacked, his body was examined carefully.

Several days after Markov's death a tiny metal ball made

from an alloy of platinum and iridium, and no bigger than a pinhead, was found embedded in his leg. Microscopic examination revealed that two tiny holes had been precisely drilled into the pellet.

The inquest into Markov's death was held on January 2, 1979. Expert witnesses testified that the pellet found in Markov's leg had probably been filled with ricin—a poison derived from the castor-oil plant and twice as lethal as cobra venom. Experts also testified

EVERYDAY KILLER The lethal weapon that killed Markov could have been a specially adapted umbrella. The murderer would fire the fatal pellet by pulling a trigger in the handle.

that it was possible that the lethal pellet had been fired through the tip of an umbrella by a device hidden inside. In the light of the evidence the court returned a verdict of unlawful killing.

The Markov attack was not unique; Vladimir Kostov, the former head of the Bulgarian state radio and TV network, who had defected to the West in 1977, had been attacked in a similar way in Paris a few weeks before the Markov attack. As Mr. Kostov emerged from the Arc de Triomphe station on the Paris Métro he was hit in the back by a pellet identical to the one used on Markov. Then in October 1978 a Bulgarian exile, Vladimir Simeonov, died in London in mysterious circumstances.

Was Zhivkov's regime in Bulgaria delivering warnings to potential defectors overseas? The Bulgarian authorities of the time denied any involvement with Markov's killing, but

OTHER VICTIMS Markov's friend Vladimir Kostov (left) was shot by a pellet identical to the one that killed Markov. Vladimir Simeonov (right) died mysteriously in London only a month after Markov.

after the overthrow of the regime in 1989 the new government accepted that the murder had been performed at the request of the old communist regime. Oleg Kalugin, a former KGB chief, has also stated that the Russian authorities furnished the Bulgarians with the necessary equipment with which to conduct the assassination.

Despite these new leads, headlines in 1991 which trumpeted the imminent arrest of the killer proved false. Precisely who killed Georgi Markov is still a mystery, and the file at Scotland Yard remains open.

THE STRANGER-THAN-FICTION WEAPONS OF SECRET ASSASSINS

The poisoned umbrella that killed Georgi Markov was just one among many ingenious weapons devised for assassination in the 20th century. During the Second World War, Britain's Special Operations Executive invented various tools for its secret agents which were worthy of "Q" from the James Bond movies: a gas gun disguised as a fountain pen, and even an exploding cowpat for saboteurs to place in the path of oncoming tanks.

In 1954 a trained Soviet assassin who had been sent to kill the leader of a Russian exile group in Germany gave himself up instead to the man he was supposed to kill. Concealed in the battery of his car were a variety of murder weapons, including a gold cigarette case that silently fired poisoned dumdum bullets when it was squeezed at the base.

In 1961 another member of the KGB execution squad defected and brought Soviet secrets to the West. His name was Bogdan Stashynsky, and he confessed to the murders of two anticommunist exiles: Lev Rebet in 1957 and Stefan Bandera in 1959. Both appeared to have died of heart attacks, but the assassin told how he had killed them with a finger-thick metal tube, about 7 inches long. It fired a spray of prussic acid into the victim's face, causing death when the vapor was inhaled but leaving no trace in the body. The killer protected himself by taking an antidote just before the attack and another afterwards.

DEADLY DEVICE An artist's reconstruction shows how the murder weapon may have worked.

As the piercer released the gas the pellet would have been fired

Poison pellet

Release catch

Tensioned spring propels the piston hammer forward when released

Piston hammer

Gas cylinder

Piercer

Screw-on gun barrel

POISON PELLET Two tiny holes in the pellet are believed to have contained deadly poison.

THE SUSPICIOUS DEATH OF "GOD'S BANKER"

THE BODY OF ROBERTO CALVI HUNG UNDER A BRIDGE AMID THE RUINS OF HIS FINANCIAL EMPIRE

On the evening of Saturday, June 12, 1982, Italian television's main news bulletins announced that the financier Roberto Calvi had disappeared. Calvi was the head of Italy's most important private bank—Banco Ambrosiano—and had for some time been the subject of rumor. At the time he was awaiting an appeal against a four-year prison sentence for currency offenses. He had also been exposed as a member of P-2, an out-

GOD'S BANKER   Roberto Calvi's Banco Ambrosiano had loaned millions to companies owned by the Vatican.

lawed masonic lodge. Calvi's vanishing act was newsworthy enough; what followed astonished the world.

The following Friday, Roberto Calvi's body was discovered in London, dangling from scaffolding under Blackfriars Bridge. The corpse hung from a nylon rope which had been noosed around the neck and fastened to the scaffolding by two half-hitch knots. A false passport bearing the name Gian Roberto Calvini was found in his pockets, which were also stuffed with $8,000 in cash, in a range of currencies. More than 10 pounds of broken bricks were crammed in his pockets and down his trousers. They had apparently acted as weights to guarantee the financier his death.

The gruesome discovery precipitated the collapse of the already faltering Banco Ambrosiano, a financial disaster which not only shook the international banking system but also rocked the Vatican.

Banco Ambrosiano and the Vatican Bank (IOR) were intricately connected. Calvi had been, it was said, "God's Banker." Even the bank's balance sheet carried the words "Thanks be to God."

Ambrosiano had channelled hundreds of millions of dollars, loaned from banks around the world, to hollow "front" companies in Central and South America. The companies were rumored to be involved in money laundering for the Mafia and were controlled by the Vatican via a holding company. But the money simply disappeared, and Banco Ambrosiano began to sink under the pressure of the loans.

There were allegations that the missing millions had been channelled into Italian political parties, into the sinister P-2 freemasons,

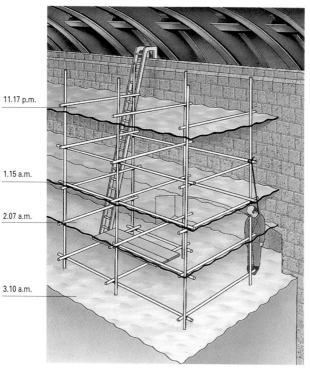

11.17 p.m.

1.15 a.m.

2.07 a.m.

3.10 a.m.

DUBIOUS SUICIDE   The changing height of the water with the tides made nonsense of some of the suicide theories. The plank that Calvi was assumed to have walked along would have been under water at 2 a.m.

and even into the Polish trade union Solidarity (a cause close to the heart of the Pope). Calvi's struggling bank could be saved only if the Vatican agreed to repay some of the money lent to the companies. But the Vatican refused to be held responsible for the financial activities of companies simply held in its name.

Against this infinitely complex backdrop, the human drama of the financier's death posed one immediate question. Did Calvi hang himself? Or was he dropped from the bridge by unknown hands?

Had Calvi taken his own life?

From the outset the police in London treated the case as a suicide, and this was also the verdict of jurors at the inquest held in July. There was no sign of violence on Calvi's body, nor any evidence that he had been drugged. The motive seemed obvious: the financier had seen the ruin of his empire and was probably facing a four-year prison sentence. He had reportedly made a previous suicide attempt in police custody.

It was not impossible to believe that he succumbed to despair in London. But clambering across scaffolding in the middle of the night was an odd way for an overweight

THE RECENTLY DECEASED Calvi's body, photographed minutes after he was found and cut down from his modern-day gibbet.

Italian banker who suffered from vertigo to kill himself. Why go to Blackfriars Bridge anyway when he had enough barbiturates in his hideaway in Chelsea to kill himself privately and without the risk of pain? Calvi's family was convinced that he had been murdered, and they insisted that Calvi had not been depressed in his last days but had been frightened for his own safety and that of his family. People were threatening him, they said, perhaps people who wanted to silence him before his appeal hearings in Italy. In order to save himself and his bank, Calvi had told his family that he was willing to "name some names."

The arguments of Calvi's family and complaints about the thoroughness of the first inquest had an effect; in June 1983 a second London inquest examined the case over a period of 11 days in far more detail. The suicide verdict seemed increasingly unlikely. Calvi's wristwatch, which was badly damaged by water, had stopped at around two o'clock in the morning, and at that time the Thames tides would have made the approach to the place where Calvi died extremely tricky, involving clambering over the upper part of the scaffolding. Expert witnesses testified that it was "possible" but very difficult. How much more difficult carrying a load of

BEHIND BARS A Calvi associate, Sicilian swindler Michele Sindona, on trial in Milan for complicity in a murder.

bricks? However, at 2 a.m. the water would have been at the perfect height for a small boat to approach the scaffolding and for a body to be strung up. The damage to Calvi's neck was insufficient for a free-fall when he dropped from the scaffold. The water must have been at a height to break his fall. More expert testimony made it seem possible that the banker might have been drugged after all, perhaps by inhalation. With the evidence mounting against suicide, the jury returned an open verdict.

In Italy in 1989 a court took things further, recording a verdict of murder. If Calvi was murdered, there is no shortage of theories as to who did it and why.

The Freemasons

Calvi had headed the financial wing of the outlawed P-2 Masonic Lodge, and it was

THE SHADOWY HAND OF THE MAFIA

Often in 20th-century mysteries of death or disappearance, research hints at a Mafia involvement. It has been discerned in cases as different as the Calvi affair, the Kennedy assassination and the murder of Sir Harry Oakes. The Syndicate's interests extend from gambling, narcotics and prostitution into the worlds of high finance, show business and big government.

The Mafia began in Sicily as a network of gangs, or "families," hired by local landowners to protect their estates. Members began to operate protection rackets among fruit-pickers, taxi drivers and other

tradesmen, demanding regular payments to allow people to earn a living. Mafia families were bound by *omerta* (manliness), a code of honor and silence. They came to the U.S. as an invisible presence among the poor Sicilian immigrants who streamed across the Atlantic in the late 19th and early 20th centuries. There Mafia gangs developed interests in gambling and in labor unions and, in particular, in the bootleg liquor industry during the Prohibition years. After fierce feuding ended in a bloody purge in 1931, a new nationwide Mafia emerged, based on cooperation between mobs.

The Second World War brought an unlikely alliance with U.S. intelligence. Sicilian gangsters and American spies shared a mutual interest in eradicating Benito Mussolini, and the Mafia cooperated with the Allies in the invasion of Italy. These links were revived in America's postwar struggle against communism—both the CIA and the Mafia wanted to see Castro ousted from Cuba (the Mafia wanted to develop gambling on the island).

Within the United States, the Mafia flourished under the name of *Cosa Nostra* (Our Thing). However, little was known about the hierarchy until 1963 when former gangster Joe Valachi (right), broke the code of silence and told all he knew. Cosa Nostra, it emerged, was run by five bosses: Vito Genovese, Carlo Gambino (above left), Giuseppe Magliocco, Joseph Bonnano and Gaetano Lucchese. Despite detailed knowledge of the organization's structure, however, convictions remain rare.

In the United States the Mafia remains a powerful force, and in Italy its influence is a national scandal. The extent of its influence was exemplified in 1995 when former premier Giulio Andreotti was brought to trial for alleged Mafia dealings.

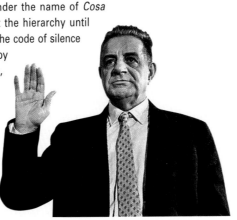

1952 Married Clara Canetti

1965 Made president of Banco Ambrosiano

1975 Made chairman of Banco Ambrosiano

1982 Found hanged — first inquest

1989 Italian court returns murder verdict

1996 Gangster confesses to Calvi's murder

CALVI CONNECTIONS Left to right: Bettino Craxi, Italian premier at the time; Archbishop Marcinkus, president of the Vatican Bank; Flavio Carboni, convicted of illegal possession of Calvi's briefcase.

rumored that he was involved both with exiled Italian fascist groups and with South American arms-trafficking through Freemasonry. There were several hints of masonic ritual about Calvi's death. A black friar is said to be the symbol of the P-2 Lodge; broken bricks (such as those found in Calvi's pockets) symbolize a discredited or failed Freemason; and the initiation of a new Mason is said to include a symbolic noose around the neck and a vow which threatens that he will be killed and left "where the tide regularly ebbs and flows twice in 24 hours," should he break the code of silence. Had Calvi been discovered a few hours later, his body would have been soaked twice by the Thames tides.

The Vatican connection

Calvi told his lawyers that he had channelled $50 million to the Polish trade union Solidarity on behalf of the Vatican. "If the whole thing comes out," he said, "it'll be enough to start the Third World War."

Not only that, but his daughter maintained that Calvi was in London to do a deal to bail out his struggling bank and to get back at the "priests" who he felt had let him down. *Opus Dei* (God's Work), a small right-wing Catholic organization, was a prime candidate for such a deal, which would have had repercussions on the balance of power within the Vatican. Clara Calvi, the victim's widow, maintained in the newspaper *La Stampa* that her husband's murder was engineered by a left-wing Catholic faction which was hostile to his connection with Opus Dei.

The Mafia theory

An odor of the Mafia lingered about Banco Ambrosiano affairs. Calvi had for many years had close dealings with the Sicilian tax lawyer Michele Sindona, who was later convicted of perjury, misappropriation of funds and murder. Sindona was also heavily implicated in money-laundering for the Mafia. He had introduced Calvi to the Vatican Bank—a lucrative connection—but when Sindona's own bank in Milan had collapsed, losing the Vatican millions of dollars, Calvi had managed to distance himself from the affair and would not help Sidona, thus making a powerful enemy.

In 1991, a reliable Sicilian informant under the protection of the U.S. government testified that a prominent Mafioso living in Britain "killed Calvi with his bare hands" and rigged up his body under the bridge. The witness, Francesco "Mozzarella" Mannoia, said that the financier was murdered for playing fast and loose in a Mafia money-laundering operation.

The case is still wide open years later

The affair simply refused to die. One of its puzzles was the disappearance of Calvi's briefcase, from which he was normally inseparable. It was reputed to contain bunches of keys to safe-deposit boxes, as well as incriminating documents.

Incredibly, the briefcase turned up in Italy in 1986 when two Rome "businessmen" attempted to sell documents from it to a minor Vatican official, who reportedly was prepared to pay millions for the contents.

The courts later heard that the briefcase had appeared via Flavio Carboni, a Sardinian businessman who had acted as a "fixer" for Calvi and had been one of the last people to see him alive in London. Carboni was convicted of illegally possessing the briefcase and was also sentenced to 15 years in jail for irregularities relating to Banco Ambrosiano's final collapse with huge debts.

In 1994 the case came alive again when the Socialist leader Bettino Craxi —a former Italian prime minister—was sentenced in his absence by a Milan court to eight-and-a-half years' imprisonment. The charges related to $7 million paid by Calvi's bank to a Swiss account controlled by Craxi. The prosecution alleged that the payment was made to reward politicians for helping Calvi's bank to obtain a loan from a state energy holding.

In 1996 newspaper headlines trumpeted the solution to the death of Roberto Calvi. Frank "the strangler" Di Carlo, a Corleone gangster, had reportedly confessed to murdering Calvi for the Mafia. However, an arrest was never made.

Top churchmen, Socialists, Fascists, Freemasons, Mafia leaders and international arms dealers . . . all move like shadows through this affair. The collapse of the Banco Ambrosiano brought many unsavory realities to light, but the secrets of Calvi's death are still lost forever, and as far as the London police are concerned the case remains open.

INVISIBLE EMPIRES

THE SECRET NETWORKS AND INTERCONNECTIONS THAT RUN UNKNOWN THROUGH EVERYDAY LIFE MAY NOURISH SINISTER AIMS AND HIDDEN AGENDAS

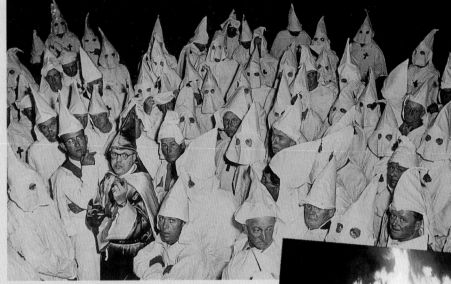

When the body of Italian banker Roberto Calvi was found dangling from scaffolding under London's Blackfriars Bridge, many investigators suspected a Masonic involvement. The secret society to which Calvi belonged is in some countries as much a part of the establishment as organized religion. Yet its aims and work are mysteries which are surrounded by tales of strange rituals. Many aspects of Calvi's death bore marks of Masonic ritual.

During the initiation rites a new recruit stands in his shirt with his left breast bared, the right sleeve rolled up past his elbow and his left trouser leg pulled up past the knee. On his left foot he wears a shoe, on his right, a slipper, so that he limps as he is led through the temple door by a hangman's rope noosed around his neck. Later he is made to swear with a dagger at his bared breast that he will not betray the secrets of the movement, on penalty of "having my throat cut across, my tongue torn out by the root and buried in the sand of the sea at low water mark."

Freemasonry is thought to have developed out of the guilds formed by medieval stonemasons to protect the secrets of their trade. The masons' lodge was originally their workshop and place of assembly, where news was exchanged and grievances discussed. Modern Freemasonry dates from 1717 when a Grand Lodge was established in England, and the movement subsequently spread to continental Europe and to America. Today there are thought to be about 9,250 lodges around the world.

KKK TRADITION Ku Klux Klan meetings are full of ritual drama, such as burning crosses and wearing sinister disguises.

Although its declared aims are to promote good works and spread brotherly love in the name of the "Great Architect of the Universe," the movement has long provoked criticism from outsiders for acting as a secret interest group responsible to no one but itself.

The Fiery Cross

The same criticisms have been leveled at other sinister secret societies which wield power independent of democratic control. The Ku Klux Klan in the United States sprang up in Nashville, Tennessee, after the American Civil War, to prevent blacks from using their newly won right to vote. Cloaked and hooded Klansmen directed by a "grand wizard," burning fiery crosses, rode out by night to lash and lynch their victims. Known as the "Invisible Empire of the South," the movement won widespread support and reduced the Black vote, restoring White control over local government. The Klan promoted white Protestant interests in public life against Catholics, Jews and immigrants as well as Blacks, and its influence spread outside the South. A Klan involvement was suspected by some in the 1922 Lovers' Lane killing.

In 1923, 30 New York City policemen were exposed as Klansmen. During the 1950s and 1960s the Ku Klux Klan opposed the civil rights movement and, despite many prosecutions of members for acts of violence, the movement is still active in the South.

OLD ORDER New Masons endure much the same ritual now as they did in the 1800s (above). A 19th-century cartoon (right) mocks the grand master.

WHO KILLED JONBENÉT?

THE MURDER OF A CHILD THAT UNLEASHED SUSPICION AND HATE IN BOULDER, COLORADO.

Her blue eyes stared out from the tabloid covers and captivated the nation. On December 26, 1996, six-year-old JonBenét Ramsey, the precocious beauty pageant contestant with the golden hair and angelic face, was found murdered in the basement of her parents' sprawling Boulder, Colorado, home. JonBenét's mother, Patsey Ramsey, had called 911 at 5:52 a.m. that morning, claiming that her daughter had been kidnapped. Earlier in the morning she had found on a back stairway a rambling three-page ransom note from "individuals that represent a small foreign faction," demanding $118,000 for their daughter's return. "You and your family are under constant scrutiny, as well as the authorities," the letter warned. "Don't think that killing will be difficult. Don't underestimate us." Local police arrived at the house shortly before 6 a.m. and waited anxiously with the family for the kidnappers to call.

As the hours flew by, JonBenét's father, John, a wealthy businessman, grew impatient and began to search the house. At 1:05 p.m., he found his daughter's body in the basement wine cellar, wrapped in a white blanket, with her wrists tied above her head, her mouth covered with duct tape, and a nylon cord around her neck. Autopsy reports revealed that the cause of JonBenét's death was a violent blow to the head that left an eight-and-a-half inch fracture, coupled with strangulation from the cord. There was possible evidence of sexual molestation and an autopsy photograph revealed marks on JonBenét's body that one investigator suggested were left by a stun gun. Investigators

found a shoe imprint on the floor of the wine cellar, a palm print on the door, and a scuff mark on the wall, but none of these clues identified anyone in particular. A photo of JonBenét's bedroom taken the day after the murder revealed a white teddy bear that seemed unfamiliar to family members; could it help point to the killer?

THE VICTIM AND THE SCENE OF THE CRIME   Child beauty queen JonBenét Ramsey (top) was found brutally murdered in the basement of her upper-class suburban home (above), with a lengthy ransom note (left) taped to a staircase in the house.

The tabloids swarmed all over the story, rabid with speculation, and the nation was besieged with images of the adorable

JonBenét, performing at a pageant in sequined cowboy boots and hat, posing innocently with a bunny for an Easter photo. The police soon realized that they would have to solve this case roasting in the media spotlight, and quickly fell into two camps about the suspect's identity. One group of detectives held the theory that the killer entered the Ramsey's home the night of the murder, and then exited unheard and unseen. The other group maintained that the killer was someone already inside the house—a family member. Various pieces of evidence supported each of these theories. None of the forensic evidence pointed to a family member's guilt, nor did any of them have a conceivable motive. Also, neither the roll of duct tape nor the remnants of the nylon cord were found inside the house, leading investigators to conclude they were brought from outside. The "inside the house" faction countered that there were no signs at all of a break-in; pry marks found on a door leading to the kitchen were said to have come from an earlier incident. In the middle of the night, the large and labyrinthine Ramsey home would not have been easily navigable by someone unfamiliar with its layout, and the family heard no stumbling. The wine-cellar was not a room guests had access to; even the family's housekeeper claimed not to know it existed. In an interview after the murder, the housekeeper also revealed a doubt that the blanket in which JonBenét's body had been wrapped was the one on her bed the night of the murder. If not, only someone intimately familiar with the house could have retrieved it from the out-of-the-way basement cabinet in which it was kept.

Many of the detectives seemed to lean toward this second theory, and early suspicion fell heavily upon JonBenét's parents. On New Years Day, the Ramseys went on national television to deny any involvement in the murder. "We have to find out who did this," demanded Patsey, staring intently into the camera. They offered a $100,000 reward for information leading to the capture of their daughter's killer. But a month later, the Boulder District Attorney publicly labeled the Ramseys as "the obvious focus of the investigation," and nearly a year later, though DNA evidence seemed to suggest otherwise, the D.A.'s office reported that the parents "remain[ed] under an umbrella of suspicion." Patsey in particular was singled out as a possible culprit. A family friend recounted that the day after the murder, Patsey walked around the house mumbling something like, "We didn't mean for this to happen." Some speculated that Patsey might have hit her daughter over the head in anger, and then, fearful that she had killed her, staged her death as a murder by strangulation. The Colorado Bureau of Investigation, through handwriting analysis, concluded that "there are indications that the author" of the ransom note was Patsey, "although there is not enough evidence to conclude that definitely." When questioned, Patsey could be extremely cooperative, charming detectives with her Southern-style graciousness. But she could become violent when pushed too hard to answer questions she found objectionable. Was this evidence of a darker side

FEEDING FRENZY The Ramsey case took over the front pages of the tabloids for months as in the *Enquirer* at left. Above, John Ramsey looks on as wife Patsey struggles to answer a question from the media at a press conference.

capable of doing harm to her beautiful daughter?

As weeks turned into months, the investigation seemed stalled. The police department and the Colorado district attorney's office, under intense scrutiny from the national media, came under fire for mishandling evidence. The Boulder District Attorney complained that the police were so determined to prove the Ramseys' guilt that "they've never been able to look at the evidence objectively." Alternative suspects should have been considered more vigorously—members of the Ramseys' church, or an employee of John Ramsey's company who owed him a considerable sum of money. Many police officers believed that the district attorney's office was actually guilty of protecting the Ramseys; they were allowed, for instance, to walk about the house before the body was found, when they were perhaps able to destroy incriminating evidence.

A new detective was put in charge of the case in September 1997, promising to invigorate it with an improved "focused and aggressive" approach. Evidence was resubmitted for forensic testing, and more interviews were conducted, but a suspect with a convincing motive has yet to emerge. The Ramseys escaped to Atlanta, where John and Patsey met and married, where JonBenét was born, and where she is now buried. They continued to deny vehemently any involvement in the murder. Meanwhile, the Boulder, Colorado grand jury began to weigh evidence, the tabloids continued to offer their wild speculations and the nation was left with the haunting image of those piercing baby blue eyes.

UNDER FIRE The Boulder, Colorado police and D.A. were under constant pressure to solve the case—at any cost. Spokesman Mark Beckner (right) responds to the press with City Manager Dave Rhodes looking over his shoulder.

BRUTAL MURDER AT THE GORILLA CENTER

WHO KILLED DIAN FOSSEY IN HER REMOTE CABIN HIGH IN THE MOUNTAINS OF RWANDA?

FOREST COMPANIONS At home among the gorillas, Dian Fossey experienced greater problems in human company.

The republic of Rwanda is the smallest and possibly the most inaccessible country in Africa. It lies buried in the heart of this vast continent, encircled by high volcanic mountains. Here, in December 1985, Dian Fossey was apparently hacked to death in a deeply puzzling murder case. Fossey was a scientist known worldwide for her work with the rare mountain gorillas of Rwanda's damp, green highlands. She was also, by temperament, a difficult woman: tough, sometimes arrogant, and very much a loner. Dian was the focus of a worldwide conservation effort to preserve the mountain gorilla and lived in the research center of Karisoke, high amid the Virunga mountains. And it was here that her body was found; she had been brutally murdered in her cabin.

A fellow American researcher named Wayne McGuire was charged with the crime. He was alleged to have killed Dian to steal her research notes and so complete his own thesis. In this he was said to have been aided by a Rwandan tracker named Emmanuel Rwelekana. The case against them was based on evidence supplied by a Paris police laboratory. Hair found in the murder victim's hands was Caucasian, but not Fossey's own. Blood matching Fossey's was found on Rwelekana's shoes.

An escape and a suspicious death

However, very few members of Rwanda's scientific community believed the official version of events. The idea that McGuire killed Dian for her research notes seemed absurd. In fact, he was allowed to escape the country and went on to pursue his studies at an American university. That the Rwandan authorities seem to have made little effort to stop him leaving and even less to extradite him is suspicious.

The tracker Rwelekana was never brought to trial either—he was found hanged in his prison cell under suspicious circumstances. Although he was allegedly found hanged with his own shirt, the autopsy stated that the cause of death was a broken neck—a feature more common to executions than suicides—and records of his interrogation indicate that he maintained his innocence with dignity throughout, despite being tortured for information. He could only explain the Caucasian-type hair found in Dian's fist, and the blood on his own shoes, by saying that someone was trying to frame him.

Journalist Nick Gordon, who made a detailed study of the Fossey case, exposed a number of anomalies. For example, Dian Fossey was supposed to have been hacked to death with a native panga, or hatchet. Blows from a panga would have left

THE SCIENTIST After fifteen years at Karisoke, Dian Fossey was a respected expert on the world's largest living ape.

MIDDLE OF NOWHERE A light in Dian's cabin at twilight. The remote Karisoke camp is habitually shrouded in heavy mist.

blood spattered everywhere, and the blood in the hut was concentrated on the floor around the body. There was a strong suspicion that she had been strangled first, then

GORILLA GRAVEYARD Dian visits the graves of victims of Rwanda's gorilla poachers. She was buried here among her friends.

hit with a panga after she was dead. It was odd that a panel from the side of her hut had been broken down, apparently for the murderer to gain access. McGuire had keys to the building and would not have needed to make so noisy an entrance. If anyone had broken in in this way, Fossey would have had time to get her gun and defend herself. Had the panel been removed to fake a violent entrance?

Nick Gordon's investigation led him to conclude that certain prominent Rwandans were seriously implicated in both the murder and a subsequent cover-up.

Making powerful enemies

In Rwanda, Dian Fossey had come upon evidence of gorilla poaching on a large scale and had campaigned vigorously to stop the barbaric trade. The gorillas that she worked with were highly prized by zoos around the world, and a healthy young specimen might fetch as much as $32,000 on the illegal market. The heads, hands and feet of gorillas are valued as souvenirs and trophies. Dian had

confronted local poachers many times and was not afraid to use force to protect the gorillas on the mountain. She had also compiled a report naming almost 100 poachers and describing their operations.

Had her investigations led her to know more than was good for her about the illegal traffic in gorillas? Nick Gordon suggests that

CONVICTED The graduate student Wayne McGuire was convicted by a Rwandan court, in his absence, of Fossey's murder.

a highly placed Rwandan named Zed was responsible for Dian Fossey's death. Zed was the brother-in-law of the Rwandan president and was involved with his sister, Agathe, the president's wife, in a lucrative gorilla business. Perhaps the murder was set up to look like the work of local poachers, but the plan misfired when it was discovered that the intruders had stolen no valuables—only Dian's notes. The thieves were looking for incriminating documents relating to the gorilla traffic. The story about McGuire and the theft of the research notes was quickly concocted as a cover-up.

There was certainly one cover-up. A feeling was widespread among scientists working in Rwanda that to re-open the Fossey case and provoke hostility from the Rwandan authorities would damage the efforts of conservationists in the country. And so no one created a fuss, not even the U.S. State Department, which failed to institute an inquiry into Fossey's death. A mist was quietly allowed to descend over the whole affair, as impenetrable as the mists which habitually fall upon the lush Virunga mountains where Dian Fossey lived and died.

1963 Dian Fossey first visits Africa

1967 Dian returns to Africa

1985 Dian Fossey murdered
1986 McGuire and Rwelekana arrested

A RUN FOR HIS LIFE— THE TRIAL OF THE CENTURY

O.J. SIMPSON STANDS TRIAL FOR THE BRUTAL MURDER OF HIS EX-WIFE AND HER FRIEND.

WILD RIDE June 17, 1994, police arrested O.J. Simpson (below) at his Brentwood home, after a low-speed Bronco chase (left) on the San Diego Freeway .

On the night of June 17th, 1994, TV viewers were treated to one of the defining and more shocking spectacles of the 1990s: a white Ford Bronco speeding down the San Diego Freeway, with a bevy of police cars trailing cautiously behind, seeming to escort the vehicle rather than chase it. In the back seat of the Bronco was Orenthal James (O.J.) Simpson, a star running back for the Buffalo Bills, who, after a glorious football career in the 60s and 70s had become a popular actor, sports commentator, and product spokesperson. Spectators lined the roadway and crowded on overpasses, holding up hastily made signs reading "Go O.J. Go," as if Simpson was still on the NFL playing field, breaking tackles and racing toward the end zone.

But this was a very different O.J. from the confidant, charming athlete cheered on the gridiron. This O.J. was desperate and suicidal, a fugitive from the law, wanted by the LA police for the double homicide of his estranged ex-wife, Nicole, and her friend, Ronald Goldman. For over an hour, America watched the scene unfold, as Simpson sat in the backseat, a revolver in one hand, a cell-phone in the other, threatening to kill himself. Only an hour, and sixty miles, later, after the Bronco pulled into the driveway of his Brentwood mansion, did O.J. surrender himself to the police. But the story was far from over. The most outrageous, exhausting, and captivating celebrity mystery of the century had just begun, and America would be captivated by its legal pyrotechnics, tawdry details, and over-sized personalities for the next several years.

Investigators pieced together a timeline for the night of the murder. On Sunday, June 12, after attending her daughter's dance recital (which O.J. also attended),

HAPPY COUPLE O.J. and his wife Nicole, with their two children in happier times.

Nicole and friends ate at a restaurant in Brentwood. After leaving with her friends, at around 9:30 p.m., Nicole apparently realized that she had left her prescription sunglasses behind, and Ron Goldman, her friend and a waiter at the restaurant, agreed to bring them over to her luxury townhouse. At around the same time, O.J. and a houseguest returned to O.J.'s mansion with take-out food from McDonald's, each eating in his own room. At around 10:15 p.m., Nicole Simpson's neighbors reported hearing a "dog's plaintive wail." Meanwhile, at around 10:30 p.m., O.J.'s limo driver arrived at his estate, and buzzed him through the intercom. After waiting for more than twenty minutes, at around 11 p.m., the driver finally saw O.J. emerge from his house with five packed bags. The limo driver took O.J. to the Los Angeles airport, and at 11:45 p.m., O.J. flew to Chicago. Then at 12:10 a.m., Nicole's neighbors were led to the murder scene by her Akita dog, which had been found hours earlier, agitated and with blood on its paws.

O.J., immediately the prime suspect in the eyes of the police, pundits, and talk-show hosts, vigorously maintained his innocence, and assembled a "dream team" of legal counsel, led by the evangelical Johnnie Cochran, to defend him in court. Though prior to his arrest Simpson had never been embraced as a black role model, he was now also defended by many African-Americans, who firmly believed in his innocence, and saw the trial as form of persecution. The nation had just recovered from the most violent riots of the century, sparked by the acquittal of Los Angeles police officers caught on videotape beating a twenty-five year old black man named Rodney King. Thus, the trial proceedings, which began on January 24th, were from the start plagued by racial tension.

Much of America, however, was convinced of O.J.'s guilt, and the prosecution's case seemed extremely convincing. Simpson had been arrested before for hitting his ex-wife, and a tearful 911 call by Nicole, accusing him of domestic abuse, was played before the court to great effect. Most damning was a trail of blood, which lab tests revealed to be O.J.'s, leading from the murder scene to Simpson's estate. There was blood on Nicole Simpson's back gate, blood in O.J.'s driveway, blood in his front hall, and blood on his white Bronco. Nicole's blood was also found on a sock in O.J.'s bedroom, and a glove smeared with the blood of both victims was found by a detective behind

Simpson's house. Marcia Clark, the LA county prosecutor, called this sanguinary evidence "devastating proof of his [O.J.'s] guilt." The prosecution also attempted to demonstrate that there was enough time for O.J. to commit the murder at his ex-wife's townhouse at around 10:15 p.m., and then race back to his own home to be picked up by his limo driver forty-five minutes later.

In response, the defense team did not attempt to counter this evidence by showing that O.J. could not have possibly committed the murder. Cochran planted seeds of doubt within the jurors by challenging the credibility of the police and the prosecution's expert witnesses and claiming that there was a conspiracy to convict O.J. within the LAPD, motivated by racism. The defense's crowning moment came with the revelation that the detective who found the bloody glove, Mark Fuhrman, was an unapologetic racist. The defense also challenged the incontrovertibility of the DNA evidence, providing what the prosecution thought to be O.J.'s genetic fingerprints, found at the scene of the crime. Though one expert witness testified that the odds of the blood coming from someone other than Simpson were one in 170 million, the defense insisted that the blood could

COURTROOM DRAMA The Simpson trial revolved around the lawyering of the prosecution team, headed by Marcia Clark, and the "Dream Team" defense, headed by Johnnie Cochran.

have been planted at the scene, or could have been contaminated during lab tests.

On the morning of October 3, 1995, the nation waited impatiently as the jury convened to deliberate on the verdict. The trial had lasted nine months, involving 120 witnesses, 45,000 pages of evidence, and 1,110 exhibits. But the jury, which had been sequestered for 266 days, took only four hours to reach a conclusion: not guilty. O.J. mouthed the words "Thank you," and hugged his supporters, while the family of Ron Goldman wept tears of disbelief. They would, however, achieve some vindication sixteen months later, when on February 4, 1997, O.J. was found liable in civil court for the deaths of Nicole Simpson and Ron Goldman and ordered to pay their families $8 million in compensatory damages and $25 million in punitive damages. O.J. was forced to auction off his mansion, his golf clubs, and even his old football trophies. Bankrupted, he still maintained his innocence. And the nation continued to split along racial lines over the case; even after the civil trial, polls revealed that the majority of whites believed O.J. to be guilty while the majority of blacks believed him to be innocent. For many, however, the gruesome Brentwood double murder remains a mystery.

THE VERDICT Simpson, Cochran and defense consel F. Lee Bailey were jubilant at the not guilty verdict (top), as were O.J.'s relatives watching the trial on TV. The Goldman family (above), however, convinced of O.J.'s guilt, was devastated.

MYSTERIOUS DROWNING OF A TROUBLED TYCOON

ROBERT MAXWELL'S BODY WAS FOUND FLOATING IN THE ATLANTIC OCEAN NEAR TENERIFE

CAP'N BOB Maxwell in the stands at a soccer match with pop star Elton John and (below) with a copy of one of his newspapers.

He was one of Britain's most flamboyant tycoons: a billionaire publisher, newspaper proprietor and friend of the rich and famous. Robert Maxwell's charisma was matched by a reputation as a bully and cheat. When his 300-pound corpse was winched from the sea by helicopter in 1991 the shock waves rippled around the world for years afterwards. Maxwell rose to become a figure of national importance in July 1984 when he bought Mirror Group Newspapers Ltd. for $150 million. Through a ruthless modernization program "Cap'n Bob," as he was dubbed, made the company highly successful. He also headed several notable charities and indulged his love of soccer by buying his local team, Oxford United.

But the tycoon overreached himself in his desire to create a global communications empire through purchases which included the *New York Daily News*. Colossal debts began to accumulate. Meanwhile a curious story began to circulate in the press, alleging that Maxwell was an agent of Mossad—the Israeli intelligence service. It had a damaging effect on the already tumbling value of Maxwell company shares.

In the autumn of 1991 the ruin of his business empire threatened, and Robert Maxwell flew south for a break on his boat, the *Lady Ghislaine*.

He spent Sunday, November 4, swimming and taking business phone calls. That night Maxwell dined in Santa Cruz, Tenerife, before setting out to sea again. He was still awake at 4:25 a.m.; a crew member saw him, dressed in his nightshirt on the stern deck, and 20 minutes later he rang to ask the bridge for the air conditioning to be turned down. But the next morning, though the ship was searched, and searched again, Robert Maxwell had vanished.

A body is found in the Atlantic

His family was informed, and a satellite distress signal was put out. At 5:55 p.m. a body was sighted in the sea to the east of Tenerife, and within the hour a helicopter had located Robert Maxwell's weighty corpse, floating naked, face-up in the water. How had he died? Was it an accident, suicide or murder?

The verdict of the autopsy carried out on Gran Canaria stated that Maxwell had died of a coronary thrombosis or heart attack. But it was not clear whether the tycoon had first succumbed and then fallen into the water, or fallen first and had a heart attack in the sea.

Then in January 1992 the French magazine *Paris Match* published the verdict of a second post mortem conducted in Israel. A video recording of this examination appeared to reveal bruising on Maxwell's face and body. Two French forensic experts who studied the video concluded that the tycoon had received several heavy blows before his death, which had fractured his nose and torn his ear. British pathologists, however, dismissed all talk of foul play.

The question was of critical importance because Maxwell's

ALL ABOARD Maxwell looking every inch the billionaire aboard his luxury boat, the *Lady Ghislaine*, at Cannes in April 1987.

SUNK WITHOUT TRACE Robert Maxwell seemed to have everything—family, fame and fortune. But his rags-to-riches fairytale ended in tears.

1923 Maxwell
born in
Czechoslovakia

1945 Maxwell
awarded MC during
Second World War

1984 Maxwell
buys Mirror
Group

1989 Maxwell
found dead in the
sea near Tenerife

1994 Trial of
Maxwell's sons
begins

life was insured for $35 million, and the insurance companies refused to pay out without evidence that his death at sea was either accidental or murder. The policies did not apply in the case of death by natural causes or suicide.

Dr. Iain West, a leading pathologist was called in to investigate the case for the insurers. He believed it more likely that Maxwell had died by drowning than of a heart attack. This meant that the four possibilities now were:

Accident: Maxwell might have had a dizzy spell, slipped and fallen into the sea where he drowned. However, it was a calm night and there was a railing round the deck.

Heart attack: Maxwell was under severe stress, hugely overweight and suffered from a lung complaint. However, it is likely that after a seizure he would have fallen to the deck, not into the water.

Suicide: Dr. West identified injuries to Maxwell's left hand and a tearing of the left shoulder muscles. This, said Dr. West, was a common pattern of injury among some people who kill themselves by jumping from high places. They "will gradually ease themselves over the edge and hold on for a time with one or both hands before letting go." The scale of the disaster facing Maxwell's empire should not be underestimated;

$700 million were missing from pension funds. On his return to London he might have faced imprisonment.

Maxwell had been uncharacteristically indecisive before his death, first wanting his sons to fly to him to discuss business matters, then countermanding the order to give himself more time to think. Did he conclude that there was no way out? On the last day he had called for his private jet to circle round the yacht as if in a last proud flypast. He had locked his stateroom on the yacht before venturing onto the deck for the last time. Why lock the door if he was only going out for a breath of air?

The final possibility

Dr. West did not dismiss the possibility of murder—he simply found no evidence either for or against it. The injuries on the body could be explained by it striking either the ship or floating objects in the water.

Maxwell had no shortage of enemies. No suspicions attached to the crew, but it would not be impossible for a hit team to stalk the undefended yacht by night. Any powerful victim of his business malpractices would

THE END Though Robert Maxwell lived in Britain, his funeral was held in Israel at the Mount of Olives in Jerusalem.

have had the means and motive. Maxwell's interests included arms dealing, and if he were an agent of Mossad, his weapons traffic in the Middle East could have made him a target for Arab assassins.

There are other shadowy possibilities. Since his death it has emerged that Maxwell had been investigated several times by the FBI on suspicion of spying for the Soviet Union. The files were censored so that it is impossible to say whether conclusive evidence was found against the tycoon, but this contributes yet another dimension to the mystery of Maxwell's death.

AFTERMATH In 1994, three years after their father's death, Maxwell's sons Kevin (left) and Ian (right) were tried for conspiracy to defraud.

HISTORIC EVENTS

A GIANT LINER SUCCUMBS TO SUSPICIOUS FIRE IN WARTIME . . . AN AMERICAN PRESIDENT IS KILLED BY AN ASSASSIN WITH SUSPICIOUS MOB TIES. . . THE FINAL DAYS OF THE ROMANOVS ARE SHROUDED IN MYSTERY . . . TWO AFRICAN PRESIDENTS DIE IN A MYSTERY PLANE CRASH. THE NEWSWORTHY EVENTS OF THE RECENT PAST ARE NOT ALL CUT-AND-DRIED CASES. ELEMENTS OF UNCERTAINTY STILL WEAVE TANGLES OF DOUBT INTO THE ROUGH FABRIC OF 20TH-CENTURY HISTORY.

SIBERIA'S COSMIC CATASTROPHE

THE FIREBALL THAT BLASTED A HOLE IN THE FORESTS OF SIBERIA REMAINS A MYSTERY TODAY

In 1908, while the tsar still ruled over a Russia seething with revolutionary unrest, a disturbance of a wholly different kind rocked northern Siberia. In the remote Tunguska Basin, a blast estimated to be equal in energy to the detonation of 30 million tons of high explosive devastated the

WRECKED FORESTS The devastation at Tunguska testifies to the awesome power of the mystery blast. Leonid Kulik (above right) investigated the impact site.

inaccessible forests. The fireball which appeared suddenly in the sky materialized not long after dawn on June 30, with a monstrous flash and bang that caused villagers as far as 200 miles away to run in terror through the streets. Some inhabitants of the sparsely populated region were badly burnt or hurled through the air by the shock waves. Within a radius of some 40 miles, forests were laid to waste and herds of charred reindeer lay among the uprooted trees.

Although the facts were reported at the time, the region was so bleak and remote

that the actual site of the mystery blast remained uninvestigated by scientists for many years. Only in 1927 did a Soviet research team arrive at the scene, and its members were mystified by what they saw. As they approached the center of the oval-shaped blast area, the investigators expected to discover evidence of a meteorite collision. But they found no hunks of meteoritic rock. Whatever had exploded at Tunguska had vanished like a bomb, instead of breaking into fragments as meteors do. Nor was there a central crater; the trees at the heart of the blast area were relatively undamaged.

Extraterrestrial activity

What happened at Tunguska has fascinated both scientists and students of the paranormal. According to some reports, the soil in the devastated area was highly radioactive, and in 1946 a Russian author, Alexander Kazantsev, proposed in a science-fiction story that the disaster resulted from a nuclear explosion in an atomic-powered alien spacecraft flying overhead. This fanciful theory has lingered on among UFO aficionados, although it is wholly unsupported by any evidence. In the 1970s, two British physicists, A.A. Jackson and M.P. Ryan, suggested in

the science journal *Nature* that a mini black hole, no bigger than an atom, entered the Earth's atmosphere. Colliding explosively at Tunguska, it may have passed through the planet and emerged on the other side, in the North Atlantic (although there is no evidence of a corresponding explosion here). Objects known as "antimatter meteorites," originating beyond the Milky Way, have also been suggested as culprits.

A more orthodox theory—and the current favorite among scientists—proposes that the disaster was caused by a comet exploding overhead. Consisting of ice and dust, with a luminous, trailing gas cloud, a comet would have left no meteoric fragments after detonating. However, because a comet is normally seen coming from some distance away, and because it is not certain that an exploding comet would change radiation levels, the Tunguska event provokes continued debate.

WITNESS TO DISASTER Ilya Potapovich, of the local Tungus people, observed the effects of the explosion and, in 1927, guided Kulik's team into the blast region.

1900   2000

1908 A fireball blasts Tunguska   1917 The Russian Revolution ends the rule of the tsars   1927 Leonid Kulik leads a scientific expedition to Tunguska   1946 Russian author Kazantsev proposes the exploding spacecraft theory

THE RIDDLE OF THE MONEY PIT TREASURE TROVE

DESPITE FORTUNES SPENT ON EXCAVATION, THE MONEY PIT HAS YET TO YIELD A SINGLE DOUBLOON

In a prospectus issued in 1909, New York engineer Henry Bowdoin asserted that treasure estimated at over $10 million was buried on Oak Island off Nova Scotia, probably by pirates, and that by using modern equipment it would be "easy, ridiculously easy" to retrieve it. To attract potential investors, Bowdoin invented the figure of $10 million—but the Oak Island enigma had a very real historical pedigree, and its allure was sufficient to attract the future president Franklin D. Roosevelt among other backers. However, Bowdoin was to drill 26 boreholes

TREASURE HUNTERS Dan Blankenship, fortune seeker, and M.R. Chappell, Oak Island's owner, survey maps of the site.

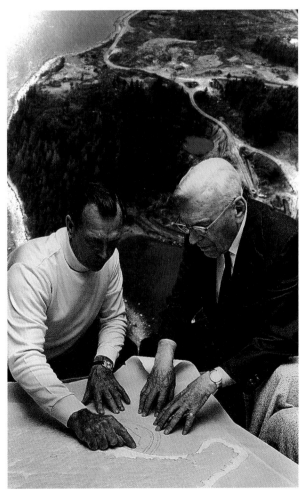

around the island without finding anything. And his successors have not had much more luck in what has proved to be one of the most enduring mysteries of the 20th century.

Booby-trapped booty?

The story began in 1795, when three local farm boys exploring the uninhabited island discovered a depression in the ground, a few yards in diameter, at the foot of an old oak tree. Thinking that someone might have buried something there, they fetched tools and helpers from the mainland, and discovered a man-made shaft sealed at intervals with oak-log platforms. About 30 feet down, the youths abandoned their excavations, but early in the following century a syndicate of local businessmen took up the quest. The searchers got 90 feet down, through further layers of log platforms, and reached a stone slab covered with cryptic symbols which were later decoded to reveal the message: "Ten feet below, two million pounds are buried." However, when attempts were made to reach the treasure itself, the shaft flooded with seawater—and the same calamity occurred when searchers angled a second shaft towards the base. It appeared that whoever made the Money Pit (as it was dubbed) had also booby-trapped it with flood tunnels dug from the ocean's edge.

Oak Island's fame spread with these and all subsequent attempts to unlock its secrets. In the 20th century new attempts were made on the treasure with heavy bulldozers, rotary drills, turbine pumps and crawler cranes. The original shaft was so damaged by flooding, digging and cave-ins that it became a huge, maimed crater, and both flood tunnels were destroyed. Meanwhile, hundreds of new shafts and boreholes pitted the 128 acre island, for the belief spread that the Money Pit itself might simply have been a decoy on an island honeycombed with interlocking tunnels. In 1965 a causeway was built to the island, and in the 1980s two separate visitor centers were set up by rival treasure companies.

The irony is that, despite its name, the Money Pit has to date disgorged not a single penny. Some skeptics have claimed that the labyrinth of tunnels in fact consists of sink-holes naturally formed in limestone and filled up by tide-borne debris;

BOX OF TRICKS?
This wooden box is one of the tantalizing clues that has been dug up on Oak Island.

the rest, they say, can be explained by self-delusion and the wilful fakery of such objects as the hieroglyphic stone slab.

But the quest continues to the present day. In 1995 newspapers published photographs taken in one borehole some 235 feet deep. Treasure-seeker Dan Blankenship lowered a video camera into the murky abyss and found what he believes to be clear evi-

WHO BUILT THE MONEY PIT?

Serious researchers have dismissed the idea that the Money Pit could have been the work of pirates. For, although Carbon-14 dating of its timbers has suggested that it might have been built during the 16th century, it would have required a more disciplined workforce and more advanced engineering skills than buccaneers could have mustered. Other equally improbable theories have suggested that it was built to conceal Marie Antoinette's jewels or even a cache of Shakespeare's plays.

dence of at least two chests at the bottom of the hole. Meanwhile, plans were launched by the Oak Island Exploration Company to fund an investigation to solve the mystery "through the application of scientific analysis and historical research." Experts have already been brought in from the Woods Hole Oceanographic Institute—the respected body that located the *Titanic*—to help resolve this most tantalizing of riddles.

1909 Henry Bowdoin issues prospectus for Oak Island exploration

1965 Causeway construction encourages tourists to Oak Island

1995 Video camera lowered into borehole

MYSTERIES OF THE *TITANIC*

HI-TECH EQUIPMENT CONTINUES TO UNCOVER THE SECRETS OF A GREAT SHIP'S WATERY GRAVE

"God Himself could not sink this ship," a crew member is reported to have said of the liner *Titanic*. Pride of the White Star fleet, she was the largest ship afloat and was equipped with luxurious fittings that ranged from elevators to a swimming pool, a squash court, a gymnasium with the latest exercise equipment from Germany, and a French "side-walk café." Yet in the early hours of April 15, 1912, the great ship struck an iceberg in the Atlantic south of Newfoundland, and not even her specially constructed steel hull could save her from disaster. The *Titanic* went down with the loss of more than 1,500 lives.

FLYING THE FLAG The *Titanic* **was the pride of the White Star fleet.**

Several mysteries surrounded her grim fate, and some were not solved until after September 1, 1985, when world headlines proclaimed that the wreck of the *Titanic* had been found. On that morning, using deep-sea sonar search aids, Dr. Robert D. Ballard and a joint French-American team located the lost ship on the floor of the Atlantic. The massive, rusted hull lay 2½ miles down on the ocean bed, and in the summer of 1986 Ballard's team went down in a three-man submarine named *Alvin* to explore the ghostly wreck. Landing on the deck of the great liner, Ballard obtained close-up photos by sending out a robot camera named Jason Junior as a "swimming eyeball" to explore the Grand Staircase and the state rooms. From the depths of the ocean came photographs of the giant liner's silverware and of glass chandeliers that still hung in place. In ten further descents, Ballard and his team explored much of the ship and the debris field around her broken hull.

SAD SOUVENIR A postcard commemorates the tragedy that claimed more than 1,500 lives.

How had the iceberg caused such damage? For safety, the *Titanic*'s hull had been constructed in 16 watertight compartments; survivors of the disaster, who had seen where the water entered the ship, reported that the damage to the hull extended from the first to the fifth of these sections.

The ship goes down

Many historians believed that the impact of the ice must have torn a long gash in the hull. However, Ballard's investigation showed this to be unlikely. Although much of the damaged area was buried in the mud, bits that could be seen revealed hull plates

1912 The *Titanic* is struck by an iceberg and sinks. An inquiry is launched

knocked apart intermittently at their seams. There was no single ice wound. What had happened was that the ship's starboard bow plates had buckled under the impact of the collision with the iceberg, the rivets had popped from their sockets, and water had rushed in through cracks between plates no more than a few inches wide.

Again, conventional views about the disaster held that, flooded at the prow, the great ship sank head-first and intact into the Atlantic. Indeed, two inquiries in 1912 concluded that the ship went down in one piece. Some eye-witnesses had reported, how-ever, that the ship had in fact broken in two: the bow plunged while the stern briefly righted itself before turning almost ver-tical and then sinking at speed. These witnesses were proved right by Ballard's findings. The hull was found snapped in two on the ocean floor, the segments 1,970 feet apart and pointing in different directions. Their posi-tion clearly indicated that the liner had bro-ken apart at or near the surface.

Yet again, many historians had assumed that when the bow reached a certain angle,

LATEST NEWS A London newsboy gives details of the disaster.

DOOMED COLOSSUS Only 705 people survived the *Titanic* sinking. Afterwards, new laws demanded that liners should have one space on a lifeboat for each passenger.

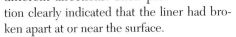

the boilers broke loose from their fittings and crashed headlong through the hull, hastening the descent. Ballard's findings sug-gested that this was highly unlikely.

Based on a careful study of the evidence, we can now reconstruct how the liner, flooding at the prow, began to lurch downwards. As the stern rose out of the water, the hull snapped under the intolerable strain of the tilt and the two segments sank independent-ly, spilling a wealth of debris from the shattered midsection. Finds have included tons of coal from the breached boiler rooms, thou-sands of bottles of wine and champagne, kitchen utensils, light fixtures, bathtubs, chamber pots and silver serving trays.

The empty safe

Are there greater riches to be recovered? In 1980, five years before Ballard located the liner, Hollywood had produced a film called *Raise the Titanic*, in which assorted treasure-seekers tried to recover rare minerals from the wreck. The theme echoed a widespread belief that—given the wealth of many passengers—for-tunes in gold and jewelry await discovery on the ocean bed. For Ballard, a moment of great excitement occurred when his head-lights picked out a ship's safe. However, when *Alvin* lifted the box, the box's bottom was missing—and there was no sign of any contents on the ocean floor. It appeared to be a safe from the second-class purser's office and had perhaps never held anything of great value.

It is known that some items of exceptional value were carried on the *Titanic*, among them a gold-covered copy of the *Ruba'iyat of Omar Khayyam* which had more than 1,000 precious stones studding its binding. Perhaps more research will reveal treasure. For future investigators the problem is not only a technological one; it has moral and legal dimensions. Attempts have been made by the United States government to declare the wreck an international memorial and to

UNDERSEA IMAGES In 1985 a joint French-American team located and photographed the wreck 2½ miles below the surface of the Atlantic.

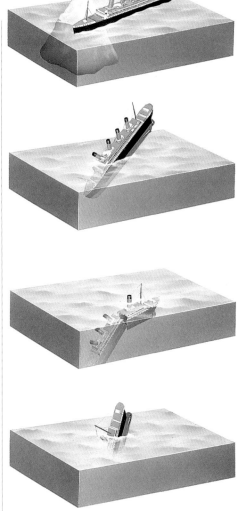

BREAK-UP Investigators believe that the hull snapped in two before the great ship plunged deep underwater.

leave it unmolested, but expeditions contin-ue to this fascinating relic. James Cameron's hit movie version of the story won 11 Oscars in 1998 and earned more than $2 billion at the box office, a testimony to the story's con-tinued hold over our imagination.

WAS MATA HARI GUILTY?

HOW THE FATE OF AN EXOTIC DANCER CAPTURED THE IMAGINATION OF A WORLD AT WAR

Oriental mystique, intrigue and sexual allure . . . all were united in the figure of Mata Hari, history's very archetype of the glamorous female spy. Arrested by the French during the First World War, the exotic

EXOTIC ALLURE Dutch-born Mata Hari cultivated one legend that she was a half-caste Javanese and another that she was the daughter of an Indian temple dancer.

dancer was tried for espionage and died in front of a firing squad in 1917. But a certain unease about her case lingered on. In 1925, an article published in France stated doubts as to her guilt. Was Europe's most famous courtesan really a German agent?

Born Margaret Geertruida Zelle in Holland in 1876, she married disastrously—a Dutchman of Scottish extraction named Rudolph MacLeod. He was a violent drunk, and the marriage only lasted 11 years. But

while living with him in Java she had become fascinated by the local dancing girls and their erotic arts. When she returned to Europe, she took the name of Mata Hari ("Eye of the Day," or "Dawn," in Malay) and appeared in Paris in 1905 as a "temple dancer," purportedly trained by Hindu priests in either Java or southern India, and dedicated to the god Siva. Her dances, she said, demanded nudity.

Scoring an instantaneous hit by dancing naked but for a few bangles, Mata Hari became a famous courtesan whose reputation spread to all the capitals of Europe. Princes, dukes, ministers and generals paid court to her, and she commanded immense fees for her favors. In 1914, when war broke out, she happened to be in Berlin where she was seen by French agents in the company, or so they said, of the chief of police. This was not especially sinister. The policeman was an old friend who had first made her acquaintance when investigating a complaint about her naked dancing and who had found ways to help her get around the law.

Code name H21

French prosecutors were later to claim that by this time Mata Hari was already a German spy with the operational number of H21 (H being short for Holland, where she lived for a few months in 1915). By the time she returned to France towards the end of 1915, she was shadowed everywhere: not only in Paris but also on visits to other European cities. However, for another year, Allied counter-intelligence services could find no grounds for arresting her. It was true that she had many male friends in diplomatic circles, including neutral Dutch, Swedish and Spanish attachés through whom she could pass information to the Germans. But there was no proof that she did so. The plain fact was that the courtesan had male friends in many important circles.

Threatened in 1916 with deportation from France, Mata Hari vehemently protested that she had never spied for the Kaiser— but that if the French wanted to employ her, she knew many high-ranking Germans from whom valuable information might be gleaned. Captain Georges Ladoux of the Deuxième Bureau, the French intelligence service, pretended to believe her, and together they discussed an assignment in which she would travel to German-occupied

THE COURTESAN Mata Hari made no secret of her profession. "30,000 marks was the fee for my services," she admitted at her trial.

1901 Mata Hari returns from the East to Amsterdam

1914 Dancing in Berlin

1917 Mata Hari arrested in February, sentenced in July and executed in October.

PRIM POSE The artiste appears modest enough in this photograph—but her dances, Mata Hari claimed, required nudity.

FIRING SQUAD Sentenced to death on July 25, 1917, Mata Hari faced her executioners with silent courage.

Belgium and seduce the German Crown Prince in return for a reward of a million francs. Mata Hari never made it to Belgium that year, but on a journey to The Hague via Spain and England she was detained when the ship on which she was travelling docked at Falmouth (on the tip of England's SW coast) in November 1916. The exotic dancer was taken to Scotland Yard in London, where she was questioned by Sir Basil Thomson, chief of Special Branch. To him Mata Hari admitted being a spy, but said that she was working for French intelligence. Skeptically, Sir Basil replied: "Madame, if you will accept the advice of one nearly twice your age, give up what you have been doing."

"Traitress, never!"

From London, Mata Hari moved to Madrid where she seduced the German military attaché, Major Arnold Kalle. He gave her some worthless gossip and disinformation, which she hoped to pass on to her new spymaster in Paris. On her return to Paris on January 3, 1917, Mata Hari intended to collect a reward from Ladoux, but instead she was arrested at the Elysée Palace Hotel by the French police on February 13, 1917. During her interrogation and subsequent trial she was questioned closely about the 3,500 pesetas she had received from Kalle. The prosecution alleged that it came from German Intelligence. Mata Hari, on the other hand, claimed that it was her fee as Major Kalle's mistress.

"Harlot yes—but traitress, never!" was Mata Hari's bold line of defense at her court martial, held in camera, in July. The money given to her by high-ranking Germans were payments for nights

THE MATA HARI FILE

In 1915, the Italian Secret Service telegraphed officials in Paris to warn that Mata Hari was returning to France—thereafter she was shadowed everywhere as a suspected spy:

"While examining the passenger list of a Japanese vessel at Naples we have recognized the name of a theatrical celebrity from Marseilles named Mata Hari, the famous Hindu dancer, who purports to reveal secret Hindu dances which demand nudity. She has, it seems, renounced her claim to Indian birth and become Berlinoise. She speaks German with a slight Eastern accent."

INTERPOL Sir Basil Thomson from Scotland Yard interrogated Mata Hari in 1916.

of love, she claimed. And for every German that the prosecution named, she countered with an exalted Frenchman. Jules Cambon, the secretary-general of the French Ministry of Foreign Affairs, had been one of her lovers and was even called as a witness for the defense.

"I am not French," declared the courtesan, "so what is to prevent my having friends of any nationality I choose?" After several heated exchanges, Mata Hari delivered a final statement: "Please note that I am not French, and that I reserve the right to cultivate any relations that may please me. The war is not a sufficient reason to stop me from being a cosmopolitan. I am a neutral, but my sympathies are for France. If that does not satisfy you, do as you will."

The prosecution case rested on little more than suspicion. It may well be that Mata Hari did dabble in espionage, but whether she was a genuine secret agent, code-named and committed to the German cause, remains much more doubtful. What is certain is that she was unlucky to have been apprehended at a time of national unrest, when France was facing mutinies at the front and fears of subversion at home. In this climate, despite a desperate fight by her lawyers for a reprieve, Mata Hari's fate was sealed. Found guilty and sentenced to death, she was taken to the barracks at Vincennes early in the morning of October 15, 1917. There, she placed herself against a stake where a cord was knotted around her waist. Mata Hari comported herself with great courage as the firing squad assembled, and refused the bandage for her eyes.

1964 Film of *Mata Hari, Agent H21*

1976 A statue of Mata Hari is erected in her birthplace, Leeuwarden, Holland

THE FATE OF THE TSAR'S FAMILY

DID ANY OF THE ROMANOVS ESCAPE ALIVE FROM THE FIRING SQUAD AT EKATERINBURG?

The Romanov dynasty which had ruled Russia for more than four centuries ended in a brutal massacre after the Revolution of 1917. Following the Bolshevik seizure of power in October that year, Tsar Nicholas II and his family were moved with a small number of courtiers to the town of Ekaterinburg in Siberia. On July 16, 1918, at the house there of a wealthy merchant called N.N. Ipatiev, Nicholas, his wife Alexandra and their son and four daughters were reportedly herded into a room and raked

FAMILY PORTRAIT Tsar Nicholas and the Empress Alexandra with their son and four daughters grouped around them.

INFORMAL GATHERING The tsar's daughters Olga, Tatiana, Marie and Anastasia take a stroll in the forest on a search for wild mushrooms.

with bullets by their guards. Those who did not die at once were finished off by blows with rifle butts and bayonets.

The Romanovs met their gruesome end at a time when civil war was still raging between Tsarist and Bolshevik armies in Russia. Not long after the massacre Ekaterinburg fell to counterrevolutionary forces, and Tsarist investigators explored the site to try to determine precisely what had happened to the royal family. They concluded that, after the killings, the corpses were hauled off to a secluded pine forest where they were dismembered, soaked in gas and burnt. Sulphuric acid was poured on the remains, which were dropped down a deep shaft at the nearby Four Brothers Mine. From the pit, the investigators recovered a handful of charred bones and one severed finger, along with bits of clothing, an emerald cross, women's corset stiffeners, diamond-studded shoe buckles, a doctor's false teeth and glasses, and more. The jewellery was easily identified as that of the Romanov women, and the searchers also found brass buttons with coats of arms that had belonged to Nicholas and his hemophiliac son Alexis.

A train with the blinds down

However, certain puzzles have continued to surround the Ekaterinburg findings. For one thing, the few human remains discovered at the mine did not suggest that the whole family and their servants—11 people—had been disposed of there. Bodies do not simply turn to ash when burned in petrol and soaked in acid. Where were the rest of the skeletons?

For a long time, serious researchers were convinced that some members of the royal family, at least, had escaped death because they were needed as bargaining counters in secret talks between the Bolsheviks and the German government. Alexandra was a relation of the German Kaiser and, so they argued, she and her children were to be exchanged for certain revolutionaries and then imprisoned in Germany. These clandestine negotiations are well documented. As late as September 10, 1918— long after the supposed massacre

1901 Birth of Anastasia, the tsar's fourth daughter
1904 Birth of Alexis
1914 Germany declares war on Russia
1917 The Bolsheviks seize power
1918 Execution of the tsar's family

THE CAPTIVES Interned by the Bolsheviks, the tsar and his family soak up the sunshine on the rooftop of a Siberian greenhouse.

—the German consul in Moscow reported: "I talked with Radek [a Bolshevik leader] again today about releasing the Empress and her children." In October, Sir Charles Eliot, the British High Commissioner in Siberia, reported the rumor that: "On 17 July a train with the blinds down left Ekaterinburg for an unknown destination, and it is believed that the surviving members of the imperial family were in it."

Spice was added to the possibility of escape by the fact that if any of the tsar's family did survive, they might inherit fabulous riches. At the time of the Revolution, the Romanovs' wealth was estimated at an incredible $9 billion—the present-day equivalent of $48 billion. How much of this was saved from Bolshevik hands was a mystery in itself, but rumors were rife of huge gold shipments out of St. Petersburg during the Tsarist regime's last days. Fortunes were reputedly hidden away in private accounts at banks in London, Paris, Berlin and New York. And with such an inheritance, there was no shortage of pretenders to the tsar's estate. Over the decades

that followed the Revolution, scores of treasure-seekers, fantasists and downright maniacs came forward, asserting that they were royal survivors of the Ipatiev house massacre.

Anna Anderson and others

The most famous claimant was a woman named "Anna Anderson" who was rescued in 1920 from a suicidal drowning attempt in a Berlin canal. After a long period in a hospital where she was reluctant to say anything about her past, she claimed to be the Grand Duchess Anastasia, the tsar's youngest daughter. She had, she said, been spared death at Ekaterinburg and sent off by train with her mother and sisters to another place of imprisonment. In the course of three escape attempts, she said, she was beaten and raped. Eventually, she got free and travelled incognito, with help from a Russian soldier, in a farm cart to Bucharest.

Some of the relatives, friends and staff of the Russian royal family, brought to meet "Anastasia," became convinced of her authenticity,

including the Grand Duke Andrew, the tsar's cousin. Others were more dubious; Prince Felix Yusupov called her "an adventuress, a sick hysteric, and frightful play-actress." Anna was the subject of a famous play, Ingrid Bergman and Lilli Palmer movies, a Lynn Seymour ballet, several books, countless newspaper articles and a 32-year-long lawsuit in

Germany. She died in February 1984 with historians no more certain of her identity than they had been 60 years earlier.

Many other claimants appeared. It has been said that in Siberia after the massacre, every town had its clutch of grand duchesses and sons of the tsar – all of them obvious frauds. Among the female hopefuls, pretenders to be Anastasia have been the most numerous, although there were others who claimed to be her sisters Olga, Tatiana or Marie. Nor was there a shortage of men asserting themselves to be the Grand Duke Alexis, the Tsar's only son. One of these was Colonel Michael Goleniewski, a Polish Army Intelligence officer who defected to the United States in 1960 after feeding the American CIA with microfilm secrets for two years. Not long after his defection had hit the headlines, Goleniewski began to make public claims to be Alexis. His story was astonishing – that the whole family had been smuggled out of Ekaterinburg. In Goleniewski's account, Tsar Nicholas lived on until May 1952, when he died incognito in Poznan in Poland and was buried in the cemetery of Wolsztyn.

The secret grave

The claims of many Romanov pretenders were shattered by dramatic developments in 1989. In that year, with the *glasnost* spirit of free enquiry spreading in the Soviet Union,

SLAUGHTER HOUSE The building in Ekaterinburg where the Romanovs met their end belonged to a successful merchant called Ipatiev. Below: the room where the family were raked with bullets by their captors.

BURIAL SITE It was at this spot, in the birch swamp outside Ekaterinburg, that the remains of several Romanov family members were located in 1989.

investigators announced that they had found skeletons of the Russian royal family in a birch swamp 12 miles outside Ekaterinburg. The location had been revealed in notes left by Jacob Yurovsky, the commander of the Bolshevik execution squad at the Ipatiev house.

The case is reopened

On the orders of the Russian president, Boris Yeltsin, an official investigation of the burial site was later carried out. The grave yielded nine skeletons, and in September 1992 remains were sent to British forensic science laboratories for DNA testing. Meanwhile, blood samples were taken from relatives of the Russian royal family who

included Prince Philip, Duke of Edinburgh (a direct maternal descendant of Alexandra's sister). A year later, it was officially announced that the mystery of the Romanovs was just about solved. Combining historical evidence with the DNA results, it was possible to identify the nine bodies in the grave as those of Tsar Nicholas II, the Empress Alexandra, three of their daughters, Dr. Botkin (the family physician), a footman, maid and cook.

Fascinatingly, two figures remain unaccounted for. Remains of the tsar's son, Alexis, were not present in the grave and one of the Romanov daughters was missing (although experts disagree as to whether this is Marie or Anastasia). Were their lives spared? Or were they butchered like the others and buried elsewhere for reasons now forgotten? The answer continues to baffle, though the evidence from the birch swamp grave has debunked the claims of many a pretender to the identity of the Grand Duchess Olga or Tatiana. It also makes nonsense of Goleniewski's claim that the tsar died in Poznan in 1952. As for the

MYSTERY WOMAN A woman known as "Anna Anderson", photographed (left) in 1928 and (right) in 1955, claimed to be the tsar's daughter Anastasia.

fascinating Anna Anderson, historians are now satisfied that she was in fact a Polish peasant called Franziska Schanzkjowska who had endured the very real ordeals of rape, pregnancy and suicidal breakdown—but was not Anastasia.

> ## THE FINAL HOURS
>
> Pavel Medvedev was commander of the guard keeping watch on the royal family at the Ipatiev house. In 1919 he was interrogated in Ekaterinburg on charges of conspiracy and murder. This is his evidence:
>
> "I, Pavel Spiridonovich Medvedev, 31 years of age, am Orthodox, literate, have never been charged with breaking the law, am of peasant origin...I took up duty the night of 16 July, and around 8 o'clock the same evening, Commander Yurovsky ordered me to confiscate all the Nagant revolvers in the detachment, and to bring them to him. I took revolvers from those at their posts and from some others, a total of twelve revolvers, and brought them to the commandant's office. Then Yurovsky said to me "Today we'll have to shoot everybody. Warn the detachment so they won't worry if they hear shots." I guessed that Yurovsky was talking about the shooting of the entire royal family and the doctor and servants who lived with them ... Around 2 o'clock in the morning the tsar, tsaritsa, four royal daughters, the maid, doctor, cook, and footman came out of their rooms. The tsar carried the heir in his arms. The sovereign and heir were dressed in soldiers' shirts and caps. Her Majesty and the daughters were in dresses with no outerwear and uncovered heads ... None of the members of the imperial family asked anybody any questions in my presence. There were no tears, no sobbing, either. Having descended the stairs leading from the second entrance hall to the lower floor, we went into the courtyard and from there through a second door (counting from the gates) into the inner lodgings of the lower floor. Yurovsky showed the way. They were brought into the corner room on the lower floor adjacent to the sealed storage room. Yurovsky ordered that chairs be brought ... It seems that all of them suspected the fate that was about to befall them, but no one made a single sound. Simultaneously, eleven people walked into the same room ... Yurovsky sent me out, saying "Go to the street, to see whether anybody's there and whether the shots will be heard." I walked out into the courtyard enclosed by a tall fence, and I heard the sound of shots before I had reached the street. I immediately returned to the house"

In July 1998, the Russian government staged an elaborate burial ceremony transporting the Romanov remains to St. Petersburg. But with the fate of two Romanovs still unknown, the tsar's family is unlikely to rest in peace.

MK-ULTRA

WERE GOVERNMENT ASSASSINS TRAINED WITH MIND-CONTROLLING DRUGS?

O n November 28, 1953, Dr. Frank Olson, an army scientist and chemical specialist, threw himself out the window of the Statler Hilton in New York City. It was only twenty years later that Olson's family learned of the events that led to his suicide, receiving an apology from President Ford and $570,000 in compensation. Nine days before his death Olson had attended a three-day retreat for a group of CIA and Army technicians in the secluded backwoods of Maryland. One evening, Dr. Sidney Gottlieb, the head of the CIA's Technical Service Staff (TSS) spiked Olson's after-diner cocktail with a dose of LSD, a powerful hallucinogenic drug. Olson reacted violently to the drug, experiencing increasingly severe bouts of depression and paranoia, and soon after, jumped to his death.

Gottlieb's ill-conceived experiment was one shameful chapter in the history of the CIA's top-secret program, MK-ULTRA. In the 1940s, the American government heard rumors that POW's in Korea were being brainwashed by communist intelligence groups and, enthused with Cold War ardor, was determined to develop a mind-control program of its own. Begun in April 1953, MK-ULTRA was its solution. MK-ULTRA was kept out of the limelight, deemed too sensitive to share with the public. Its chief architect, Richard Helms, a young newspaper executive and a future CIA director, kept the project—and its 149 "sub-projects"—hidden from all but the CIA's top brass.

By researching mind altering drugs and experimenting with techniques of narco-hypnosis—the combined use of drugs and rigorous hypnotic programming to gain control of a subject's mind—project leaders hoped to find methods of improving the resistance of American troops to interrogation, and of improving their own ability to extract information from enemy solders. The U.S. government began offering pharmaceutical companies large sums of money for their services as MK-ULTRA sponsored scientists routinely tested the effects of marijuana, heroin, sodium pentathol (the so called "truth drug"), and especially LSD, on

POPULAR SCIENCE Brainwashing—getting people to perform acts involuntarily—has always captivated public audiences, as on a 1950s British TV show (above). Some think Sirhan Sirhan (right), Robert Kennedy's assassin, was a subject of brainwashing.

subjects both witting and unwitting. The inmates of California's Vacaville State Prison were tested, and prostitutes were recruited to help administer drugs to their unsuspecting clients. An estimated 1,500 U.S. soldiers

GUT REACTION A character played by Frank Sinatra involuntarily lashed out at a Korean butler in the film "The Manchurian Candidate."

also participated in LSD research, many of whom later stated that they did so only after being pressured by their superiors.

MK-ULTRA scientists also researched psychoelectronics, testing the possibility of influencing the mind from afar with electrical forces, and with radio and microwave waves. One Yale University neurophysiologist, whose experiments were funded by the

Office of Naval Research, concluded that by implanting a small probe in the brain, "humans can be controlled like robots by pushing buttons." This possibility was MK-ULTRA's ultimate objective; one ominous CIA memorandum dated January 1952 asked, "Can we get control of an individual to the point where he will do our bidding against his will and even against the fundamental laws of nature such as self preservation?" If so, the CIA could create a class of spies, couriers, and assassins— "Manchurian Candidates" of John Frankenheimer's chilling 1962 film— all the more ruthless and effective for not knowing that they were in the government's service. Some conspiracy theorists asserted that Robert Kennedy's killer, Sirhan Sirhan, was actually such an assassin gone haywire, and wondered how many other convicted killers, languishing in prisons across the country, might have been casualties of MK-ULTRA research.

The CIA jealously guarded the secrecy of the project, but as details leaked, it began to come under attack from the public. MK-ULTRA was officially terminated in 1973, when Richard Helms quit the CIA and destroyed most of the project's files. But some people believe that the CIA continues to sponsor mind control experiments. They shudder at the prospect that the government has access to the ultimate private property— our minds.

THE CRASH OF THE HINDENBURG

WHY DID AN AIRSHIP THAT HAD BECOME SUCH A SYMBOL OF HITLER'S NEW GERMANY EXPLODE?

It is one of the most moving commentaries in the archives of recorded sound. The date was May 6, 1937, and radio journalist Herbert Morrison was reporting for WLS Chicago on the arrival in New Jersey of the giant German airship *Hindenburg*. The great Zeppelin with 97 people on board had been circling Lakehurst naval base for some time, waiting for storm clouds to pass, but at last it moved towards the mooring mast. "Here it comes, ladies and gentlemen, and what a sight it is, a thrilling one, a marvellous sight," Morrison told his listeners before suddenly breaking into an anguished scream. "Oh, oh, oh . . . It's burst into flames! . . . Get out of my way please, oh my this is terrible . . ."

The rear of the ship had exploded in a mass of incandescence and begun to sink groundwards, while passengers and crew jumped for their lives, screaming so loudly that they were heard by spectators on the ground. Herb Morrison broke down in tears, and a newsreel photographer muttered "Oh my God, oh my God" over and over as he tracked the flaring ship's descent. In just 32 seconds the whole flaming ball of hydrogen had completely burnt out, leaving only the twisted metal frame and a charred remnant of the swastika-emblazoned tailfin. Altogether, 20 crew members, 15 passengers and one member of the ground staff died.

SAILING THE SKIES Before the crash, Zeppelins epitomized luxurious air travel.

End of an era

What had caused the catastrophe? The great airship carried nearly 7 million cubic feet of hydrogen, a highly inflammable gas with obvious hazards. Nonetheless, safety precautions implemented on the *Hindenburg* were stringent, and the airship had already made many perfectly safe trips back and forth across the Atlantic. The best guess of baffled inquiry officials was that the hydrogen had been ignited after the thunderstorm by a freak discharge of static electricity known as St. Elmo's Fire. However, some of the ground staff believed that one of the *Hindenburg*'s engines was sparking badly, and that this might have ignited the gas.

Sabotage has also been suggested as a possible cause. The luxury airship was a

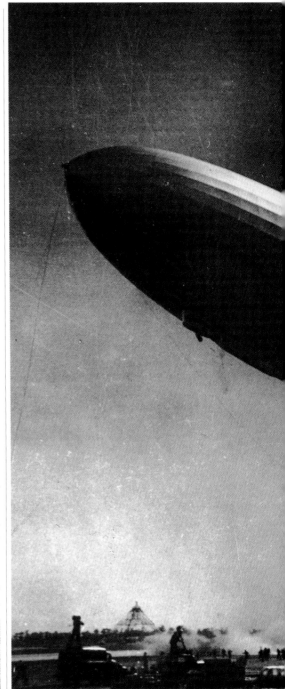

prestige product of Hitler's Germany, and as such a prime target for enemies of Nazism. Crew members had heard a bang like gunfire just before the ship burst into flames, and some of them suspected deliberate destruction. In his book about the disaster, published in 1972, Michael Mooney made the

FLY PAST At about 3 p.m. on the day of the crash, the *Hindenburg* passed over Manhattan en route to the Lakehurst landing ground. Far left: a luggage label.

1900 Count Ferdinand von Zeppelin flies over Lake Constance in a powered balloon, or airship

1909 Zeppelin inaugurates the world's first commercial airline

1929 A Zeppelin crosses the North Pole

1937 Crash of the *Hindenburg*

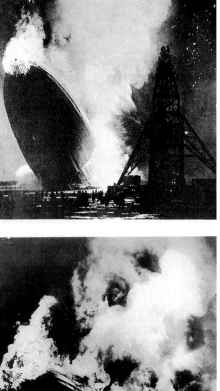

specific claim that the airship was sabotaged by crew member Eric Spehl. The 25-year-old German rigger had, it is alleged, placed an incendiary bomb on board as an act of anti-Nazi terrorism. This was due to explode after the ship had landed, but Spehl's plan went awry because of the delay caused by the storm. Mooney further claimed that German and American officials agreed to a cover-up to avoid an international incident.

True or not, the *Hindenburg* disaster had the historic consequence of putting an end

DISASTER STRIKES The giant dirigible crashes in flames following an explosion that occurred just as the airship was about to be moored to her mast.

to the age of airships. Powered balloons had, until then, been thought more suitable for passenger transport than winged aircraft, being more spacious and virtually silent. In the wake of the mystery crash, public feeling turned against them and airplanes became the preferred form of passenger flight.

1972 Michael Mooney
publishes *The Hindenburg*

THE NORMANDIE DISASTER

WAS IT SABOTAGE OR SIMPLY AN ACCIDENT THAT CAUSED THE FIRE THAT SANK THE PRIDE OF FRANCE?

The majestic *Normandie* was the pride of France's passenger fleet during the 1930s. The largest of the inter-war Atlantic liners, weighing 83,000 tons, she could carry 2,170 passengers and traveled at a mean speed of 31.2 knots. This won her the Blue Riband award for the quickest Atlantic crossing by a recognized shipping route.

When France fell to the Germans in 1940, the *Normandie* was in New York harbor where she was placed under restraint by the U.S. authorities. After Pearl Harbor, when the United States entered the Second World War, she was expropriated by the U.S. Maritime Commission for conversion into a troopship. The plan was to relaunch her as the USS *Lafayette*, and more than 3,000 workmen began the task of refitting her.

On February 9, 1942, a catastrophic fire engulfed one of the lower decks. For 12

OUT OF ACTION The flame-charred hull of the *Normandie* lies on its side at the Hudson River Pier in New York, presenting the U.S. Navy with a mighty salvage job.

hours the flames roared, and while the asphyxiating fumes and smoke blackened parts of New York City, the liner capsized at her pier and sank into the harbor mud, with her funnels poking above the water.

A subsequent investigation concluded that an acetylene torch had ignited a pile of kapok—the waterproof cotton-like stuffing

UNDER RESTRAINT The French passenger liner SS *Normandie*, at the pier in New York, was due for refitting for troop transport when the disaster occurred.

used to fill life jackets. But the timing of the disaster was suspicious. The accident occurred just one day after the *Normandie* had been turned over to the U.S. Navy. Why did the fire spread so quickly? Why did it take so long for the New York fire ser-

vice to be alerted? And why were the ship's hose fittings being changed at the moment the blaze broke out? Some blamed sabotage, either by Germany or by French Nazi-sympathizers, for the loss of the vessel, and the controversy endures to this day.

1932 The *Normandie* is launched at the Saint-Nazaire shipyard in France
1940 France falls to the Germans
1942 The *Normandie* sinks in New York harbor

THE KATYN GRAVES

THE FATE OF 15,000 POLISH SOLDIERS HAS REMAINED A MYSTERY UNTIL THE LAST FEW YEARS

On April 13, 1943, Berlin radio announced that the bodies of some 10,000 Polish officers had been unearthed from seven mass graves in a forest at Katyn, near the Russian city of Smolensk, which was occupied during the German advance. The figure was an exaggeration—in reality, the dead numbered about 4,500. But the discovery bore witness to what was undoubtedly one of the worst atrocities of the 20th century. All the signs pointed to a massacre: the officers, hands bound, had mostly been shot in the back of the head. The Nazis blamed the Russians for it, and the Polish govern-

COLD-BLOODED SLAUGHTER Mass graves uncovered in the Katyn forest in 1943 contained the bodies of 4,500 Polish soldiers.

ment-in-exile broke off diplomatic relations with the Soviet Union. In 1944, when the Red Army recaptured Katyn, the Russians countered with the claim that the Nazis had been responsible for the atrocity.

Gunshots were heard

With Europe still gripped by war there was no way of proving anyone culpable, but the evidence suggested that Stalin was the guilty party. In 1939, the Red Army had occupied part of Poland and transported some 15,000 Polish officers and intellectuals from their sector back to three labor camps in Soviet-occupied territory. Most of these men remained in the camps until April 1940 when they mysteriously disappeared. It was reported that 4,500 prisoners from the camp at Kozielsk were shipped by cattle train to Katyn. Day after

UNEASY ALLIANCE Stalin greets von Ribbentrop during the 1939 Nazi-Soviet pact. Both sides later blamed the other for the Katyn massacre.

day in the early months of 1940, local peasants saw men spilling out of the wagons and being driven into the woods. Soviet troops with picks and spades were also seen, and gunshots were heard. It is believed that the victims were lined up in rows while the Russians shot them one by one before rolling them into a pit.

In 1990 the Soviet Union admitted responsibility for the massacre of all 15,000 Poles; according to a news bulletin, the killings were "one of the greatest crimes of Stalinism." But although this ended speculation about one of the great unsolved crimes of modern times, it failed to locate the whereabouts of the remaining bodies. Are there other mass graves waiting to be found?

1939 15,000 Polish men transported to Soviet-held territory
1943 The Germans announce discovery
of the mass graves

1985 Gorbachev becomes
leader of the Soviet Union
1990 Soviets admit
to Katyn massacre

HOW DID HITLER DIE?

RECENTLY RELEASED ARCHIVES SOLVE SOME OF THE PROBLEMS SURROUNDING HITLER'S FINAL HOURS

On the evening of May 1, 1945, Hamburg Radio announced the death of Hitler who had, it was said, fallen that afternoon fighting "at the head of his troops." Like much of the information that issued from Germany's wartime propaganda machine, this was, in fact, a lie. At the close of the war in Europe, as the Allies advanced through the bombed-out rubble of the Reich, the Führer was not at the Front but in a Berlin bunker, ranting about the betrayals that had brought him down.

In that bunker, the history books now record, he killed himself. But throughout the summer of 1945, rumors circulated that the Nazi leader was still alive: he had found refuge at Innsbruck, or in a moated Westphalian castle. He was sighted living as a shepherd in the Swiss Alps, as a recluse in a cave near Italy's Lake Garda, and as a casino croupier at Evian in France. Hitler was living in custom-built underground quarters at a German-owned hacienda in Argentina,

INSIDE THE BUNKER

As the Allies approached Berlin in 1945, life in Hitler's bunker became increasingly fraught. The bunker was built on two levels, connected by a spiral staircase. On the upper level were the servants' quarters and the dining area, and on the lower level 18 rooms including the map room, a conference area, the generator, toilets and the bedrooms of Eva Braun, Goebbels and Hitler himself. The ceilings were low, the corridors narrow and conditions cramped. Condensation dripped from the walls, and, as Hitler became increasingly nervous, the body odor for which he was well known got worse.

with a stone-walled entrance operated by photo-electric cells...

In September 1945, an official inquiry into Hitler's death was set up by the British to establish the truth. It was led by Hugh Trevor-Roper, a young army major who was also an historian by training. Having tracked down witnesses from the Führer's last days, he concluded that Hitler had committed suicide in the Berlin bunker—a suite of rooms 50 feet beneath the gardens of the Reich

Chancellery. At about 3:30 pm on April 30, 1945, the Nazi leader had put a pistol in his mouth and pulled the trigger. Eva Braun, his mistress whom he had married the day before, had taken a cyanide capsule and died with him. Trevor-Roper's report, published in 1947 as *The Last Days of Hitler*, became the classic work on the subject.

MASTER OF LIES   A newspaper falsely proclaims Hitler's death in battle: Hitler and Eva Braun probably committed suicide.

But the all-important question of Hitler's remains was still an unresolved mystery. According to the reports, the corpses of Hitler and Eva were taken up to the

WAR'S END Investigators in 1945 found fragments of Hitler's clothing among Eva Braun's possessions, and explored the wreckage of the Berlin bunker (below).

The attitude of the Soviet authorities compounded the mystery. The Russians were the first to reach Berlin, and were known to have dug up a number of bodies in the Reich Chancellery garden. Among the remains were said to have been Hitler's teeth—identified by a woman who was assistant to the Führer's dentist—but for more than 20 years, the Soviets refused to comment on any such finds. Then, in 1968, a book written by a Russian journalist, Lev Bezymenski, described how in 1945 Soviet troops had recovered the charred bodies of Hitler and Eva Braun from a bomb crater in the Reich Chancellery garden. Doctors, he claimed, had identified them by their dental work and carried out autopsies. The smell of bitter almonds emanated from their bodies, indicating poisoning by cyanide.

Recent revelations

More sensational revelations were yet to come. In 1992, in the new climate of freedom in Russia, a researcher named Ada Petrova was given access to six secret files on Hitler's death, which had been hidden in the KGB archives. These revealed that, at the war's end, the Russians had taken extraordinary pains to find out precisely what had hap-

Chancellery garden, doused with gas and set alight so that they should burn, as the Führer had ordered, "until nothing remained." However, Trevor-Roper himself acknowledged that although a gas fire might char the bodies beyond recognition, the bones would have withstood the heat. Hitler's bones have never been found. What had happened?

Some continued to doubt whether the Führer was dead at all: Hitler sightings continued for decades after the report was published, and as late as 1992 a Canadian newspaper reported the death of the Führer in Latin America. Even among those who accepted the idea of a suicide in the bunker, there was controversy. Did Hitler really shoot himself in soldierly fashion? Or did he take poison—an act perceived to be a coward's way out? There were some discrepancies in the reports, and, with no remains available for analysis, these questions remained open to debate.

pened to the Nazi leader. Some 800 people were interrogated, and 70 were brought back to Russia for long-term questioning, along with a mass of material from the bunker. Stalin, it is known, had been skeptical about Hitler's death and wanted to be absolutely certain that the Führer had not escaped. Among the material in the Soviet archives were Hitler's uniforms, his photograph album and 42 watercolors by the Nazi leader. There were also pictures from the Chancellery of a man bearing a striking resemblance to Hitler, who seemed to have been shot through the forehead. This was not Hitler himself but his double—a man named Gustav Weler who was employed in the Chancellery and occasionally wheeled out in suitable costume to stand in for the Nazi leader. He either shot himself, or was shot, in the last days before the fall of Berlin. When the Russians

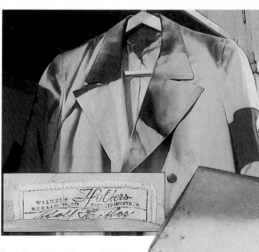

NEW FINDS Hitler's fire-scorched uniform (with his name sewn on the inside of the armband) and a sketchbook, containing 42 watercolors painted by the Führer, were among the relics that came to light in the 1990s, when the KGB archives were opened up.

AFTER THE FALL Soviet ministers and officials visit what was left of Hitler's Bunker in May 1945.

first came upon his corpse they mistook him for the Führer himself.

Crucial among the finds in the Soviet archives were fragments of what was alleged to be Hitler's skull, burnt at the edges, with

MACABRE RELICS Using dental records, researchers believe that they have identified fragments of Hitler's lower jaw (right) and upper jaw (far right). A bullet-hole is clearly visible in a piece of his skull (below).

the exit wound of a bullet hole clearly visible in one of them. This astonishing relic indicated that the Führer had, indeed, shot himself. Piecing together the evidence, researchers proposed a theory in which the Nazi leader had taken poison *and* shot himself, placing a cyanide capsule in his mouth before firing a pistol through the underside of his chin.

Some critics have doubted the authenticity of the finds, suggesting that the forensic evidence was faked, perhaps by Soviet bureaucrats who were under consid-

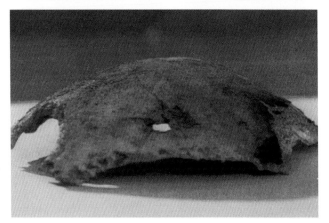

erable pressure to convince a deeply suspicious Stalin that his old rival really was dead. Why, if the finds were genuine, did the Russians not make them public sooner? The answer may lie in their discovery that Hitler did shoot himself; Stalin would have preferred a coward's death for the Nazi leader. Besides, the Soviet secret services were notoriously secretive about everything. Who knows whose interests the silence best served?

DETECTION AND DNA

Is the "Hitler skull" in Moscow truly a relic of Germany's wartime Nazi leader? A DNA analysis could help to resolve this problem, just as it has helped to clear up mysteries surrounding the last Russian Tsar's family, and many criminal cases besides. Genetic fingerprinting has revolutionized forensic science in the late 20th century. The technique derived in the 1980s from research into DNA, an acid in the nucleus of every living cell which carries genetic information. This determines a person's individual characteristics, such as the color of hair and eyes, and the structure is different in everybody (except identical twins). As a result, a person's DNA profile is as distinctive as his or her fingerprint.

To obtain a specimen, scientists work from a tiny sample containing some human cells: a spot of blood, for example, or a single hair. To produce a visual record, the genetic information is translated into a series of bars on an X-Ray film; the result resembles the bar code printed on a consumer product. There is enough cellular material in human saliva to take a reading from a cigarette butt left at the scene of a crime, or an envelope licked by a blackmailer.

The technique can be employed in paternity disputes, because the DNA of father and child match more closely than the DNA of unrelated individuals. It is through surviving relatives of Hitler that identification of "his" skull could be achieved. The remains of another prominent Nazi, Josef Mengele, have already been analyzed with the help of DNA fingerprinting. In 1985, the supposed body of this notorious concentration camp doctor was exhumed from a grave outside Sao Paulo in Brazil. DNA samples from the body closely matched samples from Mengele's son and, combined with dental and skeleton analysis, helped to fix the corpse's identity as that of Josef Mengele, Auschwitz's "Angel of Death."

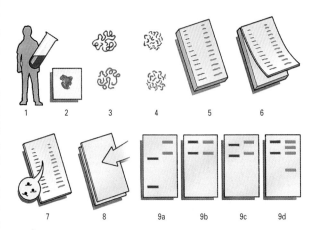

GENETIC FINGERPRINTING Blood is taken from the suspect (1) and from the crime scene (2). DNA is extracted (3) and cut into fragments (4), which are sorted by length (5). The DNA fragments are transferred to a nylon membrane (6). Light-emitting probes locate the fragments of interest (7), and these are photographed (8) for comparison (9). Only 9b matches.

Forensic evidence

In 1995, an independent Russian expert, Professor Viktor Zyagin from the Federal Center of Medical Forensic Examination, declared himself 80 percent certain that the skull was Hitler's. He even deduced, from the color of the pieces of skull, that its owner had been a vegetarian—as Hitler was. But the story need not end there: an absolute confirmation could still come from DNA fingerprinting. Some relatives of Hitler are still alive, and tests on them could be matched against analysis of the skull bones to see whether genetic material is common to both. One way or another, such an investigation could help to answer one of the most enduring mysteries of modern history.

DOUBLES FOR DECEPTION

IN THE INCREASINGLY SOPHISTICATED WORLD OF DELUSION AND DISINFORMATION, LOOKALIKES ARE USED AS DECOYS

Lieutenant M.E. Clifton James was at his desk at the Royal Army Pay Corps in 1944, when he received a telephone call from film star Colonel David Niven, who was serving with the Army Kinematograph section during the Second World War.

The call was the first thread in an elaborate web of deception intended to draw attention away from the imminent Allied invasion of Europe. James, who had fought in the trenches during the First World War, was a peacetime actor who happened to bear an extraordinarily close physical resemblance to General Montgomery, the victor of El Alamein and the commander-in-chief of all ground forces for the Normandy landings of 1944. Security chiefs hatched a plan which involved using James to impersonate Monty. Monty's double was then to be dispatched to Gibraltar and North Africa in order to delude the Germans that Monty was going to lead an invasion from southern France, rather than from Normandy.

Under conditions of the utmost secrecy, James was posted as a Sergeant of the Intelligence Corps to Monty's staff so that he could study the general's voice, gestures and mannerisms: the way he saluted, for example, clasped his hands behind his back, or pinched a little roll of his cheek when thinking. As an actor, James had little

I WAS MONTY'S DOUBLE Lookalike Lieutenant Clifton James (left) was asked to impersonate Britain's General Montgomery (right) during the build-up to the D-Day landings in 1944.

difficulty in mastering Monty's every movement, but he was more worried about his ability to capture Monty's personality. "It was so unique and overpowering," he wrote in his classic *I Was Monty's Double*, "that I despaired of ever *being* him. It was one thing to ape the outside of a man, but quite another to acquire something of his fire and forcefulness."

James underestimated his abilities. After several rehearsals, he flew as General Montgomery to Gibraltar, where he was greeted by the British Governor and introduced—as if by chance—to several of Hitler's known secret agents. A similar performance was then repeated in Algiers, where he was cheered by Allied troops. News of "Monty's" whereabouts traveled fast—transmitted by enemy agents back to the German High Command. James's performance was as fine as any he ever gave and contributed in no small way to the success of what his British Secret Service handler described as "one of the greatest plans of deception that has ever been attempted."

The German leader, Adolf Hitler, also employed a double. The man's name was Gustav Weler and he was an employee at the Reich Chancellery in Berlin, occasionally brought out to stand in for the Führer. When Russian troops discovered Weler's corpse in 1945, they believed, at first, that they had found Hitler's body.

In more recent years it has been widely reported that the Iraqi leader, Saddam Hussein, uses a double as a decoy to foil would-be assassins. His 1990 invasion of Kuwait and his savage repression of Shi'ites and Kurds have made him a prime target; he is known to have survived at least 12 attempts on his life.

HITLER'S DOUBLE The body of the Führer's impersonator, Gustav Weler, was found in the bunker beneath the Reich Chancellery garden with a bullet hole in the forehead.

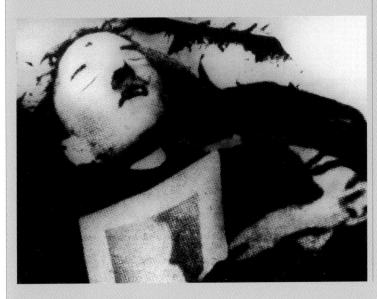

THE DEATH OF STALIN

DID THE SOVIET DICTATOR'S POWER-HUNGRY POLITICAL RIVALS ALLOW STALIN TO DIE?

On January 13, 1953, the Russian newspaper *Pravda* announced that security police had arrested nine distinguished doctors and accused them of conspiring to kill Soviet leaders. The prosecution alleged that the conspirators were agents of Zionist and Western intelligence organizations, and among them was V.N. Vinogradov, until recently personal doctor to the Soviet leader, Joseph Stalin.

The trumped-up charges suggested to foreign observers that Stalin was raising the curtain on a new terror, comparable perhaps to that of the 1930s. Particularly disquieting was the fact that six of the nine doctors named were Jewish, provoking concern about a coming pogrom. But all senior party figures must have quivered at the announcement; no one knew who would be accused next.

The dying days of a dictator

Long years of despotic rule had made Stalin suspicious to the point of paranoia, but he had good reason to feel uneasy at this time. He was 73 years old, and ailing in health. Other, ambitious men were waiting in the wings; Stalin had even come to doubt the loyalty of old comrades such as Lavrenti Beria, the Soviet secret police chief, and Nikita Khrushchev, head of the Party secretariat. Early in 1953, Stalin started elevating younger men to positions of authority in order to dilute the power of the old guard.

It was against this backdrop of suspicion and menace that, on March 1, 1953, Stalin suddenly collapsed, apparently from a stroke. At about 10:30 p.m. an anxious bodyguard broke into his rooms where the Soviet leader was found lying on the carpet, partially paralyzed and unable to speak. Asked what was wrong, he replied with an incoherent buzzing sound. His pocketwatch and a copy of *Pravda* were lying on the floor beside him. Stalin was moved to a couch and, while Beria and other colleagues were summoned, word was also sent to his family. Stalin's son Vasily had no doubt about what had happened; while the dictator lay dying he raged around the apartment shouting in a drunken voice: "They've killed my father!"

Was Stalin murdered—and if so, by whom? If there was foul play, the sinister Beria, who—as well as running the internal security services—administered the Soviet Union's labor camps, or "gulags," has been singled out as the likeliest candidate for the role of assassin. It took Stalin more than three days to die, and throughout the long

HARD MAN Notorious for his ruthless repression of dissent, the Soviet leader was born Joseph Djugashvili. Stalin (Russian for "man of steel") was an adopted name.

1900 Stalin joins a Georgian revolutionary organization

1917 The Russian Revolution

1922 Stalin becomes General Secretary of the Communist Party's central committee

1934 Murder of Kirov and the start of the purges

1941 Germany invades Russia, precipitating the Soviet Union's entry into the Second World War

HEIRS APPARENT Marshal Bulganin (above, left) and Nikita Khrushchev (above, right) came to prominence when Stalin died. Beria (right) was tried and executed.

ordeal of waiting, while others wept or lay slumped in states of exhaustion around the apartment, the secret police chief was torn by conflicting emotions and interests. As Khrushchev later remembered: "As soon as Stalin showed signs of consciousness, Beria threw himself on his knees, seized Stalin's hand and started kissing it. When Stalin lost consciousness again and closed his eyes, Beria stood up and spat . . . spewing hatred." It was not long, however, before Beria conspicuously took control, behaving as if he were heir apparent to the vast Soviet empire.

LYING IN STATE Top Soviet statesmen, jockeying for power, conceal their differences at Stalin's death watch.

Long after Stalin's death, rumors of a top-level conspiracy persisted, and indeed the Soviet politician Anastas Mikoyan later confided to the Albanian leader Enver Hoxha that he and others had discussed killing Stalin. However, there is no evidence that he was murdered by anything so compromising as, for example, poisoning or lethal injection. It is more likely that Stalin suffered a stroke, and that arrangements were subsequently made to deny medical care to the ailing despot. Beria arrived at Stalin's apartment at about 3 o'clock in the morning on March 2, with the Soviet politician Georgi Malenkov. Doctors did not arrive until 8:30 or even 9 a.m. By then Stalin had been left untreated for at least ten hours. Had Beria been keen for a recovery, medical help would certainly have arrived much sooner.

The struggle for power

The end came for Stalin at 9:50 p.m. on March 5, 1953. According to his daughter Svetlana, who defected to the West in 1967: 'The death agony was terrible. God grants an easy death

---

REIGN OF TERROR

On December 1, 1934, Sergei Kirov, a rising star in the Communist Party and a potential rival, was assassinated—almost certainly at Stalin's instigation. The murder heralded waves of "show trials" and purges, in which as many as 20 million Russians lost their lives—more than twice the number who died in the Holocaust.

---

only to the just. . ."

A savage power struggle ensued immediately. Police chief Beria made the early run-

PERSONALITY CULT A propaganda poster of 1939 proclaims: "Our army and our country are strengthened with the spirit of Stalin!"

ning, ordering tanks and flame-throwers to seal off Moscow and prevent unrest at the dictator's funeral. One of Stalin's top aides later disappeared, and key members of the Politburo were ousted from their posts. But it was Khrushchev who emerged victorious in the end. Beria was accused of conspiracy in July, tried secretly and executed in December. As for the famous doctors' plot, the whole affair was pronounced a "criminal hoax" and quickly forgotten. Within a month of Stalin's death, the accused physicians were fully rehabilitated and reinstalled in the Kremlin Medical Service.

1953 Stalin dies
Khrushchev consolidates his power and is
appointed First Secretary of the central committee

WAS DAG HAMMARSKJOLD MURDERED?

HOW THE MYSTERIOUS DEATH OF ONE MAN THREATENED THE FUTURE OF THE UNITED NATIONS

No one who becomes Secretary-General of the United Nations can expect an easy life. Sweden's Dag Hammarskjold, who took up the post in 1953, plunged into the anguish of Cold War confrontation, the Suez Crisis of 1956 and the Hungarian rising against Soviet control, also in 1956. In 1960 a new crisis developed in the Congo (later Zaire) where a bloody civil war broke out on the granting of independence to the former Belgian colony in central Africa. While the rebel statesman Moise Tshombe led the secession of the copper-rich Katanga province, Prime Minister Patrice Lumumba was deposed and murdered. Hammarskjold himself faced criticism for the way the United Nations had handled the transition to independence, and condemnation was particularly loud when UN troops from Sweden, Ireland and India were

INDEPENDENCE DAY Patrice Lumumba became the first prime minister of an independent Belgian Congo.

involved in fighting while attempting to end Katanga's secession.

This was the turbulent background to Hammarskjold's last flight. In September 1961 the secretary-general received an invitation from the rebel Tshombe to meet for peace talks at Ndola in neutral Northern Rhodesia (now Zambia). The idea was that Hammarskjold should fly from the capital of the Congo, Leopoldville (now Kinshasa), in a DC4 Skymaster plane, but he switched at the last minute to a DC6 airliner in order to evade the crowds of waiting newsmen. The plane took off in the middle of the afternoon, and after about four hours the pilot contacted the control tower at Ndola airport announcing his intention to descend for landing. Oddly, though, the four-engined DC-6B failed to come down at the expected time of arrival. It was not until two and a half hours later that the airliner began to approach the airfield, and when it did so it came in from the southwest, flying from deep inside Rhodesian territory. The assumption was that it had overshot its target by some distance and was now backtracking. There was nothing, however, to suggest any difficulty as the DC6's Swedish pilot radioed that he had the runway lights in sight and was coming down.

As ground staff peered into the darkness, they saw a burst of flame and watched in horror as the burning aircraft crashed, incandescent, into the jungle beyond the runway. When rescue workers reached the wreckage, they found that 13 of the 14 passengers were dead, including Hammarskjold, his body sprawled in the aisle.

Accident or assassination?

It might have been an accident. The DC6 was a UN plane which had been peppered by Congolese anti-aircraft fire on the day before it took off on the fateful flight. It had been only hastily fixed afterwards, and maps detailing the approach to Ndola were missing from the pilot's flight-briefing book. Moreover, the altimeter was faulty, and would have given an incorrect reading of the plane's height above the ground. A Rhodesian inquiry concluded that the crash

FINAL FAREWELL Dag Hammarskjold (left) confers with an Italian representative at the United Nations, only weeks before his funeral (above).

was indeed an accident, and put it down to pilot error. According to the official version, the plane struck a tree with its wingtip as it turned for its final approach.

But such a crash, in the midst of sensitive negotiations, raised inevitable suspicions of foul play. In New Delhi, the Indian Prime Minister Pandit Nehru was among the first to suggest that the plane might have been sabotaged. And it was certainly true that there were people on both sides of the civil war who might have wanted to see the peace talks fail. Dag Hammarskjold was not universally

SMOLDERING RUINS Rescuers work amidst the wreckage of the airliner that crashed in the African bush, 8 miles from Ndola, killing 13 passengers including Hammarskjold.

A puzzling detail was supplied by the sole survivor of the disaster, Harold Julian, an American security officer with the United Nations. Terribly burned, and suffering from broken bones, he was to recover consciousness only for a brief period after the crash.

Unanswered questions

Questioned at his bedside about the missing two hours, when the plane seemed to have overshot Ndola airport, the injured man answered that "Mr Hammarskjold told us to turn back, he didn't say why," and that, moments later, a series of explosions had preceded the crash. Police at Ndola saw a "huge flare in the sky, seconds before the crash."

Harold Julian died without being able to elucidate further. Had the secretary-general

admired. Soviet leader Nikita Khrushchev had dubbed him a "bloody-handed lackey of the colonial powers," and in the United Nations, the Russian delegate dissociated his government from a communiqué which praised Hammarskjold's leadership. When Khrushchev called for his removal, Hammarskjold responded by claiming that "by resigning I would ... at the present difficult and dangerous juncture, throw the organization to the winds."

In the twisted wreckage of the DC6, scraps of evidence hinted at something more than pilot error. Tucked into the lapel of Dag Hammarskjold's jacket, for example, was a playing card—the Ace of Spades, the mark of death. How did it get there? A revolver was found in the wreckage only a few feet from Hammarskjold's body. There were bullet holes, too, in the fuselage. Were these relics of an earlier attack on the plane, or had there been a gunfight in the cabin? Had someone tampered with the altimeter so that it gave false readings? And how to explain one witness's report of hearing jets whistle above the airport just before the airliner plunged burning into the forest?

HOMEWARD JOURNEY The coffin holding Dag Hammarskjold's remains is borne by federal policemen towards a plane for its return from Salisbury, Southern Rhodesia, to Sweden.

suddenly doubted the wisdom of the meeting? Had he been warned of something by a fellow passenger? Questions like these torment researchers, and history furnishes no clear answers. Although the Rhodesian inquiry settled for pilot error, the UN's commission declared the crash "unexplained."

REBEL LEADER Moise Tshombe, who headed the breakaway province of Katanga, was imprisoned in Algeria where he died in 1969.

WHO KILLED PRESIDENT KENNEDY?

CONSPIRACY THEORIES STILL SURROUND THE MURDER THAT SENT THE WORLD INTO MOURNING

The assassination traumatized the United States, wrenching at the psyche of the world's most powerful nation with such shocking force that the American Dream has never truly recovered.

On Friday, November 22, 1963, cheering crowds lined the streets of Dallas, Texas, as the young President John F. Kennedy moved in a motorcade through the metal-and-glass

conservative elements within Texas's Democratic Party, and he hoped to raise funds and political support for his presidential re-election campaign the following year. The crowds were enthusiastic as he waved from his open limousine. "Mr Kennedy, you can't say Dallas doesn't love you," said Mrs Connally, wife of the Governor of Texas, who was also in the car.

Then, as the motorcade moved slowly through Dealey Plaza just after 12.30 p.m., several shots rang out in quick succession. Kennedy lurched; in front of him Governor Connally was hit in the chest and head; there was more gunfire and the president jerked backwards, his head partially exploding in a shower of blood. Jackie Kennedy, in

MORNING NEWS A Dallas newspaper announces the shooting. Vice-president Lyndon Baines Johnson swiftly succeeded to the presidency.

the Kennedy shooting, a second murder was reported. A police patrolman had been shot dead a couple of miles from Dealey Plaza, and a young man was arrested in a nearby movie house. The suspect, said to have a pistol in his waistband, was hustled out of the theater. He was charged in due course not only with the patrolman's murder but also with the assassination of President Kennedy.

The young man's name was Lee Harvey Oswald, and over the next two days he faced

IN THE FRAME A film taken by Dallas dress manufacturer Abraham Zapruder (right) is the most accurate record of the assassination. Lee Harvey Oswald (below) was presumed to be the assassin.

FATEFUL MOTORCADE A smiling President John F. Kennedy, with Jackie at his side, rides through Dallas only moments before his assassination on November 22, 1963.

city sweltering in summer sunshine. The president had been apprehensive about his visit, for Dallas was politically hostile territory, but he needed to reconcile liberal and

a blood-spattered pink suit, cradled her husband as the driver raced the car to nearby Parkland Hospital. There Connally's life was saved. But there could be no hope for Kennedy. "The president is gone," Mrs. Kennedy was told.

Numb with the shock of the assassination, a worldwide audience was to follow its aftermath with disbelief. Only 45 minutes after

1917 Birth of John F. Kennedy

1943 Kennedy heroically rescues a burnt crewman when his torpedo boat is sunk by a Japanese destroyer in the South Pacific

1

2

3

4

5

6

7

8

9

10

11

12

13

14

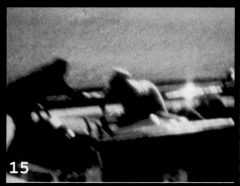
15

1950   2000

1952 Kennedy is   1960 Kennedy is elected president   1979 The House Select
elected a senator   of the United States, the youngest ever   Committee on Assassinations
for Massachusetts   1963 President Kennedy is assassinated   reports its findings

IN THE MATTER OF SACCO AND VANZETTI

WERE TWO INNOCENT MEN EXECUTED BECAUSE OF THEIR RADICAL POLITICAL BELIEFS?

On April 15, 1920, two gunmen, described by witnesses as "short, dark, foreign types," robbed and fatally wounded a guard and a paymaster of the Slater-Merrill Shoe Company in South Braintree, Massachusetts, escaping with $16,000 in employee wages. One month later, state police raided a "safe house," suspected of sheltering fugitive political terrorists, in nearby Staughton. Among those taken in the raid were Nicola Sacco, a shoemaker, and Bartolomeo Vanzetti, a fish peddler, two Italian immigrants who had come to the United States twelve years before. Sacco and Vanzetti, their names forever linked in the annals of American history, were both outspoken advocates of anarchism, as well as fiery union organizers. Though both men had sound alibis, they were quickly arrested and charged with the shoe factory murder. Police found a .32 Colt pistol in Sacco's possession, which ballistic experts later testified was the type of gun used to kill the paymaster. Vanzetti was also carrying a loaded .38 Harrington and a Richardson revolver. Witnesses to the crime identified the two men as the culprits, and others came forward to claim that they had seen Vanzetti behind the wheel of the getaway car. The two were brought to trial in the Dedham County Court, and on July 14, 1921, were found guilty of armed robbery and murder. The presiding judge, Webster Thomas Thayer, unimpressed by their claims of innocence, sentenced both men to death.

At first, the pair, with their thick accents and suspect politics, had few defenders outside of radical circles. But their lawyer, William Thompson, skillfully postponed the execution date, publicizing the perceived injustice of the court, and drawing attention to the case's symbolic importance. Soon Sacco and Vanzetti's innocence became a cause célèbre, especially among liberals and intellectuals, who claimed that the conviction was a form of political persecution, motivated by the basest forms of xenophobia and the rampant fear of anarchism. Sacco and Vanzetti's advocates pointed out the political and racial biases harbored by various members of the prosecution team, including the Attorney General Mitchell Palmer, who had campaigned for the deportation of alien radicals the year before. By late 1925 a national "Sacco and Vanzetti Defense Committee" had been organized, and mass demonstrations were held in several major American cities. The movement's efforts were furthered considerably in 1926, when a convicted killer awaiting execution confessed to participating in the robbery and fingered another Italian gang as the killers.

THE DEFENDANTS Sacco (right) and Vanzetti were, in spite of their radical political views, mild-mannered and soft-spoken.

RALLYING TO THE CAUSE The Sacco and Vanzetti case was a rallying point for political protest across America.

SPEAKING FOR THE DEFENSE

William Thompson, Sacco and Vanzetti's legal counsel, described his final conversation with Vanzetti on the day of their execution. "I told Vanzetti that although my belief in his innocence had all the time been strengthened both by my study of the evidence and by my increasing knowledge of his personality, yet there was a chance, however remote, that I might be mistaken; and that I thought he ought for my sake, in the closing hour of his life, when nothing could save him, to give me his most solemn reassurance. . . that while, looking back, he now realized more clearly than he ever had, the grounds of the suspicion against him and Sacco. He felt that no allowance had been made for his ignorance of the American points of view and habits of thought, or for his fear as a radical and almost as an outlaw, and that in reality he was convicted on evidence which would not have convicted him had he not been an anarchist, so that he was in a very real sense dying for his cause. At parting he gave me a firm clasp of the hand and a steady glance, which revealed unmistakably the depth of his feeling.

1920 Two gunmen rob the Slater-Merrill Shoe Company, killing a guard

1927 Sacco and Vanzetti are executed for the crime

Sacco and Vanzetti's cause was also championed by Harvard professor Felix Frankfurter, who wrote a scathing denunciation of Thayer's decision in Atlantic Monthly, calling the trial a "farrago of misquotations, misrepresentations, suppressions and mutilations." The president of Harvard, A. Lawrence Lowell, was so moved by the article's forceful logic that he passed it on to the Governor of Massachusetts, Allen T. Fuller. Impressed by Frankfurter's arguments and conscious of mounting public unease with Judge Thayer's decision, Fuller convened a special three-member commission, with Lowell at its head, to review the case. However, after months of deliberation and investigation, the committee upheld the original verdict, advising against clemency.

The Lowell commission's decision was met with outrage by intellectuals across the country, many of who mistrusted the judicial establishment, and Sacco and Vanzetti's innocence became their rallying cry. A columnist, Heywood Broun, lambasted the commission members in the New York World, writing "we have the right to beat against tight minds with our fists and shout into the ears of the old men. We want to know, we will know, 'Why?'" Walter Lippman, in a full-page editorial in the New York World, labeled the nation's dissatisfaction with the verdict the "doubt that will not die down." The intensity of the protests increased as the date of the execution neared. Protesters camped outside the Boston courthouse; the poet Edna St. Vincent Millay was arrested during one demonstration. Writers and public figures such as George Bernard Shaw, Albert Einstein, H.G. Wells and Jane Adamms made desperate appeals for clemency, but to no avail.

As a last resort, Sacco and Vanzetti's lawyers appealed to Supreme Court Justice Oliver Wendell Holmes, whom they felt might be sympathetic to their cause. But on August 21 Holmes announced his refusal to stay the execution; he later told friends that he believed that Sacco and Vanzetti were

"THE PASSION OF SACCO AND VANZETTI" Artist Ben Shan's tribute critiqued the trial and sentence.

ANARCHISM

Since ancient times, anarchists have maintained that every form of government control is immoral, and have promoted a society based on voluntary cooperation and free association. The tactics of terror, for which they are now known, were not explicitly linked to anarchism until the ascendancy of the Russian revolutionary Mikhail Bakunin. Many American anarchists were supporters of Bakunin, as was Leon Czolgosz, who in 1901, assassinated President William McKinley. The nation quickly moved to protect itself from this new and powerful threat. In March 1910, Congress amended the Immigration Act of 1907, prohibiting criminals, anarchists, and diseased persons from entering the United States. Then on June 2, 1919, an anarchist planted a bomb on the front steps of the office of the U.S. Attorney General, A. Mitchell Palmer. Though the bomb exploded prematurely, killing only the anarchist, the incident provoked Palmer into launching the infamous "red raids," which resulted in the arrest of thousands of dissenters across the country, and the deportations of some 500 foreigners. Palmer's actions had the opposite of the desired effect. By the time of the Slater-Merrill Shoe Company murder, anarchists were truly at war with the nation. And indeed, after Sacco and Vanzetti's execution, anarchists around the country swore revenge. They made good on their promise: Six months later the executioner's house was bombed, and on September 27, 1932, Judge Thayer's house was bombed as well.

guilty. Thus, the longest deathwatch in the nation's history ended on August 23, 1927, when first Sacco and then Vanzetti were executed in the electric chair at Boston's Charleston prison. Both maintained their innocence till the very end. Vanzetti's last words stung the nation's conscience: "I have never done a crime, some sins, but never any crime…I now wish to forgive some people for what they are doing to me. Long live anarchy!"

Both men embraced the symbolic role of martyr the nation thrust upon them. Both realized that the case was larger than the question of their own guilt, highlighting as it did the danger lurking within unchecked government power. They were willing to die for a cause whose nobility they never doubted. As Sacco declared before his death, "If I was arrested because of the Idea [of anarchy] I am glad to suffer. But they have arrested me for a gunman job." That injustice has tended to divert attention from Sacco and Vanzetti's violently anticapitalistic ideology.

OUTPOURING OF SUPPORT The Sacco and Vanzetti case would become a cause for demonstration for years, as in this 1920s demonstration in New York's Union Square.

On August 23, 1977, exactly fifty years after their execution, Massachusetts governor Michael Dukakis proclaimed the anniversary of their death a state-wide memorial day. All "stigma and disgrace should be forever removed from the names of Nicola Sacco and Bartolomeo Vanzetti," declared Dukakis. But the governor made this announcement without addressing the question of their innocence. It remains a mystery to this day.

1977 Governor Dukakis declares the anniversary of the two men's deaths a state-wide memorial day.

LIN BIAO'S MYSTERY CRASH

WAS CHINA'S VICE-CHAIRMAN THE VICTIM OF A VIOLENT POLITICAL STRUGGLE?

The news did not come out of Beijing until November 1971, and when it came the details were sparse. In the early hours of September 13, the reports announced, Chairman Mao's appointed heir, Marshal Lin Biao, had died when his military aircraft crashed in the desert in Outer Mongolia. Later came announcements that Lin had died fleeing to the Soviet Union in the wake of an abortive coup.

To China-watchers everywhere, these statements were electrifying. Lin was a hard-line leftwinger who had seemed destined to inherit the supreme leadership of 800 million people and thereby stamp his personality on the whole history of the world. Yet it was known that, in recent months, he and Chairman Mao had fallen out over certain key aspects of policy. Mao, for example, favored the opening of doors to the United States. Lin Biao's sympathies, in contrast, leaned more towards the Soviet Union. Mao feared the growing influence of the army in politics; Lin, on the other hand, had strong support among the generals. Above all, Mao mistrusted the personal ambition that Lin was beginning to exhibit, which could only threaten Mao's own authority.

COMRADES IN ARMS Lin Biao (left) poses with Mao Ze-dong at a conference.

Party politics

Tension between the two statesmen had started to come into the open in the autumn of 1970, when Mao began to purge Lin's allies and to clip the wings of the military. As the moves intensified, the marshal's supporters

BOOK MEN Party workers and Lin Biao (center right) brandish copies of *Quotations from Chairman Mao Ze-dong*, the little red book that became the bible of the Cultural Revolution; it was first published in 1964.

grew desperate and Lin's impetuous son, Lin Liguo, a deputy commander in the air force, began to plan a coup d'état against the revered chairman.

Most information about the plot comes from official Chinese sources that are impossible to verify. They describe how the coup was code-named "571" which, when pronounced in Chinese, can also mean "armed uprising." According to official reports, the conspirators made various attempts on Mao's life: through poison in his food, explosives planted in his train, and even by the strafing of his mansion by air force fighters. Some commentators have doubted whether Lin would have involved himself in assassination attempts, but it is not unlikely that his hot-headed son Liguo might have done so. Certainly, the autumn of 1971 seems to have been a nerve-racking time for Mao, for he made no publicized appearances at this time and moved out of his main residence at South and Central lakes, reportedly fearing its infiltration by his enemies.

The attempts on Mao's life failed, however, and according to the official story, their collapse caused Lin and his wife to plan to flee to Moscow. However, Lin's 29-year-old daughter, Lin

CHEER LEADER Vice-Chairman Lin Biao (left) and Chairman Mao celebrate the 20th anniversary of the founding of the People's Republic of China in 1969. This was the year in which Lin was proclaimed as Mao's successor.

Liheng, balked at this proposal and tipped off the authorities. The family was staying at the seaside resort of Beidaihe at the time, and now raced to the local airport in a convoy of cars. A hostile guard, shot by Liguo, was pushed from a speeding vehicle; suspicious ground crew at the airport tried to block the aircraft's take-off by parking two trucks across the runway. Lin's Trident man-

1900

1907 Lin Biao born

1921 Founding of
Communist Party
of China

1927 Lin Biao joins
Mao's Red Army

1950

PARTY PEOPLE Chairman and Vice-chairman commemorate the 50th anniversary of the Communist Party of China in 1971. "The thoughts of Chairman Mao are always correct," claimed the sycophantic Lin Biao.

aged to take off amid gunfire, and with damage to a fuel tank that began leaking. Some 155 miles beyond the Chinese border, the plane ran out of fuel and crashed in flames just short of the Mongolian capital, Ulan Bator. Lin, his wife Ye Qun, his son and six other people on board all perished.

A thrilling tale—but it was greeted with skepticism in many quarters. For one thing, it is known that Mao had convened a top-level meeting at the Great Hall of the People in Beijing before the dramatic flight from Beidaihe, and there stripped Lin and his

supporters of office. This suggests a more active role than merely following a tip-off from Lin's daughter. Mao was out to get Lin, and the aircraft crash was a suspiciously convenient accident. "It was probably murder," wrote Ross Terrill, in his biography of the chairman. Terrill points out that Lin had not in been seen in public since June 3. He may have been arrested—perhaps executed—at the time of the meeting in the Great Hall, or even long before.

The case has many curiosities. According to Moscow, some of the nine charred bodies found at the

HISTORIC HANDSHAKE Chairman Mao welcomes U.S. President Nixon to Beijing in February 1972.

Mongolian crash site were riddled with bullet holes. Beijing confirmed this—but only after the Russians had reported the fact. Were the gunshot wounds relics of the airport shootout? Or of a confrontation inside the airborne Trident?

Accidental death?

More controversially, Moscow at first declared that none of the nine bodies was of a person over 50 years of age—implying that 63-year-old Lin was not aboard, or that he had survived the crash. This may, however, have been a mischievous assertion, designed to worry Mao with the possibility that his rival was not only alive but also was talking to the Russians; in reality, the bodies seem to have been too charred for their age or identities to be determined, and in due course the Soviet authorities quietly dropped their "under 50" assertion.

It is simply not known whether Lin died in the Mongolian wreckage or in Chinese detention beforehand; even if he was on the fateful flight, the crash may not have been an accident. What is certain is that the crisis involved a great shake-up in China. In that second week of September, not just Lin but five other members of the Politburo died violent deaths. While the huge blow-up photographs of Lin disappeared from Chinese street parades, Mao steered his vast nation, as he had planned, in the direction of a rapprochement with the United States.

In February 1972, in one of the most astonishing twists of 20th-century diplomacy, the aging chairman welcomed President Nixon into China and entertained him at his house in the Forbidden City in Beijing.

1966 Cultural Revolution begins
1969 Lin Biao designated Mao's successor
1971 Death of Lin Biao

THE KOREAN JET CRASH

WHY DID THE SOVIET UNION DESTROY A BOEING 747, KILLING 269 INNOCENT CIVILIANS ON BOARD?

Waves of horror and alarm rippled all around the world on September 1, 1983, when the Russian government admitted shooting down a civilian airliner that had strayed into Soviet airspace. A total of 269 lives—including 61 Americans—were lost in the missile attack on Korean Airlines' Boeing 747 flight KAL 007 from Anchorage, Alaska, to Seoul. And although it was night-time and visibility was poor, there was no question of an accident on the Soviet side. In the diplomatic furor which followed the tragedy, U.S. officials played a tape at the United Nations of what the fighter pilot had said on the fateful night: "I am closing in on the target . . . I am in lock-in. I have executed the launch. The target is destroyed."

Red alert

But the Soviet Union's version of events was very different from the American. According to Moscow, the South Korean airliner did not stray accidentally but was on a spying flight over sensitive military installations off Siberia. "The

DAILY NEWS

SOVIETS SHOOT DOWN JETLINER

30 Yanks among 269 victims; U.S. demands 'full accounting;' Congress angry; Ron returning

Eight pages of stories and pictures start on page 2

FIRST REACTIONS   The American press registered outrage at the shooting and the loss of American lives (61, in fact, rather than 30). Later came questions about the plane's flight path.

What was the truth? The plane had certainly swung wildly off course; it was 365 miles to the north of its intended flight path. And in straying from its planned route, it passed over a Soviet area of high security that greatly interested U.S. aerial intelligence. As KAL 007 crossed the tip of the Kamchatka Peninsula, it passed over the Soviet town of Petropavlosk, a base for

Soviet nuclear submarines with an arsenal of ballistic missiles. The Red Army was due to test a new item of weaponry at the base at dawn that very day. As the foreign airliner approached, the weapon test was cancelled and a flight of fighters was scrambled to try to compel the intruder to land. The Russian pilots went through the usual drill of waggling their wings, switching their lights on and off, and as a last resort calling up the captain on the mayday frequency. But, according to the Soviets, the Korean pilot appeared not to see the warplanes, nor to hear the emergency signals instructing him to land.

As it happened, the airliner survived this first interception. The Soviet warplanes turned back as KAL 007 stubbornly stuck to its course, clearing the tip of the peninsula and flying on over the Sea of Okhotsk. But the captain's luck ran out when he reached the far side of the Sea and approached the strategic air bases on Sakhalin Island. This time the Russian interceptors closed in—and when a burst of cannon shells failed to win the pilot's attention, the fatal Anab heat-seeking missiles were fired.

Amid the bitter recriminations that followed the Soviet action, a puzzle remained.

SOVIET FIGHTER   The MiG-23 was among the fighter planes scrambled by the Soviets to intercept the Boeing 747.

Soviet government expresses regret over the death of innocent people and shares the sorrow of bereaved relatives and friends." However, "the entire responsibility for this tragedy rests wholly and fully" with the American leadership.

THE SEARCHERS   Three Japanese villagers scour a beach at Hamatonbetsu, looking for fragments of the Korean jet wreckage 11 days after the plane was shot down.

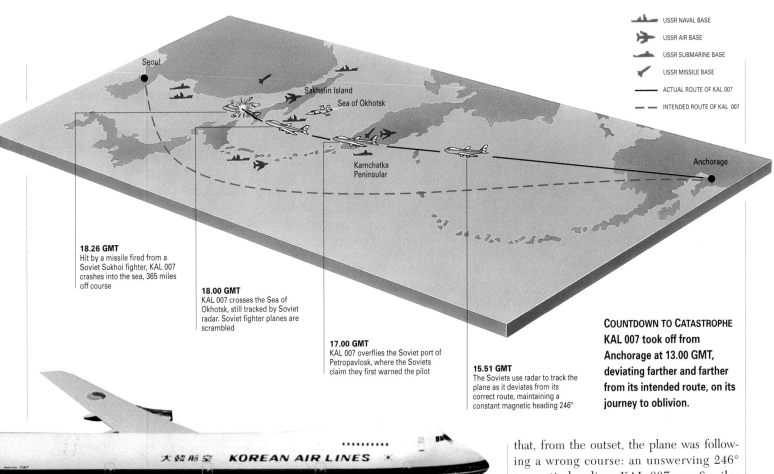

USSR NAVAL BASE
USSR AIR BASE
USSR SUBMARINE BASE
USSR MISSILE BASE
——— ACTUAL ROUTE OF KAL 007
- - - INTENDED ROUTE OF KAL 007

Seoul

Sakhalin Island

Sea of Okhotsk

Kamchatka
Peninsular

Anchorage

18.26 GMT
Hit by a missile fired from a
Soviet Sukhoi fighter, KAL 007
crashes into the sea, 365 miles
off course

18.00 GMT
KAL 007 crosses the Sea of
Okhotsk, still tracked by Soviet
radar. Soviet fighter planes are
scrambled

17.00 GMT
KAL 007 overflies the Soviet port of
Petropavlosk, where the Soviets
claim they first warned the pilot

15.51 GMT
The Soviets use radar to track the
plane as it deviates from its
correct route, maintaining a
constant magnetic heading 246°

COUNTDOWN TO CATASTROPHE
KAL 007 took off from
Anchorage at 13.00 GMT,
deviating farther and farther
from its intended route, on its
journey to oblivion.

KOREAN AIR LINES

BOEING JET This 747 jumbo jet from the
Korean Airlines fleet is similar to the one
shot down by the Soviets.

that, from the outset, the plane was following a wrong course: an unswerving 246°
magnetic heading. KAL 007 was 6 miles
north of its intended path as it left the limits
of Anchorage radar, and the discrepancy
grew steadily. Perhaps the darkness and bad
weather made the pilot unaware of the
Soviet warnings as the plane followed its
computer-controlled track to oblivion.

Why did the airliner follow such a wrong
course? The captain, Chun Byung-in, was a
veteran fighter pilot who had been in civil
aviation for 11 years, and whose flawless
record of service had placed him among the
elite eligible to fly the South Korean
President. Had he, perhaps, been briefed to
fly over the Russian bases so that U.S. intelligence could monitor the Soviet response?

Or was there a mechanical or pilot error?
The Korean airliner was equipped with a
computer-controlled Inertial Navigation
System (INS). This determines the aircraft's
position, calculates altitude and guides the
automatic pilot, all with a high degree of
accuracy. However, if even slightly wrong data
is fed into it in the first place, the error may
be magnified on a long flight. It is evident

ANGRY DEMONSTRATORS Protesters filled
the streets of South Korea's capital, Seoul,
in the days after the shooting.

1983 The Soviet
Union brings down a
Korean Airlines jet

1991 President
Yeltsin apologizes for
the shooting

MYSTERY AIR CRASHES

FROM METAL FATIGUE TO MECHANICAL FAULTS, PILOT ERROR TO POLITICAL TERRORISM, THE CAUSES OF AIRPLANE DISASTERS ARE THE SUBJECT OF INTENSE INVESTIGATION

None of the impressive technological advancements of the last century made in the field of avionics can disguise a simple fact: there is an inherent danger in flying thousands of feet in the air. A number of tragic plane crashes, many shrouded in mystery, have underscored that danger. One of the most controversial occurred on July 17, 1996, when thirteen minutes after takeoff, TWA flight 800, flying from JFK airport in New York to Frankfort Germany, crashed off the Long Island coast, killing all 230 people on board. From the moment news broke, many people suspected the crash was a deliberate attack. Some observers reported seeing a light streaking toward the plane moments before the crash, which might have been a ground-to-air missile. "It was a big event, a 747 inside the U.S. If it was an act of terrorism, if it was state-sponsored, it was an act of war," said the assistant director of the FBI. A popular theory, championed by a former White House spokesman, was that the plane was actually shot down by a Navy missile, in a botched practice session.

SALVAGE OPERATION Over 80 percent of the wreckage from Flight 800 was retrieved from the bottom of Long Island Sound.

Science began to steer investigators away from a criminal attack and toward a possible mechanical error. Investigators found no chemical or explosive residue in the wreckage or the recovered bodies that would suggest a bomb blast. A meteor shower the night of the crash was reported, which might explain the flash of light. Another theory explaining the crash was that fumes in the plane's fuel tank were heated to an explosive point by air conditioning units under the tank. To test this, the largest accident-reconstruction effort in history was conducted, costing upwards of $100 million. Investigators coordinated a set of flights, each testing a variable that might have contributed to the crash. Despite the investigators' sound arguments, conspiracy theorists refuse to reject the possibility that flight 800 was taken down by a criminal hand.

Black box

Aircraft are lost every year around the world, and if they are prestige products, or carry important political figures on board, suspicions of sabotage are often voiced. Amid the twisted wreckage of a disaster, it is not always easy to discover the cause of the calamity. For the investigators, the main puzzle-solvers are the flight data recorder and cockpit voice recorder. Known as "black boxes," they are really bright red so that they can be spotted immediately amid the debris. The flight data recorder tracks the operation of key instruments such as airspeed and altitude indicators, and the cockpit voice recorder picks up the conversation of the crew. Both boxes are walled in steel and capable of withstanding the temperatures of a crash inferno. Black boxes are generally more useful in discovering the cause of an accident than in identifying the symptoms of foul play, for evidence of sabotage is not always easy to detect.

Concordski explodes

One of the more suspicious air crashes of recent decades occurred at the Paris International Air Show in June 1973, when the star attraction, a Russian Tupolev-144 supersonic airliner, exploded in mid-air in front of 200,000 spectators. Dubbed the "Concordski," the plane had been built following a brilliant espionage coup mounted by

THE RUSSIAN CONCORDE The debris of the Tupolev-144, which exploded in 1973, damaged a French town near the airfield at Le Bourget.

Soviet Intelligence to probe the industrial secrets of the United Kingdom, France, and West Germany. This enabled the Russians to build their own version of the Anglo-French Concorde. When the "Concordski" exploded in 1973, its crew of six was killed instantly. Nine more people died and 28 were injured, as the wreckage fell to the town of Goussainville, north of Paris. Experts put the disaster down to pilot error, but widespread whispers of sabotage have never been silenced. Recent reports indicate that a French spy plane, photographing the Soviet machine, crossed the path of Concordski and forced the pilot to take evasive action, causing the crash.

The Lockerbie disaster

Foul play was certainly involved on December 21, 1988, when a jumbo jet on Pan Am flight 103 crashed onto the town of Lockerbie in Scotland, killing all 259 passengers as well as 11 people on the ground. The plane broke up in mid-air, causing bodies and debris to rain from the sky. American embassies had received a warning that the plane would be a terrorist target; the mystery in this case was: who had planted the bomb?

Two days after their arrival in Scotland, investigators found a piece of debris pitted with the tell-tale evidence of high-intensity explosives. The bomb went off in a Samsonite suitcase in the baggage area. A fragment of the timing device bore the name of a Zürich firm, declaring it to be one of a consignment delivered to a Libyan official. Also in the suitcase was a shirt that came from a boutique in Malta called Mary's Shop. When questioned, the boutique owner

CRASH SITE In a hangar (above) investigators piece together the jumbo jet's remains, which landed in and around Lockerbie (below).

recalled that in December 1988 a man with a Libyan accent surprised staff by buying a batch of clothing regardless of size or shape. FBI laboratory artists drew up a sketch of the man and matched it against photographs of known Libyan intelligence officers. He was identified as Abdel Basset Ali al-Megrahii, who had arrived in Malta with a former Libyan Arab Airlines official named Lamen Khalifa Fhimah; they had been carrying a dark Samsonite suitcase. Fhimah placed the lethal luggage on an Air Malta flight that connected at Frankfurt with Pan Am 103. In November 1991, Basset and Fhimah were charged, but Libya refused to cooperate. In April 1999, after years of diplomatic wrangling, Libya handed the two suspects over to the Scottish authorities to be tried in the Netherlands. The victims' families were at last granted the consolation of knowing that the terrorists would be punished for their heinous crime.

THE RWANDA TRAGEDY

HOW A MYSTERY PLANE CRASH SPARKED A VICIOUS ORGY OF TRIBAL BLOOD-LETTING

A horrific eruption of tribal genocide in Africa's most densely populated country, the central state of Rwanda, resulted in an estimated one million people being

EXECUTIVE WRECKAGE   A tangle of twisted metal is all that remains of the jet aircraft whose crash killed two African presidents.

killed in a single three-month frenzy. More than a million more fled as refugees from the country. Yet what triggered the calamity was a plane crash that remains a mystery to this day.

On April 6, 1994, the leaders of Rwanda and Burundi were both killed when their executive jet crashed as it came in to land at the airport at Kigali, Rwanda's capital. President Juvenal Habyarimana of Rwanda and President Cyprien Ntaryamira of Burundi had been returning from a meeting in Dar es Salaam, Tanzania, aimed at ending ethnic hostilities between members of the Hutu and Tutsi tribes. At the meeting, Habyarimana had finally given way to international pressure for democratic reform.

RWANDAN REFUGEES   Hundreds of thousands of civilians took to the roads, to flee the violence that shook Rwanda in 1994.

Early reports suggested that the airplane, a French Mystère-Falcon jet, had been shot down: a Rwandan official said that the aircraft was hit by two rockets, and Kigali residents said that they heard explosions followed by sporadic shooting, and glimpsed a small plane circling the airport in distress. But others declared the crash an accident, and United Nations officials were unable to mount a proper investigation.

SLAIN PREMIER   The Rwandan prime minister, Agathe Uwilingiyimana, was killed in the Kigali crash's bloody aftermath.

Mobs on the rampage

The violence in Rwanda was rooted in longstanding rivalries. The country had already endured a four-year civil war between its Hutu majority and Tutsi minority. But peace agreements had been signed, and there were serious hopes for a healing of the wounds at the time when the crash occurred. Though both of the dead statesmen were members of the Hutu tribe, President Ntaryamira of Burundi was a noted campaigner against tribal hatred, who had promoted Tutsis to positions of authority in his government. If the plane was shot down, the culprits may just as well have been hard-line Hutu opponents of compromise as Tutsi rebels.

Although much remains to be learned about the plane crash itself, there can be no doubt of its consequences. Suspecting a Tutsi assassination plot, mobs of youths, egged on by Hutu extremists and armed with clubs and machetes, rampaged through the streets of Kigali seeking vengeance. While parts of the armed forces tried to restore order, special units of the Rwandan army and the presidential guard, which were fiercely loyal to the late President Habyarimana, ran amok. Within days, a full-scale civil war had broken out. Rwanda's acting prime minister, the Hutu moderate Agathe Uwilingiyimana, was murdered by a mob after fleeing from the presidential palace to a UN compound; the Belgian UN peacekeepers guarding her were surrounded, disarmed and then killed. Other moderate government ministers, nuns, priests and aid workers also fell victim to the rampaging death squads. Anarchy reigned, and while the world's media began to focus its attention on terrible tales of atrocity and the plight of the refugees, both in Rwanda and in neighboring Burundi, the puzzling spark that had detonated the catastrophe—the plane crash at Kigali—was almost forgotten.

1900

1959 Rwanda gains independence from Belgium

1972 Ethnic violence between Hutus and Tutsis leaves 300,000 dead

1994 Plane crash is followed by massacres

2000

STRANGE DISAPPEARANCES

THOUSANDS OF PEOPLE GO MISSING EVERY YEAR, FOR PERFECTLY MUNDANE REASONS. PLAGUED BY FINANCIAL WORRIES OR BY UNHAPPY RELATIONSHIPS, THEY WALK OUT OF THEIR HOMES NEVER TO RETURN. OTHER VANISHING ACTS ARE FAR MORE BAFFLING, HOWEVER, AND SINISTER FORCES WERE MOST CERTAINLY AT WORK IN THE DISAPPEARANCES OF UNION BOSS JIMMY HOFFA, FOR EXAMPLE, AND THE SWEDISH BUSINESSMAN AND DIPLOMAT RAOUL WALLENBERG.

THE GREATEST AGATHA CHRISTIE MYSTERY OF ALL

MORE WHYDUNNIT THAN WHODUNNIT: A CASE THAT WOULD HAVE BAFFLED HERCULE POIROT

The story was as intriguing as the plots she so cleverly crafted for her detective novels. In 1926 the crime writer Agatha Christie disappeared from her home in Berkshire (in the south of England) for 11 days. On Friday, December 3, dressed in a velour hat, grey cardigan and green knitted skirt, the 36-year-old novelist walked out into the wintry night. The following morning her car was found about half a mile away with its front wheels over the edge of a deep chalk pit. The brakes were off and the ignition switched on; the car was empty.

Agatha Christie had vanished. And while the press speculated wildly about suicide, kidnapping and murder, the police mounted a nationwide hunt for the missing novelist (who was moderately famous at that time).

Then, on December 14, newspapers announced that the search had ended—hundreds of miles from her home. Staff at the Hydro Hotel in the north-central English resort town of Harrogate, Yorkshire, had noticed a marked similarity between a newspaper photograph of the missing Mrs. Christie and a guest named "Theresa Neele" claiming to be from South Africa. Colonel Archibald Christie, the writer's husband, was brought to the scene and there, outside the dining room—reading a newspaper report of her own disappearance—he identified the hotel guest as his wife. However, when he approached Agatha, according to the hotel manager, she seemed rather dazed and confused. Colonel Christie stated at the time that his wife did not know where she was or who she was. Colonel Christie took her home, and there doctors diagnosed that she was suffering from some form of amnesia.

"When one thing goes wrong"

Agatha always maintained that she had no recollection of how she came to be in Yorkshire. Even her autobiography makes no direct reference to it, although the book does acknowledge that 1926 was a traumatic year for her. She wrote: "As so often in life, when one thing goes wrong, everything goes wrong." First, her mother died and the writer—already feeling run down—was

QUEEN OF CRIME Agatha Christie is still one of the most widely read authors in the world, with translations into 103 languages.

MURDER HUNT Agatha's abandoned car prompted a massive police investigation.

December 3,1926 Agatha Christie vanishes
1928 Agatha Christie divorces her husband
1930 Agatha Christie remarries

reduced to a state of exhaustion clearing out her crowded house. Then Archie, her husband, confessed that he had fallen for another woman and asked Agatha for a divorce. This shattering news seems to have been what triggered the novelist's flight. And some deep psychological need was obviously answered by her escapade, for the surname she chose to live under in Harrogate—Neele

NEW LOVE In 1930 Agatha Christie married the eminent archaeologist Professor Max Mallowan. His work abroad allowed her to indulge her passion for foreign travel.

—was the same as that of Archie's new love. There was talk that the whole affair might have been a publicity stunt. But questions remained to be answered. Just how elaborate were Agatha Christie's plans? Did she drive to the chalk pit in a suicide bid, and leave the scene dazedly when the attempt failed? Or did she orchestrate a sensational disappearance to humiliate her errant husband—or perhaps even to implicate him in a murder investigation?

One aspect of the mystery that has never been revealed is the question of the three letters Agatha wrote at the time of her disappearance. Two she left behind for her husband and her secretary. The third was received in the post by her brother-in-law a couple of days later. Both her husband and her brother-in-law destroyed their letters. Her secretary handed over her letter to the police, sealed in an envelope to be opened only in the event of an inquest. The contents of all three letters remain a secret.

History records only that the Christie divorce went ahead, and that Agatha herself remarried in 1930. She shunned publicity until her death in 1976 and always refused to discuss her disappearance—the curious enigma of 1926 went with her to the grave.

MISSING PERSONS

Every year in the United States there are an estimated 932,000 reports of missing persons, according to the National Center for Missing and Exploited Children. Most of these cases (around 90% in the U.S.) are resolved—in other words, people are found, they stay missing because they want to (but have made contact to express their wishes), or are dead as a result of foul play. The exact number contained in this second category, is difficult to determine, however, since agencies do not keep records on why a missing person's file is removed from the FBI's database. Many are teenagers on the run from unhappy homes, or fugitive wives or husbands plagued by debts who—in classic cases—go out to the store and do not come back. Other people under stress have breakdowns when, for days or months on end, they forget who they are and where they live—as, perhaps, in the case of Agatha Christie.

Worldwide, no one knows just how great the problem is. Missing persons, where no crime is involved, challenge already overstretched police manpower, and there are limits to the public resources that can be expended on an individual's disappearance. Many are especially concerned with the rise in recent years of adult disappearances. Since 1995, in the U.S. the percentage of total missing persons cases that involved adults has risen to nearly 40 percent, but while there are around 50 organizations that specialize in recovering missing children, there are only a handful devoted primarily to adults.

Regardless of age, however, organizations now benefit from technology that greatly improves the chance of recovery, and expedites the search process. Police now have access to computerized databases of missing persons, and have a new technological aid at their disposal. Photosketch, a computerized machine that can "age" photographs of missing persons, produces an image of how they might look now. Photographs of the individual, and parents and siblings are fed into the machine. Because many facial features are hereditary, it has proved possible to predict how people will change as they age. First employed by the FBI in 1991, it can alter the photograph of a toddler into a teenager and then adulthood. In one early case it helped to trace a 14-year-old girl who had disappeared when she was four.

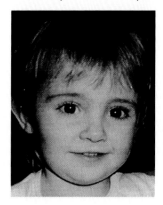

STEP ONE Last known photograph of child before her abduction at three-years old.

STEP TWO The child's photograph is scanned into the computer and stretched.

STEP THREE The stretched photo is merged with a photo of the nine-year-old brother.

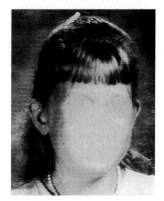

STEP FOUR Hairstyle and dress of a nine-year-old girl is taken from a reference file of images.

STEP FIVE This is merged with the missing child's aged image to produce a final result.

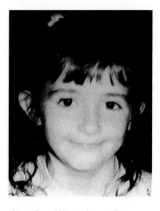

STEP SIX What she really looked like. A photo of the girl after she had been found.

1952 The Mousetrap, Britain's longest-running play, opens

1976 Dame Agatha Christie dies, aged 85

GOODTIME JOE GOES MISSING

DID NEW YORK JUDGE JOSEPH CRATER DISAPPEAR OF HIS OWN FREE WILL OR WAS HE DISPOSED OF?

In the United States to this day, the expression to "pull a Crater" means to disappear suddenly from a tricky situation. The phrase dates back to a summer's day in 1930 when Judge Joseph F. Crater hailed a taxi in New York, stepped inside and vanished.

Known in high society as Goodtime Joe, Crater had started his career as a respected law professor at New York University. But his love of money—and associating with showgirls—led him into bad company. In particular he became associated with the Tammany Hall crowd, the Democratic Party organization in New York, which was notorious for political corruption. There was some evidence that he had bought his appointment as a judge—a position of influence that soon paid off. One of Crater's coups was to act as receiver for the bankrupt Libby Hotel, which he sold to a finance company for $75,000. Two months later, the city agreed to buy it back for demolition in a street widening plan. The price was nearly $3 million. Did Crater receive a cut?

A new life

By the time of his disappearance Crater was a justice of New York's Supreme Court and a very wealthy man. While vacationing with his wife at their summer cottage in Maine, he received a phone message that called him back to New York. "I've got to straighten some fellows out," he told his wife before leaving the house.

Back in the city, on August 6, he cashed checks for over $5,000 and spent the afternoon sorting out office papers and stuffing documents into briefcases. He told an assistant he was going "up Westchester way for a few days," but did not leave immediately, for that evening he dined at a West 45th Street restaurant with a glamorous showgirl, Sally Lou Ritz. He was planning to go on to a Broadway show when, after saying goodbye, he hailed the taxi and disappeared.

Was he murdered by crooked associates who feared that he might reveal their crimes? Sally Lou Ritz herself disappeared a

few weeks after Crater, prompting whispers that she knew more than was good for her. Others believed that Crater had fled to start a new life elsewhere; sightings in Canada, Europe and the Caribbean were reported.

As late as the 1950s, Dutch clairvoyant Gerard Croiset was brought in by writer Murray Bloom to examine the mystery. When a photograph of Crater was turned face down in front of Croiset, he went into a trance and drew a map of New York City and its suburbs. Croiset believed that Crater had

MISSING PERSON A photograph of Joseph Force Crater appears against the Manhattan skyline. This picture was one of the last ever taken of the vanishing judge.

been murdered and buried at a house in Yonkers, just over the city line. When, in 1959, investigators dug a hole in the backyard of the house, no body was found.

Still unsolved, the mystery that fascinated the American public in the 1930s remains one of the most baffling on file.

1900 — 2000

1930 Judge Crater disappears

1959 Excavations at a house in Yonkers reveal nothing

CORPSES THAT WERE SPIRITED AWAY

**NOT FOR THE FAINT-HEARTED, THE MACABRE AND GHOULISH PRACTICE OF
BODYSNATCHING HAS HAD SOME UNLIKELY EXPONENTS**

T he embalmed body of Eva Perón, the glamorous wife of Argentina's dictator, Juan Perón, went missing for 16 years—an event that assumed enormous significance in the recent political history of South America. Evita ("little Eva") was worshipped by the poor, and when she died of cancer on July 26, 1952, an incredible two million people filed past her coffin.

Three years later, when roaring inflation led to her husband's overthrow, Eva's embalmed corpse vanished from its temporary resting place in the Confederacion General de Trabajadores (CGT) building in the capital, Buenos Aires. Rioting crowds demanded its return; but it was not until 1971 that it reappeared. It turned out to have been shipped abroad in a packing case and shuttled via Brussels, Bonn and Rome to a Milan cemetery where it was buried in lot 86 of the Musocco Cemetry in Milan.

SCENE OF PLUNDER Shock and speculation greeted the news that Charlie Chaplin's body had been stolen from this tiny cemetery at Corsier-sur-Vevey, Switzerland.

The plot had been the work of the military-led coup that had deposed Juan Perón in 1955. Headed by General Aramburu, the military had felt that there was

DIVINE WORSHIP In life and in death, the cult of Eva Perón was so powerful that even her corpse became an important political weapon.

much to fear in the cult of Evita. Ironically enough, a right-wing Peronist guerrilla group, the Montoneros, went on to kill Aramburu in 1970 and use his corpse as a means of trying to get Eva back. Her body was actually returned to her husband in Madrid in 1971 as part of a political deal by another military regime, and has been back in Buenos Aires since 1974 buried in a tomb 15 feet under the ground.

When the corpse of Charlie Chaplin was snatched from its grave in a cemetery in Switzerland on March 1, 1978, the motives were much less clear. For two months, speculation about the mysterious body-snatch was rife—it was even rumored that the corpse had been seized by Chaplin cult worshippers for reburial in England. It transpired that the culprits were two East European motor mechanics trying to extract a $630,000 ransom from the Chaplin family—relatives had kept silent to protect the police investigation. So inept were the kidnappers that when they were caught they couldn't pinpoint exactly where they had hidden the corpse. The police had to use mine detectors so that the body could be found and restored to its original resting place.

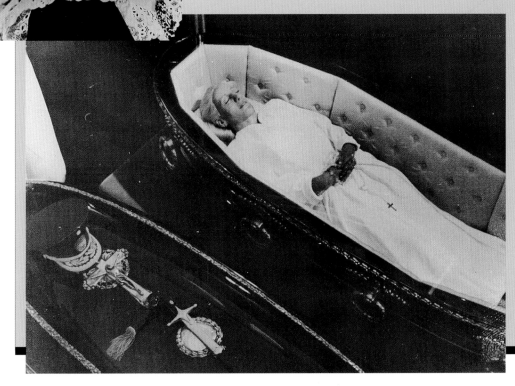

WHAT HAPPENED TO AMELIA EARHART?

LAST SEEN OVER NEW GUINEA: THE FLIGHT INTO OBLIVION OF AMERICA'S DARLING

Aparticular mystique has always attached itself to women flyers, and none is more fondly remembered than Amelia Earhart. A fresh-faced, Kansas-born

RECORD BREAKER Following her historic transatlantic flight of 1932, Amelia Earhart became the first woman to fly solo across the Pacific Ocean, in 1935.

tomboy, she was the toast of America in 1932 when she became the first woman to fly solo across the Atlantic. This adventure, soon to

be followed by many others, seemed to naturally culminate in plans for a round-the-world flight.

On June 1, 1937, Amelia set off from Oakland, California, in a twin-engined Lockheed Electra with an experienced flyer named Fred Noonan as navigator. One by one, their targets were met: Florida, Brazil, West Africa, East Africa, Pakistan, India, Burma, Singapore and New Guinea. At 10am on July 2 the pair set off from Lae in New Guinea to begin the last lap – the long haul across the Pacific Ocean.

'No landfall ... position doubtful'

Their aim was to land next on tiny Howland Island, a mere pin-prick on the vast map of the Pacific, and they took off into a headwind, with storm clouds looming, over a stretch of ocean never before flown. The crew of an American coastguard cutter, *Itasca*, waited anxiously off Howland Island, transmitting homing signals that would help the couple to locate the speck of land which was their destination.

As the scheduled time of arrival came and went, the *Itasca* and other ships picked up broken messages from Amelia: '30 minutes' gas remaining, no landfall ... Circling, trying to pick up island landfall, position doubtful ...' And then there was silence.

Despite a massive two-week search by ships and aircraft of the US Pacific fleet, the pair were never found. According to the official story, Amelia and her navigator must

HELPING HAND All flight publicity was handled by husband George Putnam: above, with Amelia in New Jersey, 1931.

have run out of fuel and drowned at sea. But this was not the only version of events. It was said that, after the aircraft had vanished, ham radio operators had picked up messages indicating that the Lockheed had landed on a coral atoll. Jacqueline Cochran, a close friend of Amelia's and an alleged psychic,

WINGS OF DESIRE Amelia's Lockheed took off from Oakland Airport in California on the ill-fated round-the-world attempt.

1932 Earhart is the first woman to cross the Atlantic solo

1937 Earhart sets off on her round-the-world flight

THE PACIFIC ROUTE Flying eastward, the Lockheed met all its targets as far as New Guinea—then just disappeared off the map.

added fuel to the controversy by insisting she could sense that the pair had ditched in the sea and were still afloat.

Later, following the outbreak of the Second World War, a startling new theory emerged. "Amelia Earhart—college head thinks flyer is Jap captive," announced the *San Francisco Chronicle* in April 1943. Dr. Brittain, president of Georgia Tech University, suggested that Amelia had been on a surveillance mission for the U.S. Government, with orders to fly over the Marshall Islands—about 650 miles northwest of Howland. She was said to have been taken prisoner while trying to discover whether the Japanese were illegally fortifying the islands.

Long after the end of the war this theory continued to fascinate. From various scattered sightings of a white female pilot or "American spy lady," author Fred Goerner claimed to have evidence that the pair had ditched at Mili atoll in the southeastern Marshalls and been taken for questioning to Saipan, Japan's military headquarters in the Pacific. There, he suggested, they had been interrogated and, presumably, executed.

More theories proliferated. One outlandish hypothesis suggested that Amelia was still alive and well and living in New Jersey under the name of Irene Craig Bolam. This myth was exploded when the real Irene Bolam sued. In 1992 an expedition to the South Pacific unearthed what were taken for historic remains: a size 9 shoe and a fragment of aircraft that was supposedly part of

TRIUMPH AND TRAGEDY Cheers greet Amelia after her 1932 transatlantic flight; inset, with round-the-world navigator Fred Noonan.

Amelia's Lockheed Electra. However, the shoe size was not a match for Earheart or her navigator—and another theory crashed.

A government agent?

The most enduring notion has been that Amelia Earhart was a spy for the U.S. government, and that officials covered up information about her secret role when she disappeared. In 1994 a book claiming to substantiate the theory was published by

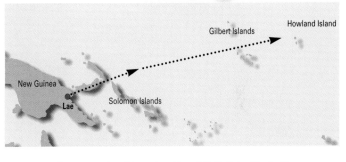

aviation historian Randall Brink. He believes that Amelia switched aircraft for the last fatal lap of her round-the-world journey, flying instead a specially fitted-out Lockheed with holes cut out of the interior to accommodate spy cameras.

Skeptics remain dubious. It is more than likely that the U.S. military supplied Amelia with substantial financial and technical assistance probably because President Franklin D. Roosevelt appreciated the flight's value in boosting national morale. If there was any element of official cover-up, though, it was perhaps to protect the public from the knowledge of Amelia's failings as a pilot. She should have delayed take-off from Lae until the weather improved; she should have kept in regular radio contact with those monitoring her progress; and she should also have carried flares.

Among all the exotic theories that surround her disappearance, the likeliest is the most dull and humdrum; for all her charisma and bravery, Amelia Earhart was a normal, mortal woman—who paid the ultimate price for human failings.

1992 South Pacific expedition falsely builds up hope that Earhart's plane has been found

THE LAST SERENADE OF GLENN MILLER

MISSING, PRESUMED DEAD: THE LOSS OF THE SWING LEGEND WAS MOURNED BY THOUSANDS

Smooth, muted brass was the instantly recognizable trademark of American bandleader Glenn Miller, whose swing tunes survive among the most evocative hits of the Second World War. In 1941 he volunteered for active service but was persuaded that he could do more for the war effort through his music. So, joining the air force, he put together a United States Army Air Force Band to entertain troops abroad.

When Paris fell to the Allies late in 1944, Major Glenn Miller and his 60-piece orchestra were scheduled to perform in the French capital. His intention was to travel ahead of the band, and on December 14 he and another officer assembled with a pilot at an airfield a few miles from Bedford in southeast-central England.

Fog had been rolling in all day but, despite bad weather warnings, they took off for France. Their plane, a single-engined Norseman D-64, then vanished with its occupants into the fog.

No one realized that the aircraft had gone missing until two days later, when the rest of the band arrived in Paris. The show took place without him, but with hope that he was still alive. After three days, when searches revealed neither plane nor wreckage, Glenn Miller was reported missing, and people began to accept that he might be dead.

A fatal crash in the sea was the probable explanation, although there were no records of a plane being shot down over the Channel on that day. According to one widespread theory the aircraft had iced up, stalled and fallen from the sky. Alternatively there may have been a mechanical failure, or the pilot may have lost his way and run out of fuel.

Did Miller reach Paris?

The shock of the tragedy, combined with the delay in official announcements, allowed alternative stories to circulate. Miller's wife refused to believe the worst and hoped throughout the war that her husband might have survived as a German POW. A later theory proposed that Miller was shot down

KING OF SWING   Some rumors had Glenn Miller being shot down by an RAF fighter; others said that he had a fractured skull from a brothel brawl in a seedy area of Paris.

in error by an RAF (British Royal Air Force) fighter, a tragic mistake that was covered up by the authorities. An even more extraordinary cover-up was proposed by an ex-RAF officer named John Edwards. He was to suggest in 1976 that Miller was not aboard the crashed Norseman at all, but reached Paris

in a Dakota and died there of a fractured skull following a brothel brawl in the seedy Pigalle district. In a variation of this story, Miller was flown from Paris to the U.S.— where he died in a military hospital.

The wreckage of Second World War aircraft have occasionally been discovered in the Channel, but the Norseman has never been located. Unless it turns up, the enigma of Glenn Miller's death will remain shrouded in suppositions as misty as the fog that engulfed southern England on that night.

1939 Miller achieves world fame as big-band leader
1941 Miller joins U.S. Air Force
1944 Miller disappears between England and France

LOST FLIERS OF THE SECOND WORLD WAR

THERE WERE OTHER VICTIMS—APART FROM AMERICAN BANDLEADER GLENN MILLER—OF PUZZLING AIRCRAFT CRASHES DURING THE SECOND WORLD WAR

Britain's best-loved female aviation pioneer and a successful movie star, a famous French novelist and the exiled Polish leader all vanished during the 1939-45 conflict.

Amy Johnson, 1941

Britain's pioneer of aviation worked for the Air Transport Auxiliary when the Second World War broke out. On January 5, 1941, while ferrying a plane, she baled out over the Thames Estuary and vanished into the waters. The puzzle was that she was 100 miles from her destination and two hours late. Moreover, witnesses thought they saw two figures drop into the waves.

Conspiracy theorists have pictured the aviator returning from a mission in France, perhaps with a secret agent. However, Johnson was flying without a radio in bad conditions. Probably, she went off course, running out of fuel in the process. As for her companion, this was probably the rear exit door—which she had to jettison to make the jump.

PEOPLE'S DARLING The British couldn't accept Amy Johnson's disappearance.

General Sikorski, 1943

Foul play was suspected from the moment news came through that General Wladyslaw Sikorski, the prime minister of the Polish government in exile, had died in an aircrash over Gibraltar on July 24, 1943. With Poland partitioned between Germany and the Soviet Union, the outspoken leader had made many political enemies—and was seen by many as a liability to the

LAST PARADE General Wladyslaw Sikorski reviews British soldiers in Gibraltar, July 1943. This was the last photograph ever taken of him.

FLIGHT OF FANCY Saint-Exupéry (right) with an air mechanic before the Paris to Saigon Race, 1936.

Allies. There was an official investigation of the crash, but nothing concrete was revealed that could prove an assassination.

Antoine de Saint-Exupéry, 1944

The great French novelist was also a pioneer aviator who had flown mail in North Africa and South America. Although he was 43 when Paris fell to the Germans, Saint-Exupéry joined the Free French Air Force.

On July 31, 1944, he took off from base at Bastia in Corsica, on a mapping mission east of Lyons, and was never seen again. Mischievous rumors at the time hinted that he had been assassinated by the Gaullists—but his disappearance was probably no more sinister than that of many others lost on wartime flights. People close to Saint-Exupéry believed that he had long been courting death. "If I disappear," he told one friend, "you can be sure it will be without regrets." He had bequeathed his chess set to another, saying: "Keep it. We'll play again on another planet."

Leslie Howard, 1943

Leslie Howard, one of Britain's best-known movie stars of the 1930s, returned from Hollywood at the outbreak of war in order to make patriotic films such as *Pimpernel Smith*. In April 1943 he flew to Lisbon to lecture on film and drama in neutral Spain and Portugal. Though his talks had no propaganda value, his business partner took the opportunity to arrange film distribution; as a result, 900 Spanish movie theaters were to show British war films. Returning on June 1, Howard took off from Lisbon on a DC3 civil airliner. As the aircraft passed over the Bay of Biscay, it was shot down by German Junkers fighters. No traces of Howard, the 12 other passengers or the aircraft were ever found. The Nazis' excuse for shooting down the plane was that the DC3 had been mistaken for an enemy bomber. But it was whispered that Howard—a potent ambassador for Britain—might have been a deliberate target.

HOLLYWOOD HEARTTHROB Leslie Howard's glittering career and life were cut short.

ON THE TRAIL OF MARTIN BORMANN

THE NAZI WAR CRIMINAL WHO WAS OFTEN "SIGHTED" BUT NEVER BROUGHT TO JUSTICE

When Hitler's top henchmen were sentenced to death for war crimes at the Nuremberg Trials of 1945–46, judgment was passed on one high-ranking SS man in his absence. This was Martin Bormann, the Führer's personal secretary since 1942, whose ultimate fate has never been completely ascertained to this day.

He is known to have served as witness when Hitler married Eva Braun in the Berlin bunker under the Reich Chancellery on April 29. The next day, when Hitler and Braun committed suicide in the bunker, Bormann was seen trying to commandeer a tank to escape the devastated capital. As he approached the vehicle, a shell burst close by. According to one witness (Hitler's

WANTED FOR WAR CRIMES Hitler's personal secretary, Bormann was sentenced to death in his absence at the Nuremberg Trials.

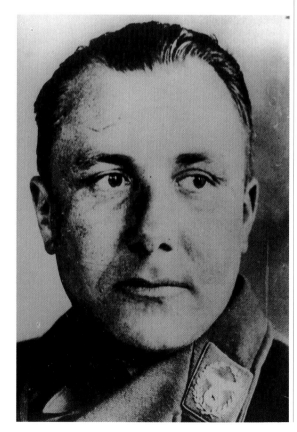

chauffeur) there was a blinding flash, and when he looked again Bormann had vanished. It was assumed that he had died in the explosion, but there were other versions of events. It was rumored that he had been spirited away and was later helped by the ODESSA organization, which was run by Nazi sympathizers to assist former members of the SS escape retribution by the Allies.

He was "sighted" time and again in South America: in Brazil, Argentina and Chile. In 1959, a grave thought to be Bormann's was opened up near Asuncion in Paraguay—to reveal only the bones of a Paraguayan named Hormoncilla. In 1967, police in Guatemala arrested a man answering the missing Nazi's description—he turned out to be an elderly carpenter named Martinez.

The bodies in the park

In 1971 new and sensational claims were made by Reinhard Gehlen, Hitler's chief of intelligence against the Soviet Union, who worked for the CIA after the war. Gehlen claimed that Bormann had been a Soviet agent and that he had escaped in 1945, and lived for many years behind the Iron Curtain, acting as an adviser on German affairs for the Russians. Few today believe this amazing claim, which was probably designed to sell Gehlen's memoirs.

Equally extraordinary is a theory put forward in 1995 by the author Christopher Creighton. He proposed that Bormann was smuggled out of the Berlin bunker on the orders of British Prime Minister Winston Churchill, taken to England and given plastic surgery. In an attempt to obtain from him the secret of hidden Nazi gold deposits, the British authorities installed him in a village on the Berkshire-Hampshire border, where he died in 1989. According to the theory, he was then buried in an unmarked grave in a local churchyard.

The simplest and most likely story of Bormann's fate is that he died on May 1, 1945, in the neighborhood of the Lehrt Station, during the bombardment of Berlin. After the unconditional surrender by Germany on May 7, 1945, the Russians found this whole area strewn with the bodies of German men, women and children, and ordered them to be buried in three mass

SINISTER SECRETS Bormann was known to be a great admirer of his Führer. A witness at Hitler's marriage to Eva Braun, he disappeared on the day of their suicide pact.

graves in a neighboring park. Bormann's body was recognized among the corpses by one of those ordered to dig the graves. The park was dug up in 1965, when a large number of bones were found. In 1972 another search near the Lehrt Station yielded a skull

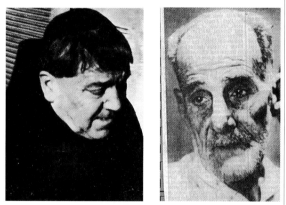

MISTAKEN IDENTITY An Italian monk named Martini (left) and the Guatemalan Martinez (right) were both thought to be Bormann.

thought by forensic experts "with near certainty" to be Bormann's. This evidence, at least, was sufficient for the authorities in Bonn. In April 1973 the West German government confirmed Bormann's death, and closed the file on the Nazi war criminal.

1900 ———————————————————————————— 2000

April 30, 1945 Bormann 1959 Grave is opened up in Paraguay
vanishes, presumed dead 1967 Man thought to be Bormann
is arrested in Guatemala

THE HUNT FOR VANISHED NAZIS

**WANTED FOR CRIMES AGAINST HUMANITY: MANY SS MEN SPENT YEARS EVADING
CAPTURE—BUT THEY RECKONED WITHOUT THE DEATH CAMP SURVIVORS**

Frederick Forsyth's bestselling novel *The Odessa File* took its name from a real-life organization operated by SS loyalists to help former members evade arrest by Allied authorities and so escape prosecution as war criminals. The acronym ODESSA stood for *Organization der ehemaliger SS Angehorigen* (Organization of former SS members). Founded in 1947 and posing as a charitable body, the organization secretly assisted Nazi fugitives with contacts, money and forged papers. Thousands of Nazis are thought to have vanished in this way. Many passed through Italy, finding aid among circles close to the Vatican, before reaching countries in South America.

Among the escapees was Adolf Eichmann, a monstrous mass murderer who never actually felt the blood of his victims on his hands. Responsible for "cleansing" Europe of Jews and any other groups deemed not to fit in with the Aryan masterplan, Eichmann was the technician who orchestrated the so-called "final solution" on behalf of the Third Reich. It was thanks to Eichmann that the horrendous scheme was made possible—from rounding-up victims to organizing the trains that took them to the Holocaust death camps.

At the end of the Second World War Eichmann was captured twice by American

THE INVESTIGATOR Simon Wiesenthal, a survivor of the death camps, has made it his mission in life to hunt down the perpetrators of war crimes.

THE EXTERMINATOR Adolf Eichmann in his Gestapo uniform in the 1940s, right, and how he looked when he was captured by Israelis in 1960, above.

troops—but both times managed to escape without being identified, despite the enormous price on his head. Subsequently he lived for four years as a lumberjack in Germany under an alias before he was able to flee via Austria to an Italian monastery, where he was issued with false papers in the name of "Ricardo Klement." Under that identity

he obtained an Argentine visa and went to live in Buenos Aires, where in 1952 his wife, Vera, and two children joined him. As far as the world was concerned, Eichmann had vanished—whereas he was actually enjoying a comfortable job under his false identity with the firm of Mercedes-Benz.

The enigma of his fate was solved in 1960 when he was tracked down and kidnapped by a team of Israeli agents. They brought him back from South America to face trial in Jerusalem, where he was convicted and hanged for his war crimes in 1962.

Eichmann had been located with the aid of Simon Wiesenthal, a prominent Austrian investigator of Nazi crimes who had himself spent three years in concentration camps. Head of the Jewish Documentation Center in Vienna since 1961, Wiesenthal has helped to track down more than 1,000 missing war criminals. However, the fate and whereabouts of others remain a mystery, including Heinrich Mueller, chief of the Gestapo; Richard Gluecks, inspector-general of the concentration camps; and Walter Rauff, who supervised the provision of gas trucks for the "final solution."

THE WALLENBERG IRONY

THE HERO WHO RESCUED THOUSANDS BUT WAS POWERLESS TO SAVE HIMSELF

It has been said that Swedish diplomat and businessman Raoul Wallenberg saved more lives during the Second World War than any single government. As part of an American plan to rescue the last remaining large Jewish population in Europe, he spent the latter half of 1944 in Hungary. There he and his helpers provided shelter in protected "safe" houses, supplied passports and even followed the trains to the concentration camps, distributing food, clothing and money. Yet the man who is credited with saving perhaps as many as 20,000 lives was powerless to save himself from a tragic fate, which remains unsolved.

Towards the end of the war, when fleeing German troops were being replaced by victorious Soviet forces in Budapest, Wallenberg decided to try to ensure the safety of his rescued Jews. He left under Russian escort en route to Debrecen (150 miles away) to negotiate with Russian military leaders in January 1945. He was never seen again.

At first, it is thought, the Russians arrested Wallenberg on suspicion of Nazi connections —because of his dealings with Eichmann in saving Jews from the camps. Later, it seems, the Russians suspected that he might have been an American spy. Whatever the initial reason for his arrest, the Russian version reports Wallenberg's death from a heart attack in Lubianka Prison, Moscow, in 1947. But no body was produced, and, over the decades, many reports from freed Soviet prisoners suggested he was still alive in a Siberian camp or elsewhere —caught in a no-man's land of denied existence because of the Cold War.

The international enquiry

In 1981 President Reagan and the Swedish Prime Minister jointly pledged to continue the search for Wallenberg. The new period of *glasnost,* or openness, in Russia strengthened hopes, and in 1989 the KGB handed over some of Wallenberg's effects. The Russians still insisted that he was dead, but this did not prevent an international

COLD WAR VICTIM Decades have been spent trying to track down the missing Raoul Wallenberg.

AFTER OCCUPATION Wallenberg disappeared amidst the chaotic legacy of booby-trap bombs and devastation left by the Germans.

commission from asserting the opposite in 1990. Their report included eyewitness sightings of the diplomat within the Soviet Union, as well as the views of the late Andrei Sakharov, the Nobel prize-winning human rights activist. "The evidence is incontrovertible that he did not die in 1947 as the Soviets claim," said the report.

Sadly, as investigation continued, it began to seem likelier that the missing diplomat did perish soon after the war's end. In 1992 a former KGB man declared on Swedish television that Wallenberg died in 1947 during interrogation, and the following year a Danish newspaper claimed that he had been executed. There are still some who believe that Wallenberg survived—but with every year that passes, the chances of finding him alive are slimmer. Wallenberg was born in 1912; he would be in his eighties by now.

ENTER THE VICTORIOUS The arrival of Soviet troops spelled saviour in Budapest, but not, ironically, for Raoul Wallenberg.

July 1944 Wallenberg arrives in Budapest
January 1945 Wallenberg leaves Budapest with Soviet escort, bound for Debrecen
1947 Official date of death, in Lubianka Prison, according to the Soviets
1990 International inquiry reports that Wallenberg is probably still alive

GLASNOST RATTLES THE SKELETONS

BURIED TREASURES AND MACABRE LONG-LOST SECRETS WERE JUST SOME OF THE
REVELATIONS OF MIKHAIL GORBACHEV'S NEW POLICIES IN THE SOVIET UNION

CRACKS IN THE ICE Talks between Gorbachev and Reagan at the Geneva Summit in 1985 heralded a new era in East-West relations.

In 1986 Mikhail Gorbachev, the new leader of the Soviet Union, sparked a massive upheaval in his country with a speech to the 27th Communist Party congress. Mincing no words, he strongly criticized the corrupt Soviet bureaucracy, its centralized economy and the record of former President Leonid Brezhnev. Prominent Soviet dissidents were released that year, and in January 1987 Gorbachev ushered in a new democratic age with a call for electoral reform and a policy of *glasnost*—or openness—in social and cultural life.

Gorbachev's democratic reforms had ramifications on politics worldwide. And as glasnost fostered a free investigative spirit within the Soviet Union, long-sealed doors were opened and secret files came to light. Many a historic puzzle was solved as a result. Through glasnost, researchers were able to locate and unearth the long-hidden skeletons of the Russian royal family and send them for DNA testing. For the first time, journalists were allowed to enter and film in the

LOST LOOT Last seen in Berlin, the Gold of Troy was among the art treasures from Germany that turned up in Moscow.

notorious *Gulag*. This Russian archipelago of labor camps and prisons is where thousands of political prisoners and exiles disappeared under Stalin and his succesors.

No certain conclusions have been reached about the fate of the missing Swedish diplomat Raoul Wallenberg, but many other wartime mysteries have been cleared up. At last, officials have admitted Soviet responsibility for the Katyn Massacre, when 4,500 Polish officers were shot and buried in mass graves in a forest near Smolensk. Many paintings, sculptures and other art treasures taken from Germany by the Red Army at the end of the Second World War have been located. They include the celebrated Gold of Troy discovered by German archaeologist Heinrich Schliemann, which had vanished from Berlin and recently turned up in the basement of the Pushkin Museum in Moscow. Perhaps the most remarkable finds, though, have been the items relating to Hitler's death, which were long kept secret from the public by the KGB.

File I-G-23, which was discovered in the State Special Trophy Archive in Moscow, turned out to comprise six buff-colored files of documents, plus charts and photographs, reporting what went on in Berlin at the

REVOLUTIONARY ART New attitudes in the Soviet Union paved the way for open expression, as in this anti-Stalin poster.

time of the Führer's death. At the same time, in the State Archive of the Russian Federation (also in Moscow), another astonishing find was made: Hitler's charred and tattered uniforms, watercolors and personal photographs, and even what appeared to be fragments of his skull. The skull had been kept in a crumbling cardboard box originally used for ballpoint pen refills.

THE FROGMAN WHO NEVER SURFACED

WAS LIONEL "BUSTER" CRABB SOLD DOWN THE RIVER BY THE BRITISH GOVERNMENT?

Much publicity surrounded the eight-day visit to Britain in 1956 of the new Soviet leaders, Nikita Khrushchev and Nikolai Bulganin. The heirs to Stalin came for talks with the British Government, and

THE MISSING MAN Buster Crabb in 1950 during work in Tobermory Bay, where he was employed to locate a sunken galleon.

arrived on the *Ordzhonikidze*, an impressive new cruiser admired for its speed and maneuverability. Accompanied by two destroyers, the warship anchored outside Portsmouth Harbor, in southern England.

On the day before the Russians arrived, April 17, 1956, a dapper little man named Lionel "Buster" Crabb checked into the Sallyport Hotel in Portsmouth. He had

served as a frogman in the Royal Navy, and his expertise in dangerous underwater work had earned him a George Medal in the Second World War. Officially at least, Commander Crabb was now a civilian employee of a company in the espresso coffee business. But speculation would soon be rife that Crabb still did underwater work—albeit of a somewhat hush-hush nature.

The day after the Russians' arrival in Portsmouth, Buster Crabb was missing from his hotel. A companion of his, who had given his name as "Mr. Smith," cleared out all his luggage, and some time later an unknown man turned up and tore out all of the April pages from the hotel register. He gave no explanation, merely cautioning the staff under the Official Secrets Act to say nothing about the visit of Crabb. When a friend later telephoned the Admiralty in an attempt to contact the missing diver, he was told that the frogman was dead.

The headless corpse

Soon it was being whispered among journalists that Crabb had come to grief while taking part in an underwater spying mission to investigate the unusual hull and rudder of the *Ordzhonikidze*. But while the sensitive Anglo-Soviet talks were going on, all inquiries about the missing frogman met official silence.

It was only after the Russian delegation left that the government admitted that Crabb had disappeared—presumed dead—while carrying out "trials with certain underwater apparatus" near the Soviet cruiser. In the House of Commons, the Prime Minister, Sir Anthony Eden, declared that it would not be in the public interest to disclose more about these particular circumstances.

The Foreign Office did acknowledge, however, that a frogman who had been sighted by a Russian look-out swimming between the two Soviet destroyers "was to all appearances Commander Crabb." They were keen to point out, though, that his presence near the destroyers had occurred "without any permission whatever and Her Majesty's

Government express their regret for the incident." Inevitably, Soviet newspapers railed against this "shameful underwater espionage," but did the Russian authorities know more than they let on? Indeed, in Britain, the absence of a body prompted speculation that Buster Crabb had perhaps been captured alive and taken back to the Soviet Union for interrogation.

In June the following year there came a sensational development: Crabb's body had reportedly been found in the sea near Chichester Harbor, east northeast of Portsmouth. The corpse lacked its head and hands, but the lower part of the body had been protected by a diver's suit, and the left leg bore what looked like a scar the missing frogman had acquired in wartime.

The coroner declared himself satisfied that the remains were those of Commander Crabb, and the body was buried at Portsmouth. But not everyone accepted this

MACABRE FIND Two fishermen, Ted Gilby (left) and D.L. Randall (right), found Crabb's supposed—and headless—corpse.

1910 Lionel "Buster" Crabb is born.

verdict. Was it not strange that the head and the hands, which would have provided a truly positive identification, were missing? Was it not all too convenient?

Was the body planted?

Suspicions inevitably deepened when it became known that three Soviet submarines had passed through the English Channel just a few days before the corpse had made its appearance near Chichester Harbor. It was rumored that one of them could have slipped the headless body into the sea near to where it came ashore.

This hypothesis was taken up by the journalist J. Bernard Hutton, who published two sensational books about the case. He claimed to have evidence that the body washed ashore was a plant, and that the real Buster Crabb lived on as "L.L. Korablov," a frogman instructor in the Soviet Union.

Hutton's story alleged that the Russians had taken Commander Crabb back to the Soviet Union and, after interrogation,

STILL WATERS The Russian cruiser *Ordzhonikidze* (foreground), alleged to be Crabb's intelligence target, berthed outside Portsmouth Harbor with two destroyers.

offered him the alternative of death or a career passing on his submariner's skills to recruits in the Russian Navy.

Skeptics regard Hutton's version as far-fetched, but it is not inconceivable that Crabb was recovered from the water, alive or dead, and removed from the scene on that particular night in April 1956. A disastrous diplomatic incident would have put the crucial Anglo-Soviet talks—billed at the time as being conducted "in a spirit of candor and realism"—in serious jeopardy. Whether the headless corpse returned to the Channel was that of Crabb or a substitute must remain open to some doubt. What is certain is that if someone sent it floating towards Chichester Harbor—almost a year later—that person wanted the case closed once and for all.

DO SVIDANYA, BRITAIN Bidding farewell, from left to right, Nikita Khrushchev, Dr. Ivan Kurchatov (Atom Chief), Nikolai Bulganin and A.N. Tupolev (Soviet aircraft designer).

1950 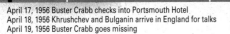 2000

April 17, 1956 Buster Crabb checks into Portsmouth Hotel
April 18, 1956 Khrushchev and Bulganin arrive in England for talks
April 19, 1956 Buster Crabb goes missing

THE MISSING PRIME MINISTER

AUSTRALIA'S HAROLD HOLT PLUNGES INTO THE SURF—NEVER TO BE SEEN AGAIN

Crowds of Australian vacationers watched and waited near a beach on the Victoria coast, while soldiers checked the sands over a 30-mile front and helicopters flew low over the waves. Hundreds of divers, including navy frogmen, searched underwater for signs of the missing statesman. The date was Sunday, December 17, 1967, and Australia's Prime Minister, Harold Holt, had vanished into the sea.

As leader of Australia's Liberal Party, Harold Holt headed a coalition government which he had been struggling for some time to hold together. Two days before he disappeared the usually ebullient politician had seemed to journalists to be tired and withdrawn. But that had not stopped him from entertaining weekend guests and playing vigorous tennis at his house in Portsea some 60 miles from Melbourne. On that Sunday morning, he and a group of friends had driven to Cheviot Beach for a swim. The waters here were well known for their treacherous currents, and most of the prime minister's friends were reluctant to go in. But Holt took the plunge and swam powerfully out to sea, followed by a young businessman named Alan Stewart.

Some distance from the shore, Stewart felt an alarming undertow and decided to turn back. Holt however, forged on ahead, swimming strongly. Back on the beach, a witness named Marjorie Gillespie became worried for the prime minister and ran down to the surf's edge. "The water became turbulent around him very suddenly. It seemed to boil and these conditions seemed to swamp him."

After that, Holt was gone. And despite a full-scale six-day search, his body was never found washed ashore.

An astonishing allegation

While President Lyndon Johnson and other world statesmen gathered in Australia for Holt's memorial service, some inevitable questions were raised. Why had the 59-year-old prime minister swum with such determi-

FAMILY MAN Keen fisherman Harold Holt and his wife, Zara, play in a speedboat with their grandson during a weekend of relaxation on the Victoria coast.

THE SEARCH CONTINUES A newspaper (above) of Monday, December 18, 1967, describes continuing attempts to find Australia's missing Prime Minister, Harold Holt, photographed in 1966 (left).

nation so far out into the notoriously dangerous waters? Some theorized that he had committed suicide as a way out of his increasingly fraught political position. Holt's coalition was shaky; he had been under pressure from protesters demonstrating against his support for the Vietnam War; it was rumored that his own party wanted to ditch him. While friends and family repudiated the idea of suicide as wholly against Holt's character, there were some in the parliamentary opposition who felt that he had showed signs of an impending breakdown.

In 1983, however, a much more controversial claim was made. In a book called *The Prime Minister was a Spy*, the British journalist and author Anthony Grey argued that Holt had not drowned off the Victoria coast at all. He swam out to a waiting submarine, was pulled down by frogmen who provided breathing apparatus, and was whisked away to the People's Republic of China. This astonishing allegation was based on unverifiable information from Chinese sources that Holt was a spy for Chairman Mao Ze-dong. He had (it was claimed) been a socialist sympathizer since the 1930s, passed information to the People's Republic of China, and made his escape when exposure was imminent.

Critics laughed at the theory, though this would not have been the only escape through a fake drowning. Britain's John Stonehouse, a former member of parliament, had apparently drowned when his clothes were found on a Miami beach. In December 1974 he turned up living in Australia on a false passport, and he was subsequently brought back to England to face charges of fraud and theft. In the case of Harold Holt, such a secret getaway seems implausible, though the lack of a body has left room for the imagination to wander.

THE VANISHED SKYJACKER

HOW A MYSTERY MAN KNOWN ONLY AS D.B. COOPER ENDED HIS DARING CAPER WITH A PARACHUTE JUMP

The quiet, clean-shaven man in dark glasses boarded a Northwest Airlines Boeing 727 at Portland, Oregon, giving his name as D.B. Cooper (which was all that was ever known about him). About half an hour after takeoff, he pushed a button overhead to call the stewardess who came with a tray to take his order for a drink. But Cooper asked for no liquid refreshment. Instead, he passed her a note warning that he had a bomb with him, and that unless he was given $200,000 in cash he would blow the plane to bits. Then he opened the canvas carrier bag on his lap to reveal the sticks of dynamite and the detonator.

It was Thanksgiving Day—November 24, 1971—a date that would long be remembered among students of 20th-century crime. For that night, D.B. Cooper pulled off a coup that led him to be dubbed the world's only successful skyjacker.

Notified of the danger, the pilot, Captain Bill Scott, managed to radio a coded alert about the hijack, so that when the plane landed some 400 miles away at Seattle, squads of police, airline officials and FBI men were already assembled on the ground. But they could see that the risk was real enough and acceded to Cooper's requests. A sack containing the $200,000 was brought to

MYSTERY PASSENGER As part of the police investigation into the identity and fate of D.B. Cooper, artists attempted to capture his likeness from eyewitness accounts.

the aircraft, along with a selection of four parachutes that he had requested in return for the safe release of the hostages. Oblivious of the dramatic events unfolding around them, the passengers on board were then allowed to leave before the plane took off once again with Cooper and the three-man flight crew.

At 8:13 p.m., 32 minutes after leaving Seattle, with the jetliner flying at 200 mph over the Lewis river, Cooper opened the rear exit door and leapt out.

His fate is unknown to this day. Cooper jumped into high altitude winds and freezing rain wearing only his lightweight lounge suit and a raincoat. Some believe that he would have perished in the air, or on hitting the thickly wooded mountains, but neither aerial searches by spotter planes nor satellite surveillance photographs revealed any trace of his parachute canopy. And the authorities were further confounded when, three weeks after the hijack, a typed letter purportedly written by D.B. Cooper arrived at the offices of a Los Angeles newspaper. "I am no modern-day Robin Hood," the writer declared, "unfortunately I have only 14 months to live. The hijacking was the fastest and most profitable way to gain a few last grains of peace of mind. I didn't rob Northwest because I thought it would be romantic, or heroic, or any of the other euphemisms that seem to attach themselves to situations of high risk."

The money in the mud

Was the letter genuine? Or a fake? It was difficult to tell since the vanishing skyjacker had started to acquire a cult following in the United States, prompting everything from scrawled graffiti to newspaper cartoons, proposals of marriage from impressionable women, and record dedications by radio disc jockeys. But as time passed, the forests of Washington

MONEY IN THE BANK Investigators dig a trench at the spot in the river bank where thousands of dollars of the skyjack loot were found by picnickers in 1980.

State began to yield some real and tantalizing clues. In 1979, a deer hunter in the woods above Kelso village came upon a plastic warning sign that came from the rear door hatch of a Boeing 727. Then, in 1980, a full nine years after his disappearing act, about $3,000 of the marked bills from Cooper's haul were recovered from the shore of the Columbia river.

For some, the implication of the muddied cash was that D.B. Cooper must have perished after all, and that his bones lay somewhere in the forest, or in the riverbed, upstream. Further searches, though, revealed nothing, and others have pictured him injured but still alive making a cunning escape from the forest with the bulk of his ransom money. No one can say for certain unless Cooper really did survive and secretly lives on, enjoying the proceeds of his audacious coup in the skies.

1900   2000

1971 D.B. Cooper disappears
1976 FBI officially close the file on D.B. Cooper
1980 Dollar bills found on bank of river

VIETNAM'S MISSING GIS

WERE AMERICAN SERVICEMEN LEFT BEHIND IN SOUTHEAST ASIA AFTER THE END OF THE WAR?

On March 29, 1973—two months after peace talks had brought the Vietnam War to an end—the last prisoners officially held by the North Vietnamese in Hoa Lo Prison (known as the Hanoi Hilton) boarded an Air Force plane at Gia Kam airfield near Hanoi. Their release prompted an immense outpouring of joy and relief from the crowds who gathered in the United States to greet them. But the trauma of this bitter and divisive war was not over yet. Still unaccounted

high in relation to the handful of released prisoners of war. Only 591 Americans regained their freedom following the signing of the Paris peace accords in January 1973. Had others been left behind?

The official silence

Suspicions were aroused in June 1973 when a North Vietnamese defector called Nguyen Thanh Son told newsmen that he had recently seen six prisoners who he believed were Americans who had not yet been released. As other Vietnamese refugees turned up telling similar stories, families of the MIAs became alarmed by Washington's seeming inactivity. Accusations of a cover-up were to be leveled against the U.S. government.

exchange for prisoners of war. But Congress had refused the aid money—so the POWs' liberty became forfeit.

One missing serviceman who did turn up was a Marine, Private Robert Garwood, who had been captured near Da Nang in 1965, when barely 19 years old. After the war he had worked as a mechanic in the motor pool of a prison camp, repairing American vehicles left behind in Vietnam. In 1979, he managed to smuggle a message out of Vietnam to the BBC via a neutral diplomat, telling the world that he wanted to go back to the United States. On his return, however, he was accused of being a turncoat who had collaborated with the enemy, been given preferential treatment in the camps, and had

on one occasion struck a fellow American prisoner. At his court martial, Garwood insisted that he had been isolated from other POWs and forced to live with his Vietnamese guards because of his gift for languages. Either way, he disproved Hanoi's claim that there were no Americans left in Vietnam.

And Garwood insisted that other GIs were still alive in Southeast Asia. He claimed to have been in a camp with other American prisoners when he heard former Secretary of State Henry Kissinger assert over the camp radio: "There are no more live POWs in Vietnam." This was a devastating blow to all of them, and their guards had taunted them with their government's desertion. Garwood claimed that he could name other American prisoners still alive in Vietnam, but was reluctant to do so because if he identified them by name they were liable to be killed by their captors.

MARINE'S RETURN Private Robert Garwood, captured in 1965, escaped from Vietnam in 1979 and brought back reports of other American POWs still alive there.

MAN WITH A MISSION "Bo" Gritz, a former Special Forces officer, led a rescue team to recover American GIs who were believed to have been left behind in Southeast Asia.

for at the war's end were more than 2,400 servicemen and civilians who had disappeared during the struggle in Southeast Asia, some 1,800 in Vietnam itself. These were the MIAs—the Missing in Action—who had been involved in combat with the enemy but had been listed neither as killed in action nor as prisoners of war.

Obviously, in the chaos of a long jungle war, many lives might be lost unaccountably. But the number of the missing was exceptionally

What possible motive could there be for government secrecy? Part of the problem was reputedly that the missing personnel included troops lost during the secret wars in Laos and Cambodia—conflicts long denied by officialdom. To acknowledge the prisoners would be to admit an involvement in covert operations. It has also been alleged that President Nixon had secretly agreed to provide more than $3 billion to help pay for postwar reconstruction in Vietnam in

A secret expedition

Another extraordinary story came to light when it was reported that a retired Special Forces soldier named Lt. Colonel James "Bo" Gritz had led a mission in 1981 to recover American servicemen left behind in Southeast Asia. The rescue team had investigated a suspected prison site, said to have been located on several satellite photographs, but had found no Americans. After a two-year silence, the Department of Defense acknowledged that Gritz had headed just such an expedition.

PUZZLE PICTURE This grainy black-and-white photograph, dated 1990, was alleged to depict three captive pilots shot down during the Vietnam War: (from left to right) Col. John Robertson, Major Albro Lundy and Lt. Larry Stevens. Relatives were convinced that the photograph of the middle-aged men, last seen 25 years before, was genuine.

The whole issue was now becoming a national scandal, and a vigorous campaign was conducted by the National League of Families of American Prisoners and Missing in Southeast Asia. Many individual cases became known to the increasingly concerned public. A Colonel David Hrdlicka, shot down

TRAGIC TOLL During a ceremony at Hanoi airport in 1985, American service personnel salute the remains of 26 MIAs handed over by the Vietnamese and returned to the U.S..

in 1965, had been photographed and was thought to have made a radio broadcast as a prisoner, but was not among the returnees of 1973. The wife of a serviceman named Captain James Grace, shot down in 1968, identified her husband as the bearded man shown on a Soviet propaganda film on prisoners made during the war. What had happened to these men, and others like them?

President Ronald Reagan himself asserted that the missing servicemen's fate was a matter of top priority for his administration. In 1986 a high-powered U.S. delegation visited Vietnam for talks to resolve the problem. Hanoi officials acknowledged that there might be some Americans still held captive in remote areas of Vietnam not fully under government control, and later that year the U.S. government agreed to help Hanoi in tracing and accounting for the MIAs.

But the mystery of the missing GIs was still not resolved to everyone's satisfaction. In January 1993, a U.S. Senate report declared that in its eagerness to see an end to the war the Nixon administration had "shunted aside" the possibility that the POWs were left behind. The same year, a report made by a North Vietnamese general, Tran Van Qang,

in 1972 was discovered in the archives of the Soviet Communist Party in Moscow. The document said that North Vietnam was

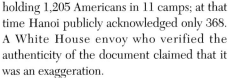

MY GOD! LOOK!

Scott Barnes, a freelance specialist in covert operations, has claimed that in the course of a CIA mission into Laos in 1981, in company with an American named Jerrold "Hog" Daniels, he saw U.S. prisoners being kept in a jungle compound:

"He assembled the cameras—one had the longest lens I'd ever seen; then radio equipment with what looked like a satellite dish . . . In a valley below, I saw what seemed like a triangular camp, surrounded by a fence, with a watchtower at three points. One building was larger than the others and was surrounded by large drums. Outside the walled compound were fields, one to the left and the other facing us, where men worked under armed guard. At the furthest point there was a kind of tunnel into the thick jungle.

"Suddenly Daniels shouted, 'My God! Look!' I took the binoculars and saw two Caucasians under armed escort, walking to the compound. He shouted, 'We really did leave them behind!'"

holding 1,205 Americans in 11 camps; at that time Hanoi publicly acknowledged only 368. A White House envoy who verified the authenticity of the document claimed that it was an exaggeration.

Its discovery did nothing to allay the worries of concerned relatives. In July 1993, President Clinton said that he would not lift a crippling US trade embargo on Vietnam unless the country did more to resolve the fate of the American servicemen still listed as missing in action. And, at the request of relatives, the former world boxing champion Muhammad Ali even visited Vietnam to try to persuade top officials to continue their investigations. The trade embargo was lifted the following year, but when, in 1995, the United States formally renewed diplomatic ties with Vietnam there was a public outcry. The uncertainties lingered on, long after the conclusion of the harrowing war in Southeast Asia.

1950

1965 U.S. government commits the first fighting American soldiers to the Vietnam War

1973 U.S. government withdraws troops; POWs returned

1979 Robert Garwood returns home
1981 "Bo" Gritz's secret mission

1994 Trade embargo lifted

2000

MICHAEL ROCKEFELLER DISAPPEARS

WAS THE ADVENTUROUS HEIR TO THE ROCKEFELLER EMPIRE DEVOURED BY CANNIBALS?

Michael Rockefeller was born into a life of extraordinary privilege. The son of Nelson Rockefeller—then the governor of New York, and soon the Vice President under Gerald Ford—and the great-grandson of the Standard Oil titan John D. Rockefeller, Michael was heir to a vast oil fortune estimated in the hundreds of millions of dollars. But though he shared his family's commitment to public service, he did not inherit his father's interest in politics, or his great-grandfather's financial savvy. Instead, Michael, endowed with the prodigious wanderlust and curiosity of a real-life Indiana Jones, developed a deep interest in archeology, anthropology and adventure. As he noted in his journal during his years at Harvard, "I want to do something romantic and adventuresome now, while there are still faraway frontiers to explore, something utterly different than anything I have experienced before."

After graduation, he had his chance. In 1961, the 21-year-old Rockefeller and a friend, Sam Putnam, joined an expedition to study the primitive culture of the Dani tribe in the Baliem Valley of Dutch New Guinea.

The region, one of the most remote corners of the world, possesses a rough but spectacular beauty, marked by lush forests, mangrove swamps, and murky rivers. Michael Rockefeller fell in love with the land and its people. Putnam recalled that his friend seemed transformed—transfixed, in fact—by the exhilarating strangeness of the place. Michael's diary bears testimony to the expedition's profound effect on him; "My New Guinea experience will not stop in its intensity," reads one entry. When Putnam and the original research team returned to the United States after six months, Rockefeller decided to remain, forging farther into the dark mystery of the New Guinea interior. He became fascinated with the local Asmat tribes, studying their society and trading chocolate, silver and photographs for the large, elaborately decorated wooden sculptures carved by their skillful artisans. Many of these sculptures are now displayed in the Metropolitan Museum of Art in New York.

ALL ASHORE Michael Rockefeller was last seen swimming ashore by Rene Wassink (left) after the raft they shared overturned. Wassink vainly tried to prevent Rockefeller from leaving the raft.

On November 18, 1961, in order to collect more artifacts, Rockefeller and a guide left from the Christian mission at Agats, on the western coast of Dutch New Guinea, to the village of Atsj. The crude catamaran on which they were traveling, overpowered by the infamously treacherous currents, was swept off to sea. Michael decided to swim for shore. He was never seen again.

Soon after his disappearance, Michael's twin sister Mary organized a desperate search through the region, aided by the Dutch Navy and the Australian Air Force. Michael, or his body, was never discovered, and the search was abandoned.

What happened to the young Rockefeller? Missionaries in Dutch New Guinea reported rumors of a headhunting and cannibalistic incident in a coastal village known to be hostile to outsiders shortly after his disappearance— Michael might have been the victim.

Michael's family and friends were disgusted by these tales,

LOST Michael Rockefeller (top) on an anthropological exploration of Dutch New Guinea (bottom). Middle: Michael's father, Nelson Rockefeller, at a news conference.

wholly unsubstantiated. His former travelling companion, Sam Putnam, summed up the feelings of many of Michael's friends: "Actually, I was appalled when I read all the rather gory hypotheses as to how Michael had died. I am quite sure that he drowned."

But there is another possibility, one more in tune with Michael's character. Is he, perhaps, still alive, living peaceably deep within the New Guinea interior? Or did he truly pay the highest price for a life of adventure?

1961 Michael Rockefeller, son of Nelson Rockefeller, disappears while on an expedition in New Guinea

WHERE ARE THEY NOW . . . REALLY?

**STRANGE DISAPPEARANCES AND SUSPICIOUS DEATHS HAVE FUELED CULT-LIKE
CONSPIRACY THEORISTS CONVINCED THAT THESE PUBLIC FIGURES ARE NOT REALLY GONE.**

After the death of some public figures, there arise rumors that they are not really dead. Usually the theory is based on some supposed reason that a celebrity might want to have faked his or her demise: to escape the limelight, or to abscond with an organization's treasury, or to avoid prosecution by the IRS. Such rumors have often been fueled by the lurid speculations of the supermarket tabloids, complete with blurred photos of supposed "sightings" of the celebrities.

The most popular deceased celebrity to be "sighted" was Elvis Presley, who died suddenly in August 1977 from complications resulting from medication he was taking for an obstructed colon—a malady that caused him to gain 50 pounds in the last years of his life. The outpouring of grief from his fans and the spectacle of his funeral and grave site, turning his lavish Tennessee home, Graceland, into a shrine to the singer, resulted in persistent rumors that Elvis was still alive. Rumors spurred witnesses to swear they had seen Elvis in a Midwestern mall. Another rock star whose death was doubted by his fans was Jim Morrison, lead singer of The Doors. Morrison died of a drug overdose six years before Elvis, but many of Morrison's fans came to believe the singer had faked his death.

In September 1996, rap artist Tupac Shakur was shot while leaving a boxing match. No arrests were made and the rapper died six days later. Funeral arrangements were so secretive that rumors arose that Tupac had faked his death to avoid prosecution by the Drug Enforcement Agency—or to escape retribution from drug dealers he had betrayed to the authorities.

More perplexing is the very real disappearance of Madalyn Murray O'Hair, famous American atheist. O'Hair vanished without a trace, along with her son and daughter-in-law, on September 29, 1995. The organization O'Hair had founded, American Atheists, claimed the three had been killed by religious groups to prevent her from picketing the Pope, who was then visiting the United States. Others believed O'Hair had absconded with millions from AA's treasury, and still others believed she disappeared to avoid a $1.5 million tax bill being levied by the IRS. Except for her daughter-in-law's car being found abandoned at a Texas airport, no trace has ever been found of the trio.

THE TEAMSTERS' LEADER

WHATEVER HAPPENED TO THE NOTORIOUS AMERICAN UNION BOSS, JIMMY HOFFA?

UNION MAN Jimmy Hoffa, the Teamsters' leader, appears at a press conference after the Union's quarterly meeting, held at Miami Beach in 1960.

At 12:30 PM on July 30, 1975, Jimmy Hoffa kissed his wife Josephine goodbye and climbed into the bullet-proof limousine waiting outside his luxury home in Orion, Michigan. The former president of America's giant International Brotherhood of Teamsters—a union of drivers, store clerks and department store workers with over 1.7 million members—was on his way to a luncheon appointment at the Machus Red Fox Restaurant in a Detroit suburb. Hoffa had told associates that he expected to meet with Anthony Giacalone, a Detroit mobster, and Tony Provenzano, a New Jersey Teamsters official with reputed mob ties, who had held a grudge against Hoffa ever since their days together in prison. But now, apparently, Provenzano wanted to "bury the hatchet."

Neither man showed up; Giacalone claimed that he spent the day at a nearby athletic club, and Provenzano insisted he was playing cards at his local union hall in New Jersey. A few hours later, an aide received a call from an irate Hoffa, demanding, "Where the hell is Tony Giacalone? I'm being stood up?" That was the last anyone heard from him, though several witnesses claimed they glimpsed Hoffa in the back seat

WASHINGTON D.C. Hoffa with lawyer George S. Fitzgerald at the August 20, 1957 Senate Rackets Committee meeting.

of a car with several men that afternoon. He was not seen again.

Hoffa was one of the most notorious figures in American public life. Appointed president of the Teamsters' union in 1957, he was to be accused of milking the organization of almost $2 million and of using vicious gangster tactics to maintain power. Hoffa became the prime target of Robert Kennedy, attorney-general between 1961 and 1964, who called his union leadership a "conspiracy of evil" and initiated inquiries that absorbed the energies of 13 grand juries, 16 lawyers and 30 FBI agents. There was no love lost between Hoffa and the Kennedys; on the day that JFK was assassinated, Hoffa wouldn't let the union flag be lowered. "I'm no hypocrite," he said, "I hope the worms eat his eyes out."

But Robert Kennedy's persistence paid off when the efforts of his "Get Hoffa Squad," as it was soon dubbed, finally came to fruition. On March 7, 1967, the Teamsters' boss was sent to Lewisburg Penitentiary in Pennsylvania for a total of 13 years on two separate convictions (with sentences to run consecutively) for jury fixing and defrauding the union's pension fund.

The abandoned car

Richard Nixon, whose presidential election campaigns in 1960 and 1968 had been generously funded by the union, commuted Hoffa's prison sentence to four years—on the condition that he should hold no union office until 1980. When Hoffa emerged from jail in 1971, however, he immediately embarked on a campaign to get President Nixon's ban lifted. And he also began maneuvering against a one-time colleague, Frank Fitzsimmons, who had replaced him as Teamster president in 1967. Hoffa recognized that challenging Fitzsim-

mons—who was even more complicit in mob illegalities than Hoffa—might make him some enemies, but he sensed his popularity among union members; indeed, a 1974 poll showed that 83 percent supported him. The months after his release might get a bit messy, but Hoffa did not seem to fear for his life. As he once remarked, "I don't cheat nobody. I don't lie about nobody. I don't frame nobody. I don't talk bad about people. If I do, I tell 'em. So what the hell's people gonna try to kill me for?"

This was the setting for Hoffa's disappearance—and there has been no shortage of theories about his fate. In one version, he was killed by the rival Fitzsimmons faction within the Teamsters' union. In another, he was murdered by the Mafia in order to prevent him from exposing details of the corrupt relationship between the union and organized crime—or even from revealing details of plots, involving the CIA, to assassinate Fidel Castro of Cuba. And still there remains a third possibility: knowing his life was in danger from his many different enemies, Hoffa staged his own disappearance.

Hoffa's car, located after an anonymous phone call to the police, offered no clues. Inside was a pair of white gloves, neatly folded on the back seat. But there was no sign of a struggle. In the months that followed, police and private citizens—encouraged by a

and Frank Fitzsimmons. A report from October 31, 1975 states: "Informed sources of the Detroit Division [of the FBI] are generally of the opinion that Hoffa was abducted and "hit" with the knowledge, consent and possible participation of the Detroit LCN family"—La Cosa Nostra, the mob's name for itself.

The secret files also reveal that much of the FBI's investigation centered around one man: Chuckie O'Brien. O'Brien, whose father was close friends with Hoffa, was practically his adopted son, and lived for a while in Hoffa's house. Hoffa navigated O'Brien through the perilous world of union politics, and secured him several cushy Teamsters jobs. However, in 1974, the two became estranged when O'Brien asked to be made president of Hoffa's old local in Detroit, one of the most coveted positions in the union. When Hoffa refused to support him, O'Brien moved on to Fitzsimmons's camp. There were also reports that O'Brien pocketed money given to him by Hoffa to pay merchants, and that Hoffa had to pay off

O'Brien's gambling debts. Just as incriminating, O'Brien had worshipped and often worked for Tony Giacalone.

Many of the testimonies collected by the FBI suggest O'Brien might have been used as a pawn—either willing or unwilling—to lure Hoffa into a trap. Since, as one interviewee claimed, "Hoffa would never enter another person's automobile unless he was certain that he could completely trust that individual," Giacalone may have pressured O'Brien into "pick[ing] up Hoffa and driv[ing] him to a nearby location where the 'hit' was handled," the FBI concluded.

Soon after the disappearance, the FBI tracked down O'Brien's car (it was actually the car of Tony Giacalone's son, which O'Brien had borrowed); police dogs identified Hoffa's scent in the back seat and lab analysis found a hair matching Hoffa's in the upholstery, as well as traces of his skin and blood. In this mire of rumor and surmise, this was the most tangible evidence the investigators would find. O'Brien's alibi was also inconsistent, with different people offering many variations. For two crucial hours, between 2:30 and 4 p.m., O'Brien could not be accounted for. These are the hours the police believed the kidnapping took place.

O'Brien denied any involvement in Hoffa's disappearance, claiming he "loved the old man." He passed a lie detector test on "The Maury Povich Show" on national TV Since then, no one has been prosecuted for Hoffa's abduction, or his murder. Officially, the FBI still lists the Hoffa case as "open," but as key witnesses grow older, and dust collects on the boxes of evidence scattered around the country, this mystery will not grow easier to solve.

$300,000 reward—searched through landfills, woods and rubbish dumps in hopes of discovering the corpse.

In 1997, twenty-two years after Hoffa's disappearance, secret FBI files were found in the bottom of a filing cabinet in the basement of a Detroit recreational facility (how they got there is perhaps as big a mystery as Hoffa's disappearance). The documents, sought after by Hoffa's family but suppressed by the federal government, represent work done by the FBI in the first five months of the investigation—and still amount to some 1,500 pages. They demonstrate a befuddled FBI, faced with a paucity of reliable witnesses and credible evidence, while at the same time deluged with outrageous claims and unsubstantiable testimonies. Compounding the agency's difficulties was the fact that the mob, usually eager to clear themselves of any charges, did not conduct its own investigation; "the street" was keeping silent. So government investigators were forced to conduct hundreds of interviews, grilling top union officials and rank-and-file members, petty criminals and mob bosses as well as politicians and influential businessmen, funeral home proprietors and motel operators. They even questioned Coleman Young, then the Mayor of Detroit, who had lunched with Hoffa the day before he disappeared. Detectives canvassed the country, traveling from Oakland County to Lake St. Clair, from northern Michigan, to Texas, to Pennsylvania, to Arkansas—following even the most outlandish tip in a vain search to find Hoffa, or his body.

The documents shed some light on the nature of the FBI's early suspicions. A few weeks after the disappearance, the FBI theorized that Hoffa was indeed killed by the mob, in a plot by Giacalone and Provenzano

ARCH ENEMIES Top: Jimmy Hoffa jabs his finger at Robert Kennedy, chief counsel for the Senate Rackets Committee, in 1959. Above: The last place Hoffa was seen alive. Right: Is Giants Stadium Jimmy Hoffa's final resting place?

1957 Hoffa elected President of the Teamsters' union

1967 Hoffa sent to Lewisburg Penitentiary

1975 Hoffa's disappearance makes him Missing Person 75-3425

WHAT HAPPENED TO SHERGAR?

THE KIDNAP RIDDLE OF THE WORLD'S MOST FAMOUS RACEHORSE REMAINS UNSOLVED

On the evening of Tuesday, February 8, 1983, armed men burst into the home of James Fitzgerald, head groom at Ballymany stud, the Aga Khan's stable in County Kildare in the Irish Republic. The intruders locked the groom's family in a downstairs room and then, at gunpoint, forced Jim Fitzgerald to identify the security stable housing Shergar, a handsome bay stallion with a distinctive white blaze, who was one of the world's most valuable horses.

Another member of the gang (police estimated that more than six were involved) required a ransom of $3 million, and then driven in a van to the outskirts of a village 20 miles away. From here he had to make his own way home—some four hours after the break-in. Shergar, meanwhile, vanished with his kidnappers into the night.

Hoax calls

Shergar's kidnapping prompted a massive farm-by-farm search. While police issued Identikit pictures of three men they wanted to question in connection with the theft, more than 100,000 farmers throughout the country combed their land, sheds and barns for traces of the missing steed. Nicknamed the "wonder horse" after winning one of Europe's most prestigious races by

that had been lined up to be covered by the Derby-winner in 1983 alone.

Reports circulated that huge ransoms had been asked for Shergar, but throughout the period of the search the police were bedeviled by hoax calls; the syndicate of 34 shareholders that owned Shergar countered such rumors by claiming that no ransom had been demanded. According to some reports, Shergar had been smuggled to Libya or the Middle East. But early in April an anonymous caller to RTE, the Irish radio and television station, indicated that the stallion was still in the country, and said that unless $2.2 million ransom was paid, the head of Shergar would be cut off and deposited at a location somewhere in Dublin.

The IRA connection

In May the horse's insurers decided to pay theft claims on Shergar—a fact indicating that they expected no swift return of the horse from the kidnappers. With the passing months, and then years, fears for Shergar's safety deepened into a widespread conviction that the horse must be dead. In 1986 a book claimed that Shergar had been killed by the IRA, and a TV drama was broadcast based on this version of events. In 1991, however, hopes for the horse were revived when the deputy chairman of Lloyd's bloodstock committee revealed that he had been contacted by a bounty hunter claiming that Shergar was still alive.

In December 1992 a former IRA police informer imprisoned in Northern Ireland claimed to reveal the definitive version of events. Sean O'Callaghan, serving a life sentence for two murders, told *Sunday Times* journalists that Shergar was killed within hours of being kidnapped. In this account, the Derby-winner was shot because he had panicked in captivity and could not be controlled by his kidnappers. The five-year-old stallion was then buried in thick woodland 100 miles from the Aga Khan's stud farm. Although this version of events has been widely accepted, Shergar's remains have yet to be located and identified.

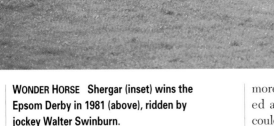

WONDER HORSE Shergar (inset) wins the Epsom Derby in 1981 (above), ridden by jockey Walter Swinburn.

reversed a scruffy light-blue or green horse-trailer to the stall, and Shergar was pushed inside, with the reluctant help of the head groom. Mr. Fitzgerald was taken back to his house, told by the kidnappers that they more than 10 lengths, Shergar was syndicated at $15 million. However, he probably could have fetched three times that amount on the open market, and had been seized only a week before the breeding season started. The Aga Khan, one of the richest men in the world, and other members of the syndicate who owned the champion stood to lose $100,000 for each of the 50 or so mares

PARANORMAL PHENOMENA

THE 19TH-CENTURY POET PERCY BYSSHE SHELLEY RECALLED HOW "WHILE YET A BOY I SOUGHT FOR GHOSTS." IN THE 20TH CENTURY, TOO, ENQUIRING INDIVIDUALS HAVE CONTINUED TO HUNT FOR SPECTRES. SPACE-AGE MAN, IT SEEMS, SHARES HUMANKIND'S AGE-OLD FASCINATION WITH REPORTS OF UNIDENTIFIED FLYING OBJECTS, MONSTERS, MIRACLES, UNCANNY PHENOMENA AND HAUNTINGS. IN OUR TECHNOLOGICAL AGE, THE DREAM OF AN OTHERWORLD STILL PERSISTS.

THE ANGELS OF MONS

HOW A PIECE OF POPULAR FICTION BEGAN A FIRST WORLD WAR MYTH THAT WOULD NOT BE EXPLODED

On August 23, 1914, during the early engagements of the First World War, British and French troops fighting near the village of Mons were overwhelmed by a larger German force and began to retreat.

In September of the same year, the writer Arthur Machen published a story called "The Bowmen" in the London Evening News. In it, he told how struggling soldiers were saved from the advancing Germans by a vision of St. George and the bowmen of Agincourt (not far from Mons). Although Machen's story was fiction it was taken for fact by a number of readers, and found its way as a true story into a number of magazines. Reports were published of winged and robed "angels" who suddenly appeared at Mons between the Allied troops and the Germans, causing the enemy to fall back in disarray. When Machen told the press that he had made the original story up, many people refused to believe him.

Enemy propaganda?

The case might be taken as a classic example of how easily people are deceived, especially at times of stress when the need to believe outweighs common sense.
And many

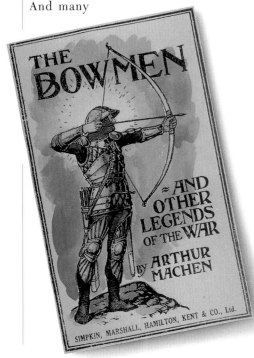

APPARITIONS "The Bowmen of Mons" as they appeared in a Christmas issue of the *Illustrated London News*, 1915.

troops who served at Mons continued to insist that they did see angels. An affidavit was sworn in August 1915 by Private Robert Cleaver of the 1st Cheshire regiment that "I personally was at Mons and saw the vision of Angels with my own eyes."

It has also been reported that weeks before Machen published his story, Brigadier General John Charteris wrote to his family that "the Angel of the Lord on the traditional white horse, clad all in white with

LEGEND COMES ALIVE Arthur Machen's fictional tale began a long-lasting controversy. Some who fought at Mons said that it was true.

flaming sword, faced the Germans and forbade their further progress."

The debate was revived in 1930 when Friedrich Herzenwirth, a man claiming to have been a member of German Military Intelligence, told a New York newspaper that German aviators at Mons had projected movie images onto the white cloudbanks over Flanders to prove that God was on their side. "What we had not figured on," he said, "was that the English should turn the vision to their own benefit." Controversy deepened when a member of the German War Office declared the story a hoax and asserted that there was no such person as Herzenwirth.

Products of propaganda? Hallucinations? False memories? Or bona fide apparitions? The Angels of Mons have not yet been explained to everyone's satisfaction.

1914 Battle of Mons
Arthur Machen writes
"The Bowmen"

1930 Claims that
Germans projected
"angels" at Mons

MIRACLES AT FATIMA

HOW THE HOLY VIRGIN TOLD HER SECRETS TO THREE CHILDREN IN A PORTUGUESE VILLAGE

Three shepherd children at the grazing ground of Cova da Iria outside the Portuguese village of Fatima reported being visited by a "Lady from Heaven." Lucia (aged ten) and her two cousins, Jacinta (aged seven) and Francisco Marto (aged nine), saw a white-clad image of a beautiful, shimmering

THE VISION The shining lady who appeared before shepherd children at Fatima told them that she was the Lady of the Rosary, who wanted to save souls and bring peace.

woman on a cloud above a small oak. The date was May 13, 1917, and the children reported that the vision asked them to come back at the same hour on the thirteenth of each month for the next six months. Ever larger crowds gathered with the children each month, but the Lady was visible only

TERRIBLE SECRET Pope John XXIII is said to have almost fainted when he learnt the third secret of Fatima.

THE WITNESSES The children who saw the vision, photographed in 1917. From the left: Jacinta, Francisco and Lucia.

to their eyes. Their claims were doubted so strongly that they were arrested and interrogated, but they stuck to their story.

The final visitation

At the final sighting on October 13, a crowd of about 70,000 people assembled in pouring rain. Once again the shining lady showed herself only to the children, who reported that she called herself Our Lady of the Rosary, and told them three secrets about the future.

After this visitation, the rain suddenly stopped. Then, through a gap in the clouds, the sun appeared and seemed to spin and plunge earthwards, giving off heat as it approached. There was considerable panic in the terrified crowd, some of whom feared that the end of the world was near. Then the sun returned to its normal position, but onlookers found that their clothes, which had been soaked by the rain, were dry.

The so-called "miracle of the sun," which lasted ten minutes, was observed many miles away, and documentation of the episode was so persuasive that, in 1927, the Catholic

Church authorized pilgrimages to the village of Fatima, which today is the site of a shrine for Our Lady of the Rosary of Fatima.

The two youngest children, Francisco and Jacinta, both died during the great influenza epidemic that swept war-weakened Europe in 1918–19. But Lucia, the oldest child, lived on to become a Carmelite nun called Lucia dos Santos, and to record in writing the

VISIONS OF THE PAST

Only a handful of 20th-century apparitions have been authenticated by the Catholic Church: Fatima, Portugal (1917); Beauraing, Belgium (1932-3); and Banneaux, Belgium (1933). Historically, the best-known visions of the Virgin Mary were seen at Lourdes in France in 1858 by the 14-year-old peasant girl Bernadette Soubirous, who was canonized in 1933. The most famous modern Visions of the Blessed Virgin Mary were reported in 1981 by children at Medjogorje in former Yugoslavia.

three secrets that the Lady of the Rosary had told to her and her two cousins. The first "secret" was a vision of hell, and the second has been taken as a warning of the outbreak of the Second World War.

The third secret has never been disclosed to the world and was known to no one but Lucia dos Santos until 1960, when it was allegedly read by Pope John XXIII. It has been reported that what the Pope read so horrified him that he almost fainted.

1917 The vision appears at Fatima

1927 Pilgrimages to Fatima are authorized

1948 Lucia becomes a Carmelite nun

1967 Lucia and Pope Paul VI visit the shrine

1981 Sightings of the Virgin at Medjogorje begin

A DISSOLUTE DEMON AT THE TSAR'S COURT

WAS THE "MAD MONK" RASPUTIN A WOMANIZING CHARLATAN OR A TRUE HOLY MAN?

Psychic energy does not submit easily to scientific analysis, yet certain historical figures have undoubtedly possessed an ability to direct others' actions—for good or evil—through a kind of personal magnetism. And few had more influence on 20th-century history than Grigori Yefimovich, who became known as Rasputin, the "mad monk" or "holy devil" of Tsarist Russia. "Rasputin" is a term meaning dissolute which Grigori, the son of Yefim Novykh, welcomed as his nickname from the local villagers in his home province of Tobolsk. Rasputin was born around 1872 into a peasant family and received no education. To the end of his life he was unable to write properly. Nonetheless, he experienced some kind of spiritual awakening, and left his native village to devote himself to religion. His adopted views were those of a sect called the Khlysty who believed that salvation could only be won through sinning followed by repentance. "Sin in order that you may obtain forgiveness" was their doctrine—and one well suited to a man of Rasputin's lusty temperament.

An uncouth, hard-drinking womanizer, he was an unlikely candidate for a divine calling. Still, he cannot have been a complete charlatan, for he made pilgrimages to Mount Athos and Jerusalem and spent some time in monasteries before returning to his village as

MAGNETIC PERSONALITY Above: Rasputin among his many lady admirers. Right: the monk with the vivid blue eyes captured the tsar's family in his spell.

1905 Rasputin
introduced at
court

1916 Rasputin murdered
1917 Russian Revolution
1918 Tsar's family murdered

a mysterious itinerant holy man. In 1903 he appeared in St. Petersburg and presented himself to the city's most revered holy man, Father John of Kronstadt. Rasputin was a compelling personality and a spellbinding preacher and rapidly made a name for himself. In 1905, certain admiring Russian churchmen allowed him to be presented at the royal court.

Trying to kill a holy man

When Alexis, the son of Tsar Nicholas II and Tsarina Alexandra, began bleeding uncontrollably, they were persuaded to call for Rasputin, who was rumored to have mysterious healing powers. Rasputin's apparent cure of her hemophiliac son made a deep impression on Alexandra, who became Rasputin's main champion.

The charismatic but illiterate holy man with the "exceptionally brilliant" pale blue eyes won immense sway over the royal family, and it was not long before he was advising the tsar and tsarina on affairs of state. In consequence he developed immense power over the Russian Government, and high offices were granted to his corrupt and incompetent hangers-on. By 1915 he and the tsarina virtually controlled domestic affairs while the tsar occupied himself with Russia's entry into the First World War.

Tales of the slovenly monk's behavior both within and outside the royal court in St. Petersburg, and of his debaucheries and liaisons with numerous mistresses, including court ladies, were rife. Rumors even circulated of an illicit affair with Tsarina Alexandra herself. But when some officials complained to the tsar, they found themselves "transferred" to remote regions of the empire. The scandalous tales about Rasputin, and his growing power, aggravated his increasing unpopularity. Finally, with the prospect of revolution

NOBLE CONSPIRATOR Prince Yusupov was an aristocratic murderer. Rasputin was poisoned, shot and beaten at Yusupov's palace.

in the air, a group of ultra-conservative noblemen decided to murder the monk in order to save the monarchy's reputation.

On December 29, 1916, Prince Yusupov, a former admirer of Rasputin, invited him to supper at his palace. Poisoned wine and cake were laid out for the unsuspecting guest and just as the conspirators planned, he helped himself—in copious quantities—to the lethal refreshments. Amazingly though, Rasputin seemed unaffected by the poison. Prince Yusupov resorted to a gun and shot Rasputin in the back. The monk then fell to the floor where he was pronounced dead.

The noblemen's plan was to dump the murdered monk in the river Neva, but when they came to pick up the body Rasputin sprang to life again. Dragging himself along on his hands and knees, he chased the terrified Yusupov up a flight of stairs. Only when he was shot twice more did Rasputin finally crumple. The conspirators then kicked and bludgeoned his apparently lifeless form, took the corpse to the river, broke a hole in the ice and lowered him in.

An unshakeable belief

The tsarina never doubted Rasputin's holiness. She had his corpse recovered from the river three days later. Incredibly, he was discovered to have lungs full of the freezing water and was reportedly making a sign of benediction, with three fingers laid across his breast. Rasputin must still have been alive when he was finally dumped—poisoned, shot and beaten—into the river.

Alexandra had a special chapel built to hold Rasputin's body and she went every night to pray at his grave.

How, other than occult powers, to account for the incredible resistance

of the "mad monk" to poison and bullets? There are rational explanations. Rasputin was a powerfully built man whose sheer physical strength may have enabled him to survive, at least temporarily, gunshot wounds and battering. Alcohol, which he drank in

TWO CHARISMATICS The Russian mystic and bon viveur George Gurdjieff (left) and the English magician Aleister Crowley (right) attracted cult followings.

prodigious quantities, can nullify the toxic effects of cyanide, and its presence in the lining of his stomach may account for Rasputin's miraculous survival of the poisoning attempt.

And what of his cure for hemophilia? Alexis's health did improve around the time that Rasputin came to court, but this could have been coincidence. There is no scientific evidence that the monk "cured hemophilia."

The deeper mystery lies in Rasputin's personal magnetism. Even his opponents paid tribute to his mesmerizing presence. "Rasputin's eyes," wrote Yusupov, "shone with a kind of phosphorescent light. From them came two rays that flowed into each other and merged into a glowing circle." When Rasputin stared at him intently, said Yusupov, he became paralyzed. The same spiritual force has been attributed to other 20th-century occultists, such as the Russian George Gurdjieff and the British magician Aleister Crowley. The great evangelists, faith healers, cult leaders and demagogues of the world all seem to tap the same inexplicable psychic energy that remains one of the greatest of all human mysteries.

THE WOLF CHILDREN OF MIDNAPORE

HOW A STARTLING DISCOVERY IN INDIA GAVE NEW CREDENCE TO OLD FABLES

From the Roman legend of Romulus and Remus—the twins cared for by wolves—to the more recent story of Tarzan—a child reared by apes—the idea of children adopted by wild animals has gripped the human imagination. From the jungles of Bengal in the 19th century came several reports of children reared by wolves, a concept which was immortalized by Rudyard Kipling in 1895 in *The Jungle Book*, a tale of a lost boy, Mowgli, who is cared for by the

AMAZING FIND Two children were found curled up with the wolf cubs in the den (above). They ran on all fours (right).

jungle animals. The most celebrated real-life case was reported by a 20th-century missionary, the Reverend J.A.L. Singh, during an evangelistic tour of the district of Midnapore (Bengal), India, in 1920. The missionary heard curious reports of two *manushbaghas* ("man-ghosts")—small, phantasmal creatures with blazing eyes who were neither human nor animal. The ghostly beings were said to frequent the forests near Denganalia and to run with the wolves, terrifying the local people.

Reverend Singh decided to get to the bottom of the curious tale, and by hiding in a tree one night he managed to glimpse the creatures at their lair, an abandoned ant-heap. From what he saw he came to the conclusion that the *manush-baghas* were in fact human children—albeit hideous in appearance—who were living with a pack of wolves and ran on all fours.

On October 17, he returned to the mound with a party of local beaters in order to dig out the wolf den. As soon as excavation began, two wolves bolted from the lair and fled. Then a mother wolf appeared and attacked the diggers in a fury; before Mr. Singh could prevent it, the beaters had killed the animal with arrows.

An amazing discovery

When the ant-heap was opened, two small children were found huddled in a ball alongside two wolf cubs. Both children were female; the elder girl was about eight years old and the younger about one and a half.

> ## I WALKED ON ALL FOURS
>
> In 1921 a "Baboon Boy" was brought in by a police patrol chasing a troop of baboons near Grahamstown in South Africa. The 12-year-old child, who then made only guttural ape-like noises, later learned to speak Afrikaans and English. In 1939, as an adult farm-worker, he told an interviewer the following:
>
> "I can recall only a few incidents of my life among the baboons. My food consisted mainly of crickets, ostrich eggs, prickly pears, green mealies and wild honey. I was kicked on the head by an ostrich while raiding its nest, and was often stung by bees while robbing their hives, and once fell and broke my leg. While with the baboons I walked on all fours and slept in the bush entirely naked. I was busy hunting for food one day with my baboon companions when two policemen shot at us with revolvers, but I was captured by one of the policemen."

The four creatures proved difficult to separate, clinging together furiously, but eventually the human and wolf children were forced apart. The tribesmen sold the wolf cubs off, and Mr. Singh took the little girls to Midnapore Orphanage, to be looked after by his wife.

Mrs. Singh named the younger child Amala and the elder one Kamala. But their newly acquired names were their only human characteristic. They astonished everyone by running on all fours, howling like wolves, and shunning daylight. They were said to be confirmed carnivores too, exhibiting a marked preference for raw meat—even carrion—over vegetable and cereal foods. The girls avoided human company and made friends with the dogs at the orphanage.

Amala died of dysentery within a year of being taken captive, but her sister, Kamala, lived for nine years and in time learned to walk upright, to eat more like a human than a wolf, and to speak 30 words of English.

Despite the copious documentation of the Midnapore case, some people doubt whether it is possible that the children were nurtured by wild animals. It has been disputed, in particular, whether Mr.

CAPTIVE CARE Mrs. Singh feeds biscuits to Kamala soon after her capture (above left). By 1926 Kamala could stand upright and would tolerate clothes (above right).

Singh really was present at the time when the children were discovered. However, the writer Charles Maclean concluded in his 1977 study *The Wolf Children*, based on diaries and eyewitness reports, that Singh's account was broadly true.

The child psychologist Bruno Bettelheim argued in 1959 that the Midnapore girls were abandoned autistic children. He suggested a number of characteristics that they shared with autistic children, such as speech difficulties and howling noises, the urges to run about naked and to bite humans, and uncontrolled urination and defecation. Bettelheim suggested that to observers who believe children to have been reared by wild beasts, any animal-like behavior is seen as evidence of an animal upbringing.

Reports of wild children have continued since the Midnapore discovery. Can children really be raised by animals or do the stories reflect a deep-rooted longing in humans for some lost harmony with nature?

REPORTS OF WILD CHILDREN

Long before 1900, children had been found whom observers assumed to be youngsters reared by animals. As far back as 1344, documents record the capture of a "wolf-boy" in the German principality of Hesse. He was allegedly seized from the wolves by hunters, ran on all fours and could jump prodigiously. Other historic characters include the 17th-century Bear-Boy of Lithuania and a Swine-Girl of Salzburg who had lived during the 1820s in a hog-sty, sitting cross-legged; according to one account: "She grunted like a hog, and her gestures were brutishly unseemly."

Were they really raised by beasts? Typical characteristics of wild children include the habits of walking on all fours, making animal-like sounds, and eating and drinking like animals. All could be the traits of retarded children abandoned by their parents. Another often-reported characteristic is an insensitivity to heat and cold. In a famous 18th-century case, Victor, the wild boy of Aveyron, would squat naked in the chill, driving rain without apparent discomfort, and could pluck hot potatoes out of boiling water. Such a remarkable resistance to extremes of heat and cold is often found among autistic children.

Where the youngsters have been reported running with packs of wild animals, the case is rather different. The wolf children of Midnapore have provided the 20th century with its most thoroughly documented case, but there have been others. In 1971 the distinguished anthropologist Jean-Claude Armen wrote of a gazelle-boy moving in leaps and bounds among herds in the Spanish Sahara; he participated in their games and knew their sign language. "I have watched him approach gazelles and lick their foreheads as a sign of recognition," claimed Armen. The anthropologist further described the wild boy as roughly ten years old, with a pleasant, open expression. His disproportionately thick ankles presumably derived from his practice of leaping with the herd, and he left footprints that hardly made any impression in the sand, "revealing a rare suppleness, the human prints blending with the rhythm of the bounding prints of the gazelles."

1959 Psychologist suggests the girls were autistic

1971 Armen reports a gazelle-boy in the Spanish Sahara

1977 *The Wolf Children* published

ABOMINABLE SNOWMEN

LOCAL LEGENDS OF HUGE APE-LIKE CREATURES HAVE PROVOKED WORLDWIDE CURIOSITY

Reports of a bizarre man-like creature in the Himalayas had circulated in the early years of the 20th century, but it was only as the "Abominable Snowman" that the creature made headlines worldwide.

In 1921 a British expedition, led by Colonel C.K. Howard-Bury, made an attempt on the northern face of Mount Everest. At about 17,000 feet they saw through their binoculars a number of dark figures moving about in a snowfield far above them. On reaching the place where the creatures had been, they discovered huge footprints, "three times the size of those of normal humans." The colonel thought the footprints were probably those of "a very large stray, grey wolf." But excited Sherpas in the group identified them as the tracks of semi-human creatures, which they called by a variety of names, including *yeti* and *mehtohkangmi* (snow or wild creature). When a journalist freely translated this local name as "Abominable Snowman," a legend was born.

Creatures of the snows

The Sherpas—mountain people of Tibet and Nepal—believe yeti to be hairy, human-like creatures that live in the mountains and forage in the valleys. Some even believe that the yeti will carry off humans. In 1913, for example, a Sherpa girl was allegedly abducted from her village by a yeti. Also, several sensational reports of attacks by the Abominable Snowman have appeared in the press in the decades following Howard-Bury's expedition.

Skeptics have explained away the numerous reported sightings as sightings of bears, large langur monkeys that live in the Himalayas, or even the hardy Hindu hermits who are known as sadhu.

Material evidence for the yeti's existence has been presented too. In 1951 the respected mountaineer Eric Shipton published photographs of what he believed was a trail of yeti footprints, found in the Menlung Basin in Nepal. One close-up revealed a foot some 13 inches long that did not belong to any recognizable creature. It has been suggested by some that snow melting around normal-sized tracks may enlarge and distort their shape and produce these mysterious tracks.

Rather less impressive was a so-called "yeti scalp" prized by certain Sherpa villagers, which turned out to be made of goatskin. Nonetheless, the idea of some unknown creature existing in the mountains has been sufficiently credible to interest serious scientists and explorers. In 1958, the Soviet Academy of Sciences sent teams to various parts of Asia where

YETI OR YAK? Many villagers living in the mountains have seen "Yeti" relics. One "Yeti scalp" turned out to be goatskin.

semi-human creatures had been reported. The team eventually concluded that some kind of primitive hominid lives in the mountainous areas of Asia.

The American Indians of British Columbia and northern California, mean-

STRANGE FOOTPRINTS The mountaineer Eric Shipton with the alleged "Yeti tracks" that he found in Nepal.

ITS HEAD WAS HIGH AND POINTED

In March 1949 a herdsman named Mingma at Pangboche in the Himalayas heard a strange, half-human cry and saw something coming towards him through the rocks. Taking refuge in a hut, Mingma observed a creature that he assumed was a yeti. He later described it to Charles Stonor, former Assistant Curator at the London Zoo:

"It was a squat, thickset creature, of the size and proportions of a small man, covered with reddish and black hair. The hair was not very long, and looked to be slanting upwards above the waist, and downwards below it, and was rather longer about the feet.

"The head was high and pointed, with a crest of hair on the top; the face was bare, except for some hair on the sides of the cheeks, brown in color, not so flat as a monkey but flatter than a man, and with a squashed-in nose. It had no tail. As I watched it, the yeti stood slightly stooping, its arms hanging down by its sides; I noticed particularly that the hands looked to be larger and stronger than a man's. It moved about in front of the hut with long strides..."

while, have their own legends of a ferocious "Sasquatch" or "Bigfoot," which appears on carved totem poles and masks. In his book *The Wilderness Hunter*, published in 1893, American President Theodore Roosevelt reported a sighting by two trappers of a "great body" with a "strong wild beast odor."

1913 Yeti allegedly carries off a child

1921 Everest expedition sees footprints

ODD SOUVENIRS A former rodeo rider called Roger Patterson caught a large, ape-like figure on film as it loped away from a campsite (below). He also managed to take plaster casts of its tracks (right).

In October 1967, at Bluff Creek in northern California, an alleged Bigfoot was caught on film by a camper named Roger Patterson. The film seems to show a giant female ambling across a forest clearing.

The Wildman of China

The small town of Wan Xian, half-way down the Chang Jiang (Yangtze River) in southern China, is the home of the Wildman Institute, where information on thousands of reported sightings of China's own version of "bigfoot" and "yeti" are collected, as well as material evidence.

The Wildman is said to be a red-haired creature, 6 feet tall. The collection at Wan Xian includes pickled hands and feet said to have been from a Wildman, but which have turned out to belong to a previously unknown species of monkey. Other relics include the skeletal remains of a small child with a skull that appears to be half human,

BUILDING STORIES FROM BONES These remains found in the Chinese highlands are supposedly the skeletons of some of the Wildmen said to inhabit remotest China.

half ape. Huge clumps of bright red "Wildman hairs" have also been collected. Analysis by electron microscope has yielded disputed results. According to one report in 1990, six out of twelve samples of the hair were found to have a different iron-to-zinc ratio from that of humans and general primates.

The Chinese take reports of their Wildman seriously. Much of the evidence supporting its existence comes from a year-long expedition in 1977 by the Chinese Academy of Science. Perhaps the creature is a descendant of *Gigantopithecus*, an ape known to have roamed central south China 500,000 years ago. Alternatively, some unknown species of ape, even

FABULOUS FINDS

Skeptics may doubt whether a large humanoid such as the Yeti could evade discovery for long, but astonishing zoological finds have been made even in the 20th century. These include the mule-sized Okapi (1901), the 12 foot Komodo Dragon (1912), the supposedly extinct Coelecanth fish (1938) and the long-nosed or Chacoan Peccary, a 100 lb pig-like creature thought to have died out 2 million years ago, which was found in 1975, roaming the wilds of Paraguay.

a group of surviving Orangutans, which were believed to have become extinct in China many years ago, could explain the consistent sightings of the Wildman.

Sasquatch, Bigfoot, Wildman or Yeti—the legends persist because we can never really know what is hiding in the mountains.

1951 Eric Shipton photographs strange footprints

1967 Bluff Creek film of "Big Foot"

1977 China's year-long search for the Wildman

1995 Second major Chinese expedition in search of Wildman

THE CURSE OF TUTANKHAMUN

ARE WARNINGS TO THIEVES CARVED ON EGYPT'S ROYAL TOMBS IDLE THREATS OR EVIL PROMISES?

When archaeologist Howard Carter finally broke into the tomb of ancient Egypt's boy king Tutankhamun on November 26, 1922, he was struck dumb by the shimmering splendors inside. There were effigies of strange animals, statues and gold everywhere. Behind, his sponsor, Lord Carnarvon, a respected amateur Egyptologist,

MAKING THE FIRST CUT The moment of the first incision in Tutankhamun's wrappings is captured on film. Inset: Carter at the tomb.

barely contained the suspense. "Can you see anything?"

"Yes," Carter breathed, "wonderful things!" They unearthed one of the most magnificent treasures ever found. But did they also unleash an ancient curse?

Months later Lord Carnarvon was bitten by a mosquito. The bite became infected and he died on April 5, 1923, in a Cairo hotel. At a news conference in Paris, a French Egyptologist and occultist, J.S. Mardus, declared that the Englishman had in fact paid the penalty for profaning the pharaoh's resting place.

Mardus said that the tomb had been protected by the ancient priests against such a

ETERNAL GAZE The death mask of Tutankhamun, who became pharaoh at the age of 11 and ruled from 1361 to 1352 BC.

violation. Thus the legend of the pharaoh's curse was born, and it grew, nourished by a widespread fascination with Egyptian mummification and by reports of strange events at Tutankhamun's tomb. It was said, for example, that on the day that the burial place was first opened, a sandstorm had sprung up and a hawk, sacred emblem of the pharaohs, had soared over the tomb and flown off to the west—the Egyptian Land of the Dead.

It was also said that, upon entering the pharaoh's tomb, the archaeologists came upon an inscription that read: "Death will come to those who disturb the sleep of the Pharaohs." No such text was ever found, but there did seem to be a large number of deaths involving people connected with the tomb.

However, on closer examination the toll was not especially high. Herbert E. Winlock, director of the Metropolitan Museum of Art in New York, calculated that of the 22 people present at the tomb opening in 1922, only six had died by 1934, some of whom were ill before visiting Egypt. Their deaths were all of natural causes, and if some victims succumbed to disease in Egypt that was hardly surprising for foreigners unaccustomed to local conditions.

Howard Carter himself scoffed at the idea of a curse and lived to the age of 66, dying peacefully in 1939. Still, the unremarkable statistics have not prevented public imagination from being captured by Tutankhamun's curse, and papers regularly report eerie mishaps connected with the treasures. Most famously, in 1966, while Egyptian authorities were considering sending the treasures to Paris for an exhibition, the Director of Antiquities, Mohammed Ibrahim, was run over by a car. Was the accident a common coincidence or an ancient Pharaoh's curse?

1900 ━━ 2000

1922 Tutankhamun's tomb opened
1923 Lord Carnarvon dies

1939 Howard Carter dies peacefully

1966 Egyptian curator killed by a car

CURSE OR COINCIDENCE?

WHEN LIFE THROWS UP STRANGER-THAN-FICTION COINCIDENCES, SHOULD THEY BE BLAMED ON CHANCE OR ON THE SHADOWY WORKING OF SOME UNKNOWN POWER?

On the seventh day of the seventh month (July) of 1977, a woman named Mrs. Severn became 77. As human beings we relish such curiosities, perhaps because they hint at the presence of inexplicable forces working behind the scenes of everyday life.

More compelling still are those coincidences with a moral dimension. When Lord Carnarvon and others died after helping to open Tutankhamun's tomb, it seemed a retribution for breaking into an ancient place of burial. The idea of a curse is darkly attractive to the superstitious mind. Perhaps we consider Fate, however stern, to be more alluring than a cold, material universe, wholly indifferent to how we behave.

Hard-headed statisticians have no difficulty in explaining coincidences in terms of the law of averages. In the case of Mrs. Severn, the odds are that once in a while someone of her unusual surname will celebrate a birthday on a date with many sevens in it. The event is less striking if set against the innumerable days on which people of the surname "Seven" or "Severn" celebrate birthdays without sets of seven in the date.

Statisticians have also denied that there is anything exceptional about the number of deaths associated with the opening of Tutankhamun's tomb. In any group of adults assembled for whatever reason, a certain number are likely to die within a few succeeding years. Deaths will follow the opening of a garden fete as surely as they will follow the opening of a pharaoh's tomb.

Stranger in its way is the famous coincidence of the *Titanic* prophecy. In 1898 author Morgan Robertson penned a novel called *Futility* which bore striking similarities to the loss of the real-life liner 14 years later. Robertson's ship was the largest vessel afloat with the most modern equipment, but it lacked sufficient lifeboats to accommodate everyone on board. The ship went down in April (like her real-life counterpart) after an encounter with an iceberg —and her name was the *Titan*. Was this prophetic fiction? Not according to the skeptics who have put

MORBID REMINDERS Lord Carnarvon's death certificate. Four months after opening Tutankhamun's tomb he was dead, having fatally infected a mosquito bite while shaving.

many details down to good research. The threat to shipping from icebergs, for example, was a known hazard of Atlantic travel, and Robertson was perspicacious (but not psychic) in observing how regulations about lifeboat numbers did not change to match the modern liners' increase in size. In one view, the only outstanding coincidence was the choice of *Titan* as a name—and even there, Roberston did not have that many options in naming his giant liner. *Emperor, Colossus, Giant* ... the odds on settling on *Titan* were not very long.

The law of averages operates in ways that may be surprising to the layman. For example, how many people are needed in a group before there is a 50-50 probability of two of them sharing the same day and month of birth? Commonsense may suggest 365 people; yet statistically this coincidence is likely to occur when only 22 people are gathered together.

Many people believe, however, that there is more to the mechanism of coincidence than blind chance. According to the pioneering psychologist, and believer in the paranormal, Carl Jung, events may be meaningfully connected, although there is no discernible cause. He called this principle "synchronicity."

Jung quoted an incident from his own life as an example

SYMBOLIC BEETLE The scarab beetle—a symbol of rebirth— played a part in developing Jung's theory of synchronicity.

of synchronicity: one day a young female patient was describing a dream to him. She had dreamt of being given a golden scarab beetle, an ancient symbol of rebirth. As the patient told the psychologist about her dream, a scarabaeid beetle (*Cetonia aurata*), the nearest thing to a golden scarab beetle that can be found in the northerly latitudes, flew into the room.

This apparently significant coincidence began the patient's healing process. It seemed to Jung that the presence of a real-life carabaeid beetle had indeed produced a real, psychological rebirth— yet more synchronicity.

BELIEVER Psychologist Carl Jung (left) coined the term "synchronicity" to describe meaningful coincidences.

THE FLYING DUTCHMAN

HOW A PHANTOM SHIP TERRIFIED SUN-SEEKERS ON A BEACH IN SOUTH AFRICA

On a blazing hot day in March 1939, about 60 people were relaxing on the sands of Glencairn beach, South Africa. Suddenly an apparition of a high-pooped 17th-century merchantman (sailing ship) emerged from the sea haze. A newspaper later reported that all her sails were billowing, although there was not a breath of wind at the time. According to the *British South*

with talk of a mirage or a mass hallucination. But the witnesses on the beach were sure that what they had seen that day was the fabled *Flying Dutchman*.

According to sea lore, the *Flying Dutchman* is the ghost of a 17th-century ship whose Dutch captain refused to find safe port during a wild gale on the Cape of Good Hope, despite the pleas of his passengers and crew.

Punishment from God

The maniacal captain lashed himself to the wheel of his ship and sang blasphemous songs, leaving the terrified passengers to throw themselves on the mercy of God. As

WAGNERIAN SCENE A German print illustrates the legend of the *Flying Dutchman*, which was the inspiration for one of Wagner's best-known operas.

Africa Annual of 1939, "The ship sailed steadily on as the beach-folk, shaken from their lethargy, stood about keenly discussing the whys and wherefores of the vessel, which seemed to be bent on self-destruction on the sands of Strandfontein. Just as the excitement reached its climax, however, the ship vanished as strangely as it had come."

Skeptics have explained the phenomenon

punishment, the captain was condemned to sail round the Cape forever, bringing bad luck to all those who saw him.

Perhaps one of the most famous sightings of the *Flying Dutchman* was that by the future King George V of England in 1881. At the time the prince was a young naval officer aboard HMS *Bacchante*. In his private journal, he recorded the appearance of a strange

POPULAR IMAGE The legend of the *Flying Dutchman* has inspired novels, poems, films, plays and even cigarette cards (right).

MY GOD, IT'S A GHOST SHIP

A ship thought to be the *Flying Dutchman* was sighted on January 26, 1923, by seamen rounding the Cape of Good Hope on a voyage from Australia to England. At about 12:15 a.m. a strange light was noticed on the port bow. Fourth Officer N.K. Stone described what happened:

"It was a very dark night, overcast, with no moon. We looked through binoculars and the ship's telescope, and made out what appeared to be the hull of a sailing ship, luminous, with two distinct masts carrying bare yards, also luminous; no sails were visible, but there was a luminous haze between the masts. There were no navigation lights, and she appeared to be coming close to us and at the same speed as ourselves. When first sighted she was about two-three miles away, and when she was within about a half-mile of us she suddenly disappeared.

"There were four witnesses of this spectacle, the 2nd Officer, a cadet, the helmsman and myself. I shall never forget the 2nd Officer's startled expression - 'My God, Stone, it's a ghost ship.'"

red light, "in the midst of which the masts, spars and sails of a brig stood out in strong relief as she came across our port bow. The lookout man reported her as close on the port bow, but there was no vestige or sign of a material ship." The phantom ship, true to legend, brought bad luck. The seaman who had first reported the *Flying Dutchman* fell from the mast later that day and was killed.

CHURCHMAN'S CIGARETTES

THE FLYING DUTCHMAN

1923 *Flying Dutchman* sighted off Cape of Good Hope

1939 Phantom ship startles Glencairn beach-folk

1957 Seen off the Indian Ocean coast of South Africa

VISIONS, ILLUSIONS AND HALLUCINATIONS

CAN YOU REALLY TRUST WHAT YOU SEE WITH YOUR OWN EYE— WHEN IT COULD BE AN OPTICAL ILLUSION, A MAGICIAN'S SLEIGHT OF HAND OR A TIRED BRAIN PLAYING TRICKS?

S keptics often explain phenomena, from shared visions of the Virgin Mary to group sightings of the *Flying Dutchman*, as "mass hallucinations." But in doing so, they employ an explanation that in itself requires some explaining. What is a hallucination? And how can a whole crowd of people participate in it? In medical terminology, a hallucination is something very different from an illusion.

Illusions result from misinterpreting real, physical events. For example, through sleight of hand a professional magician may be able to trick members of an audience into believing that they have seen him cause a playing card to disappear, when it has in fact been deftly slipped up the his sleeve. Also using trickery, Hindu fakirs (miracle-workers) have famously created great illusions of levitation.

Illusions may occur naturally, too. For example, on summer days, when the air near the ground is much hotter than the air above, light rays are often refracted, or bent, creating the illusion, or mirage, of a shimmering lake.

The effect of light being refracted by the sea can also create the illusion of a "ghost ship" by distorting the image of a real vessel which is sailing below the horizon, and therefore not visible, and making it seem nearby. Perhaps this is the physical explanation for the persistent reports of the legendary phantom ship *Flying Dutchman*.

ST ELMO'S FIRE Atmospheric electricity during stormy weather can cause a ship's mast to glow.

Hallucinations differ from illusions, arising as they do out of the private imagination. A hallucination occurs when the person mistakenly believes that he or she can see or hear something that is happening only in his or her fantasy realm. Schizophrenic patients, for example, may "hear" voices, and "see" threatening visions.

But healthy people experience hallucinations too. In a sense, everybody hallucinates when they dream, and people are also prone to hallucinate in states of deep concentration, emotional arousal, excitement, fear, ecstasy, or tense anticipation. Some religious and magical ceremonies are designed to encourage just such states, so that participants see visions and hear spirit voices.

Skeptics believe that disorientation encourages participants to hallucinate, and to mistake private fantasies for external reality. In the doubters' view, a mass hallucination could be triggered by one member of a crowd declaring that he can see a vision, prompting others who are already in a state of anticipation and arousal to fantasize along the same lines.

In a devout Catholic community, for example, the image of the Virgin Mary is so embedded in everyone's psyche that it may take surprisingly little stimulus to trigger a shared holy vision.

DECEPTION OR HALLUCINATION? Saint Giuseppe di Copertino is said to have levitated before Pope Urban VIII. Was it a hallucination or a clever variant on the famous Indian rope trick?

HARRY HOUDINI—MAGIC AND THE WORLD BEYOND

WORLDLY DEVICES COULDN'T HOLD HIM— AND COULD DEATH?

In 1920, on a tour of England with his wife Bess, the world famous escape artist and magician Harry Houdini met Sir Arthur Conan Doyle, the author of the Sherlock Holmes stories. The two quickly became close friends, bonding over their mutual interest in spiritualism. Doyle was convinced that communication with the dead was possible, and that his wife could coax the departed out of their other-worldly reticence with a process called automatic writing, in which a spirit would direct her hand to write personalized messages. Houdini was skeptical, yet fascinated. He knew enough of the prestidigitator's wiles—the skillful misdirection, the trap doors, the hidden compartments—and of an audience's active willingness to believe, to suspect any such fantastic claims. On the other hand, for years, Houdini had desperately tried to contact his dead mother with scores of mediums, without success.

Back in the United States, Houdini chose the night of his mother's birthday to test Lady's

FASCINATED BY THE UNKNOWN Born Ehrich Weiss, in Budapest Hungary, Houdini was constantly searching for a connection to the world beyond.

Doyle's powers. Houdini's wife Bess had informed him, using a secret code, that the night before Lady Doyle had extracted from her a wealth of information on his family, but he was willing to participate nonetheless. They sat together around a parlor table, a pencil gripped tightly in Lady Doyle's hand. Suddenly, she began shaking convulsively—the spirit had arrived—and her hand began to flutter around the paper. She first made a mark of the cross at the top of the page, and then began scribbling, at a furious rate, a message from Houdini's mother to her "darling boy," full of affection and happiness that she was finally able to reach him. Houdini was deeply moved. After his mother's spirit departed and Lady Doyle came out of her trance, he asked her if he himself could try automatic writing. After receiving Lady Doyle's encouragement, he took hold of the pencil and scratched out the word "Powell" on the page. Sir Doyle gasped—a friend of his named Powell had recently died and this, he believed, must be his spirit.

But Houdini's skepticism had not been defeated, only stunned, and he soon began to look critically at the séance. He discounted his own attempts at automatic writing by suggesting that "Powell" was actually a reference to a magician friend by that name with whom he had recently spoken. Secondly, he pointed out that his mother was Jewish, and would not have used the sign of a cross to begin her ghostly communiqué. Also, she was Hungarian, and never spoke English fluently, so the spirit's fluidity with the language was problematic. Doyle provided Houdini with ready responses to each of these challenges, but their friendship soon disintegrated as the mas-

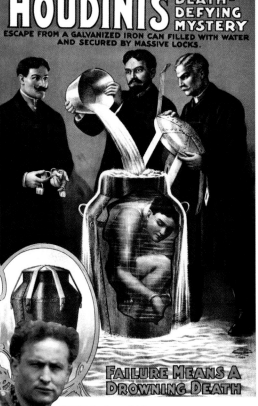

HOUDINI'S DEATH-DEFYING MYSTERY
ESCAPE FROM A GALVANIZED IRON CAN FILLED WITH WATER AND SECURED BY MASSIVE LOCKS.

FAILURE MEANS A DROWNING DEATH

ESCAPE! A world famous escape artist, Houdini writhed his way out of every contraption designed to contain him, many of which were filled with water and locked, as seen in the poster above. Houdini was locked in chains as he performed underwater feats (left).

ter illusionist intensified his efforts to unmask spiritualist chicanery. Houdini solicited letters from hundreds of informants, each describing the tricks of the medium's trade. One "revealing" letter described a medium who sewed his pants to the carpet in order to ensure his own immobility during the séance, but then walked around the room in his underwear when the lights were out. But despite these discouraging reports, he still yearned for proof of the paranormal – as long as it didn't reek of quackery.

In search of such proof, in January 1923 Houdini joined a test committee sponsored by Scientific American that promised to offer $2,500 to anyone that could produce "physical paranormal phenomena and have it recorded by scientific instruments." However, he quickly came into conflict with the other members of the committee over a celebrated Boston psychic named Margery. After a private showing, the

1926 Houdini's Death

1942 Houdini's wife declares attempts at contact a failure before she dies

committee, sans Houdini, had confirmed Margery's powers, but convinced that she was a charlatan, Houdini insisted on testing them himself. Margery consented, and during the demonstration, Houdini unleashed the full fury of his incredulity. By strapping a tight bandage around his leg, rendering it sensitive

Disillusioned with the ability of others to provide adequate proof, Houdini decided to take matters into his own hands. After all, if anyone could break the bonds of the other world and escape back to realm of the living, it was the man whom chains, padlocks, and stiff metal boxes buried meters under the ground

Bess showed those present the inscription on her wedding ring—words to a song she and her husband had once sung together on stage: "Rosabelle, sweet Rosabelle, I love you more than I can tell. Over me you cast a spell, I love you my sweet Rosabelle." After singing the song, Bess fainted.

When she revived, Fletcher explained that the strange message should be decoded using the couple's old mind-reading tricks; it really commanded "Rosabelle, believe." Bess confirmed that this was the secret password Houdini promised to give her if there was life beyond the grave. She even signed a statement recognizing the séance's legitimacy. The irony was delicious; Houdini, spiritualism's greatest skeptic during his life, had confirmed its authenticity after his death.

HOUDINI PICTURE CORPORATION

presents

HOUDINI

in

"THE MAN FROM BEYOND"

BEYOND THE GRAVE Houdini's famous promise was that he'd contact his wife from the dead with a message only the two of them knew. Above, a movie poster from Houdini's "The Man From Beyond."

to the slightest movement, he was able to catch her ringing a bell box hidden under the table, which she claimed was rung by her dead brother Walter in the other world. He also caught her moving objects surreptitiously that she claimed had been thrown by spirits. Houdini waited to expose Margery, and in the meantime, the press declared a victory for spiritualism over the great skeptic. But in the next séance, Houdini was not so restrained, constructing a special locked box in which Margery could sit that constricted the motion of her head, legs and hands.

Houdini was even accused of planting incriminating objects inside the box that could be used to discredit Margery. Houdini's tactics alienated the other members of the committee, as well as believers across the nation. Doyle called his old friend "a bounder and a cad," and even Walter, Margery's control (her partner in the spirit world), offered a vituperative otherworldly rebuke.

could not restrain. Houdini promised his wife that if he died first, he would make every effort to come back, using their old mind-reading codes as a means of communication. Houdini had a chance to test this strategy sooner than he expected. On October 22, 1926, after a show in Montreal, an overeager student surprised Houdini backstage and punched him in the stomach, hoping to test the great magician's claim to iron abdominal muscles. But the blow ruptured Houdini's appendix, and nine days later he died of severe peritonitis.

Almost immediately mediums besieged Bess, offering their services. After rejecting most as opportunistic hacks, Bess finally settled on Arthur Ford, the pastor of the First Spiritualist Church of New York, who agreed to conduct a séance on January 9, 1929. As soon as all the participants were seated around the table, Ford fell into a deep trance. Ford's control Fletcher, a boyhood friend who had been killed in WWI, spoke first, offering to help contact Houdini. After a pause, the great magician claimed to speak through Ford, who uttered the cryptic words, "Rosabelle, answer, tell, pray, answer, look, tell, answer, answer, tell." The message seemed incoherent until

But as in her husband's first experience with Lady Doyle, Bess soon grew skeptical and retracted her statement after learning that the "secret code" had been made public in a 1927 book. She condemned the Ford séance with an apostate's vehemence, and vowed to spend the rest of her life revealing the deception of spiritualism. For the next few years, however, she continued to hold séances on Houdini's birthday, Halloween. She never received a response. So frustrated was Bess with spirits and their otherworldly chatter that she promised not to return to this world once she died, even if she were able.

ENIGMA OF LOCH NESS

HI-TECH EQUIPMENT IS USED TO SEARCH FOR AN ANCIENT MONSTER IN THE PEAT-BLACK WATERS

Tales of a huge "beastie" in Loch Ness go back at least as far as 700 A.D., when St. Columba reportedly encountered Scotland's most famous monster. The legend —of a secretive throwback to a dinosaur age living in the loch—has survived, and it continues to fascinate, even as the 20th century draws to its close.

Loch Ness is the largest freshwater body of water in the British Isles. It is 24 miles long and almost severs northern Scotland from the rest of the nation. It was once thought to be bottomless, and its immense waters are so dark and peaty that underwater photography will not reveal with any clarity anything that is more than a few feet from the lens. Here is the ideal environment for a secretive monster, or colony of monsters— for if Nessie has any zoological reality, the creature must be capable of breeding.

Nessie's modern history

Modern press coverage of the monster in the loch began in May 1933 when the *Inverness Courier* reported how Mr. and Mrs. John Mackay had seen an enormous animal that rolled and plunged in the water. Publication of the story prompted many other witnesses to come forward with sightings of their own, and by the end of the year 20 or 30 reports had appeared in the press. The monster had become a focus of worldwide media interest.

From the sightings, a profile of Nessie began to take the shape of a huge, hump-backed creature with a long, flexible neck that would occasionally break the surface of the loch. The image was fixed in April 1934 when a photograph was published.

The picture, which was reportedly taken from a promontory north of Invermoriston by a London gynecologist, Robert Kenneth Wilson, showed the dark silhouette of a head

> **PATENT OF FAITH**
>
> In 1982 Mr. Duane Marshall of the Boston Academy of Applied Science took out a patent for photographing the Loch Ness Monster by means of an automatic camera attached to a trained dolphin. The camera was to be strapped to the dolphin's side, with ultrasonic equipment that would sense when it approached a large submerged object, triggering a 35 mm camera and flash unit.

and neck moving through the loch. The so-called "Surgeon's Photograph" remained one of the most persuasive pieces of evidence for Nessie's existence until March 1994, when the world learned that it had been a hoax. Just before he died, Christian Spurling, the last surviving member of the group of trick-

SURGEON'S PHOTO This shot was finally exposed as a fraud after fooling the public for 60 years. But an earlier glimpse of Nessie (inset) taken in 1933 by Hugh Gray, which has been dismissed by some as 'a dog with a stick', remains controversial.

1933 *Inverness Courier* reported sighting
1934 The Surgeon's Photograph published

sters, confessed to Loch Ness researchers how a group of conspirators had created the picture by propelling the foot-high head of a fake serpent through the water, attached to a clockwork submarine.

Telling testimonies

Nessie might be taken for a national joke were it not for the sheer number of sightings reported by people from every walk of life. Alex Campbell, the water bailiff of Loch Ness, reported 18 encounters with the monster, which he once saw fleeing trawlers. He

SCIENTIFIC SEEKER In 1975 Dr. Rines' team from the Academy of Applied Science used underwater cameras (right) to produce the grainy image above.

said: "Suddenly there was this upsurge of water . . . I was stunned. I shut my eyes three times to make sure I was not imagining things. The head and the huge, humped body were perfectly clear."

Another convincing tale was that of Father Gregory Brusey who in October 1971, watching with a visitor in the grounds of a Benedictine Abbey at Fort Augustus, saw the creature rear its head 7 feet above the water before swimming off. "We felt a sort of awe and amazement," he said.

Some believe that what these witnesses saw was a Loch Ness monster. Many people

have long favored the notion that a small breeding population of relic dinosaurs—perhaps a left-over group of long-necked plesiosaurus, which supposedly died out 65 million years ago—inhabit a network of caves and tunnels deep beneath the surface of the loch.

Doubters prefer to explain sightings in terms of giant eels or outsized otters. Motor boats could account for reports of a monster traveling at great speed. And occasionally, logs and debris floating up from the loch bed may burst to the surface in a gaseous mass that might be misinterpreted as the upsurge of a huge marine creature.

Project Urquhart seeks the truth

In recent decades all the paraphernalia of hi-tech underwater search equipment has been brought to bear on the loch. In the 1970s expeditions by the Academy of Applied Science, led by Dr. Robert H. Rines, investigated its murky waters with sonar equipment triggering a camera and strobe light. The apparatus yielded much-publicized underwater pictures that were said to show the torso, neck and head of the monster. But the latest scientific findings tend to reinforce the doubts of the skeptics.

In 1992, under *Project Urquhart*, Loch Ness was surveyed by sonar to chart its underwater topography. Vessels cruised the whole lake and, in a fan-shaped sweep of its bed, produced 7 million depth readings. The loch's lowest point was found to be a forbidding 787 feet down, northeast of Invermoriston. Computer-interpretation of the data allowed scientists to produce virtual reality images of the submarine terrain. Loch Ness proved to possess steep sides plunging to a fairly level lake bed. Labyrinthine caves and tunnels simply do not exist. Where in this stern, rock-walled habitat could Nessie have made a den?

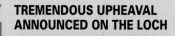

SOUNDING OUT THE LOCH The sonar room aboard MV *Simrad*, Project Urquhart's research vessel, which performed a sonic survey of the bed of Loch Ness in 1992.

THE BERMUDA TRIANGLE

IS THE WORK OF PARANORMAL FORCES BEHIND THE REPUTATION OF THIS NOTORIOUS SEAWAY?

In June 1991 the *Deep See* underwater research vessel was using hi-tech equipment to search for sunken Spanish galleons off the coast of Miami. Instead the instruments revealed five Second World War bombers stacked neatly together on the sea floor. One of the aircraft bore the same number and call-sign as the leader of Flight 19, an ill-fated bomber squadron that had set out from its base at 3:15 on the afternoon of December 5, 1945—never to return. The excited crew of the *Deep See* had expected to find treasure, not to solve one of the mysteries of the Bermuda Triangle.

Flight 19, made up of five TBM (Torpedo Bomber Medium) Avenger aircraft, successfully completed a U.S. Navy training exercise around the Bimini islands on December 5, and was due to fly back to base at Fort Lauderdale, Florida. It never arrived and a five-day search of the ocean found nothing.

Many believe that the aircraft and their occupants fell victim to the strange forces of

LOST SQUADRON   Torpedo bomber No. 28 and her crew—one of the five planes that made up Flight 19, which vanished in 1945.

the Bermuda Triangle, an expanse of sea between Bermuda, Puerto Rico and Miami. Here, it is alleged, ships and aircraft are prone to vanish eerily, instruments to fail and compasses to swing wildly. Some have blamed "interference from other worlds," while others have speculated that an irregularity in the Earth's magnetic field may account for the disappearances.

The truth behind the hype

Skeptics, however, cite the Flight 19 case as the classic example of a so-called mystery cranked up by slipshod research, misrepresentation and sensationalism.

Disquieting radio messages were allegedly received: "Everything is wrong . . . strange. We can't be sure of any direction. Even the ocean doesn't look as it should . . ." But this "quote" was actually made up by an early writer on the case. The bits of genuine radio messages that have survived indicate that Lt. Charles Carroll Taylor, leading the aircraft, reported that both of his compasses had simultaneously gone out of action. Being unfamiliar to the area he mistook his position, thinking he was near the Florida Keys when he was actually close to the Bahamas. With faulty equipment and a darkening sky he simply flew off in the wrong direction. Eventually, the lost Avengers ran out of fuel. In his final, tragic transmission, Taylor

THE WALLS OF ATLANTIS

Lying in the Bermuda Triangle, the small island group of Bimini near the Bahamas became the focus of intense interest in 1968 when aircraft pilots glimpsed what seemed to be giant submerged stonework in the sea off the north island. Divers exploring the site reported colossal blocks of square-cut masonry 35 feet underwater, which were thought to be the top of some massive wall, or perhaps the foundation of a vanished building. Were these relics of Atlantis—the lost island civilization in the Atlantic of which Plato wrote 2,400 years ago? The notion excited followers of the American psychic Edgar Cayce, who had predicted in 1940 that the drowned civilization would rise up again in 1968 or 1969, somewhere in the Bahamas.

Sadly for the enthusiasts, scientists believed that the Bimini formations were natural rock features, resulting from faulting of the seabed—though tourist maps of the holiday islands still advertise them as the Walls of Atlantis.

called for all planes to close into a tight formation and prepare to ditch into the sea: "When the first man gets down to 10 gallons we will all land in the water together."

Perhaps the question of what happened to Flight 19 is partially answered, but why

MISSING SHIP   The USS *Cyclops* disappeared without trace on a journey to the West Indies in 1918.

did two compasses which had just passed pre-flight tests fail simultaneously?

Despite the *Deep See*'s find, the final resting place of the unlucky bombers and their crews remains a mystery. The five planes found by the treasure-hunters were not the missing Avengers of Flight 19 after all. The site turned out to be an old bombing practice range, where planes had been regularly ditched between 1943 and 1945. The U.S. Navy revealed that Lt. Taylor's plane bore the same number as a plane that had already

1900 — 1950

1902 German ship *Freya* found abandoned

1918 USS *Cyclops* disappears

1940 Yacht *Gloria Colite* found drifting abandoned
1944 *Rubicon* ghost ship found
1945 Flight 19 disappears

been lost in the waters of the Bermuda Triangle long before he even took off on his own mission to nowhere.

Hurricanes take the blame

Ships and their crews have also disappeared in the Triangle, and one natural phenomenon that is certainly responsible for such mysteries is the tropical hurricane. In a famous "ghost ship" case of October 1944, the Cuban freighter *Rubicon* was found drifting off Florida's east coast. A dog was found to be the only living thing on board. What had happened to the crew? The ship was seaworthy, and everything aboard was intact but for one missing lifeboat and a broken hawser.

Light was shed on the mystery by National Oceanographic and Atmospheric Administration records. That month a ferocious hurricane had ravaged the area with winds of up to 158 mph. It is presumed that the *Rubicon's* broken hawser had secured a sea anchor that got severed in the storm. The crew panicked as the freighter ran adrift and must have taken to the missing lifeboat only

HOODOO SEA About 1,000 airmen, sailors and passengers in over 100 different aircraft and ships are alleged to have disappeared in the Bermuda Triangle.

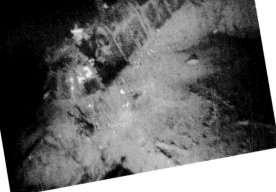

INTRIGUING FIND Captain Caloway and Graham Hawkes (left) thought they had found Flight 19 when they came across planes on the sea bed (below).

to perish in the storm-torn sea.

Lawrence Kusche, a research librarian at Arizona State University, examined many cases cited in the Triangle legend and found a natural cause for most. For example, the USS *Cyclops*, a navy cargo ship lost in 1918, went down in bad weather; a DC-3 missing in 1948 made a navigational error; another plane, a British troop transporter that disappeared in 1953, more than likely crashed in a storm some 900 miles north of the Triangle.

Patiently examined one by one, disappearances in the Triangle have not been especially mysterious. Weather conditions, equipment failure, and human error seem to be able to explain most of the tragedies, not

something from the supernatural. Even the frequency of accidents in the area is not unusual. In fact, as science fiction writer Arthur C. Clarke once said: "It is a considerable tribute to the Florida Coast Guard that there are so few disappearances in this busy area, among the legions of amateur sailors and weekend pilots who venture out across it, often with totally inadequate preparation."

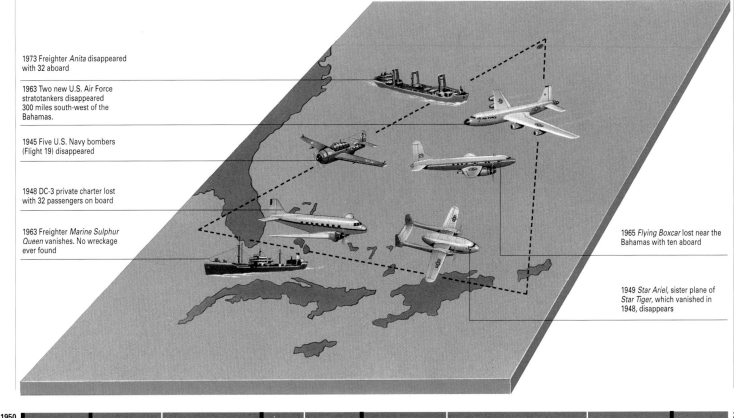

1973 Freighter *Anita* disappeared with 32 aboard

1963 Two new U.S. Air Force stratotankers disappeared 300 miles south-west of the Bahamas.

1945 Five U.S. Navy bombers (Flight 19) disappeared

1948 DC-3 private charter lost with 32 passengers on board

1963 Freighter *Marine Sulphur Queen* vanishes. No wreckage ever found

1965 *Flying Boxcar* lost near the Bahamas with ten aboard

1949 *Star Ariel*, sister plane of *Star Tiger*, which vanished in 1948, disappears

1950

2000

1950 Freighter SS *Sandra* vanished without trace

1955 Yacht *Connemara IV* abandoned

1967 Yacht *Revonoc* disappeared within sight of land

1974 Cabin cruiser *Witchcraft* and crew vanished while moored at a harbor buoy one mile from Miami

THE COMING OF THE FLYING SAUCERS

DO UNIDENTIFIED OBJECTS IN THE SKY REALLY INDICATE THE EXISTENCE OF ALIEN LIFEFORMS?

An American search and rescue pilot flying on a mission over the Cascade Mountains on June 24, 1947, had a very peculiar experience. The weather was fine, and the visibility excellent, when suddenly a flash lit the inside of Kenneth Arnold's plane. He then saw what he described as a formation of nine bright objects coming from the direction of Mount Baker, flying close to the mountain tops at a phenomenal speed. From his knowledge of the area, Arnold

FIRST-HAND ACCOUNT Arnold published a book about his experience called *The Coming of the Saucers*.

was able to calculate that they were traveling at no less than 1,200 mph—more than twice as fast as any known aircraft of his day.

Arnold described the craft as silvery on top and black on the bottom. He said that they traveled in a diagonal formation, flying "like you'd take a saucer and skip it across the water." That phrase captured the imagination of the newsmen reporting the strange encounter, and they wrote of "flying saucers" for the first time.

Earlier strange sightings

Arnold's sighting was by no means the first report of bizarre objects in the skies. References to strange celestial craft are found in mythologies from around the world. Reports even crop up in medieval manuscripts. It is recorded that on January 1, 1254, the monks of St. Albans saw in the sky "a kind of large ship, elegantly shaped, and well equipped and of marvellous color."

STRANGE LIGHT A reconstruction, based on contemporary reports, of a wartime bomber sighting one of the "foo-fighters."

During the Second World War, Allied pilots on sorties in Europe and the Pacific had reported a new, strange form of German

EVIDENCE This photograph of a classically shaped unidentified flying object was taken in 1967 at East Woonsocket, Rhode Island.

air defense, which they named "foo-fighters." Typically, foo-fighters manifested themselves as incandescent balls of silvery-white or orange-red light. The foo-fighters would follow an aircraft for a while, as if under intelligent control, and then the strange craft would turn away and vanish into the ether.

ALIENS HAVE CRASH-LANDED

In March 1993 an unusual and alarming police radio message crackled across the airwaves around Warrington in Cheshire, England. The message reported that a huge, glowing alien spacecraft had crash-landed in a field at Appleton. "Do not approach. It may be radioactive," warned the transmission. Was an alien invasion under way? Not at all: the message was put out by local police in order to trap a group of radio eavesdroppers, who had been illegally tuning in to police frequencies. The unwanted listeners were arrested on arrival at the field, and five people were subsequently prosecuted for telecommunications offenses.

The odd thing was that at the same time as the Allies were reporting the foo-fighters, so

WEIRD EFFIGY Model of a dead alien at the UFO Enigma Museum, Roswell, New Mexico—the site of a controversial UFO incident in 1947.

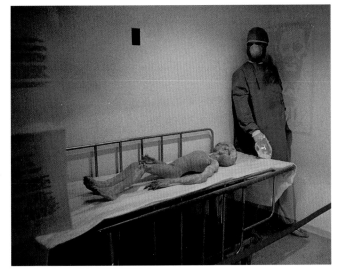

were the Germans and Japanese. Each side in the conflict assumed that the glowing spheres were instruments of war made by the enemy. No one ever found out where the foo-fighters really came from or what their mission was.

Reliable witnesses

It is thought that an unidentified flying object is sighted somewhere on the Earth once every two minutes. Hoaxes, misrepresentation and honest mistakes may account for many of these, but surely not all. Many reports of UFOs are lodged by trained, responsible observers, such as airline pilots and astronauts.

Ed Mitchell, the sixth man on the moon, said: "I am completely convinced that some UFO sightings are real. The question is not whether there are UFOs, but what they are."

The most compelling reports of aerial phenomena have been those where human eyewitness testimony is supported by other evidence. Perhaps one of the most convincing sightings occurred on December 31, 1978, in the Antipodean skies.

Following reports of UFOs by six different airline pilots over New Zealand's South Island, an Australian TV crew took to the skies in a cargo plane. The crew retraced the flight path between Wellington and Christchurch, along which unidentified lights had been seen for several weeks.

Something described by the cameraman as having a "brightly lit base and a sort of transparent dome" approached the cargo plane. The object was

INUNDATED A simulation of an eerie craft seen near Belleville, Wisconsin. The town was plagued by UFO reports in 1987.

picked up by the plane's radar, and using 16 mm color film the TV crew was able to get footage of it. Meanwhile ground radar confirmed the presence of objects near the plane at that time.

 MOON OVER GEORGIA

At least one president of the United States has witnessed a UFO. One evening in 1969, when he was governor of Georgia, Jimmy Carter was standing with about 20 other people at the town of Leary, waiting to address a local meeting, when the group saw something strange in the skies above.

Carter later said, "I am convinced that UFOs exist because I've seen one. It was the darndest thing I've ever seen. It was big; it was very bright; it changed colors; and it was about the size of the moon. We watched it for 10 minutes, but none of us could figure out what it was."

The film, which excited viewers all around the world, and its associated documentation were turned over to a U.S. Navy physicist, Dr. Maccabee, for investigation. He estimated that the strange object was about 100 feet across and was traveling at about 3,000 mph. Despite a rigorous investigation the phenomena caught on film over New Zealand could never be satisfactorily explained; they must remain UFOs.

UFO reports do not always end with strange lights and elusive blips, however. Many people have reported direct encounters with the occupants of alien spacecraft. Some of the reports have come from eyewitnesses whose testimony would be regarded as reliable under normal circumstances.

In 1964, for example, American police patrolman Lonnie Zamora claimed that he saw a blue, flaming UFO land near the town of Socorro in New Mexico. Speeding to the spot he encountered two weird figures, no more than 4 feet high, beside a glowing oval vehicle mounted on supporting legs. The figures fled inside and took off, leaving Zamora white and shaken. When another officer arrived at the scene he saw the burning brush, and also square indentations in the ground left, it was presumed, by the spacecraft's landing gear.

Another well-documented case is that of Scottish forestry worker Bob Taylor. In November 1979, while patrolling forests near the town of Livingston, he came upon a curious vehicle, like a huge spinning top, with a large flange running around its rim. As he watched with astonishment, two spiked metal balls emerged from it, bounced towards him, and seemed to tug at his legs. Taylor became aware of a strange smell, then

BAFFLING IMAGES Inset: UFO spotted on a Swiss glacier in 1952. Below: four UFOs sighted at Salem, Massachusetts, in 1952.

he blacked out. When he recovered minutes later, he felt "drained of energy" and believed he had been gassed.

The police officers assigned to the case did not doubt Taylor's integrity—his thighs were scratched, and his trousers were found to bear long upward tears consistent with having been ripped by spikes as he had described. Police officers investigated the forest clearing and discovered marks in the turf which showed that something had landed heavily. Around the marks were 40 small holes which could have been made by the spiked balls. The marks covered only this patch of turf. How had the vehicle arrived if not from above? Had Bob Taylor been assaulted by aliens?

A UFO hotspot in Scotland

The scene of Bob Taylor's frightening encounter was near Bonnybridge, a small Scottish town where there has been a wave of UFO sightings. Since 1992 about 2,000 UFOs were reported at Bonnybridge—glowing orbs, circles of lights and silver cylinders. About a third of the local

HOVERING SPACECRAFT? This UFO was photographed in daylight near Albuquerque, New Mexico, on June 16, 1963.

population claims to have experienced strange phenomena. In January 1994, a white light moving in the sky was captured on video by a Bonnybridge housewife, Lorraine Malcolm. She filmed the 18-second video sequence after her shocked husband saw the object while driving home. As news of the Bonnybridge phenomena spread around the world, U.S. and Japanese TV crews arrived, and science fiction magazines even organized trips to the town for UFO enthusiasts.

The cover-up theory

In December 1993 a draft report of the European Parliament, drily named DOC/EN/PR/233233, proposed the establishment of a special European Center for the investigation of UFO sightings. There have been at least two major investigations into UFOs in the United States since 1948. Officialdom, it seems, acknowledges the existence of unidentified flying objects.

Since modern reports of UFOs began, however, there have been accompanying theories that the authorities know far more about UFOs than they reveal to the public. The reasons for such a cover-up are as murky as the origins of the UFOs themselves. Perhaps UFOs are part of top-secret national defense systems; or maybe the authorities have proof that UFOs are alien craft and fear the

potential repercussions of making such knowledge public.

After Arnold's first flying-saucer report, eyewitnesses reported a fantastic range of aerial phenomena in the U.S. Reports of domed, winged and cigar-shaped craft, as well as flying discs and spheres, raised public concern about the number of supposed visits to the Earth by aliens.

This prompted an official investigation by the U.S. Air Force named *Project Blue Book*. From 1948 to 1969 Blue Book investigated 12,600 cases. Most could be explained quite easily, as natural occurrences misinterpreted by the observers, such as escaped

BRIEF ENCOUNTER Bob Taylor at the scene of his strange meeting with the unknown at Livingston, Scotland, in 1979.

COMPARISONS Overlaid technical drawings (below) expose the similarity of a flying saucer photographed in California in 1952 (right) and a UFO photographed by a young boy in England in 1954.

weather balloons, sightings of planets, cloud formations, or migrating birds. But 701 of the cases defied explanation and were classified as Unidentified Flying Objects—or UFOs.

The air force declared the end of *Project Blue Book* in 1969, saying that the results it was yielding were nebulous and didn't warrant continued expense. Some believe that the project is still going on, even that the U.S. Government is concealing actual evidence of the existence of alien lifeforms.

In July 1947, a month after Kenneth Arnold's historic sighting of flying saucers, newspapers reported an extraordinary discovery near Roswell, New Mexico. "U.S. ARMY TO EXAMINE A FLYING DISC" reported the *London Times*, describing how the Eighth Air Force had confirmed that an object had been found there and was being sent to the research center at Wright Field, Ohio. The Air Force's first press statement said that a flying disc had been recovered. Later it was released that it was in fact the remains of a weather balloon that had been found. Army officers who recovered

the debris were placed under strict instructions not to talk to reporters, though at least one repudiated the official story.

Some eyewitness accounts talk of discovering bodies in the desert near Roswell shortly after the crash, and of peculiar activity around the site. There is even a 91-minute video film in existence which purports to show the investigation of several dead alien bodies (without hair or facial features) and the wreckage of their craft.

In 1994, the U.S. Air Force admitted that the Roswell Incident, as it had become known, was part of a secret American atomic spying program. There is no question that the authorities were hiding something, but was it mundane espionage or a far more astonishing reality?

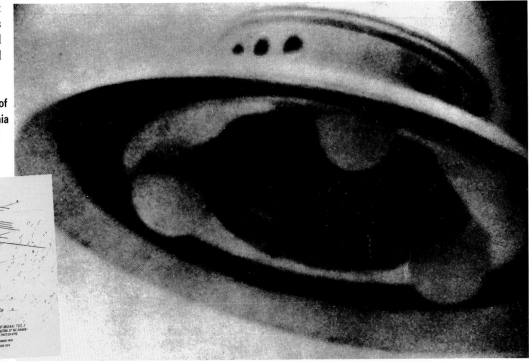

1969 Jimmy Carter sees UFO in Georgia

1978 Australian TV crew films UFO over New Zealand

1994 Lorraine Malcolm films an object above UFO "hotspot" in Scotland

THE CROP CIRCLE CONUNDRUM

TORNADOES, HEDGEHOGS, ALIEN INVADERS AND HUMAN HOAXERS HAVE ALL BEEN BLAMED FOR STRANGE PATTERNS IN FIELDS OF GROWING CORN

Inexplicable circular indentations in reed beds and corn fields have been explained by some as saucer "nests"—landing sites of alien spacecraft. Back in 1966, Australian farmer George Pedley reported three such nests in the swamps of North Queensland and claimed to have seen a blue-gray spaceship rise from the scene. Investigating the site, he found a flattened circular area about 30 feet wide, where the reeds were swirled around clockwise "as if they had been subjected to some terrific rotary force."

Skeptics dismiss the circles as the results of atmospheric turbulence. Tornadoes, in particular, have been invoked to explain them. But tornadoes move along the ground and so would leave a furrow, not a circle. Other suggestions range from irregular crop fertilization to helicopters, hedgehogs and even rutting deer.

In the late 1980s Britain seemed to be overrun by crop circles, some of them comprising elaborate patterns of straight lines as well as circles. Then, on September 9, 1991, newspapers reported the mystery solved. It appeared that making the corn circles had been the hobby of "two jovial conmen" for 13 years. Doug Bower and David Chorley, a pair from southern England, claimed to

TOO CLEVER An elaborately patterned crop circle near Hungerford in Berkshire implies either alien intelligence or a hoax.

GROWING CIRCLES Corn circles appeared frequently in south-west England in the late 1980s.

have been responsible for just about all of the classic examples. They confessed to creating the patterns with "two wooden boards, a piece of string and a bizarre sighting device attached to a baseball cap."

Immediately there were furious repudiations of the two men's claims. One expert asked: "Yesterday there were circles discovered on a prairie in Canada. Have these two guys been out there with their board?" No one could doubt that some circles were the work of hoaxers. But were they all? Dedicated circle-hunters were certainly not put off.

In 1995 Dr. William Levengood, a retired biologist from the University of Michigan, announced a method for distinguishing fake circles from authentic ones. He claimed that plants in genuine crop circles undergo changes including a swelling of the nodes, the knuckle-like joints on the plant stems—an effect that no hoaxer could reproduce.

Dr. Levengood believes that genuine crop circles are caused by unstable vortices of ions originating in the atmosphere, which reach the ground rather like lightning discharges. In the brief burst of heat that results the plant nodes swell up while the crops are whirled round and laid flat.

THE BESTSELLING TALE OF BRIDEY MURPHY

CAN PEOPLE UNDER HYPNOSIS RE-EXPERIENCE THEIR LIVES IN PREVIOUS INCARNATIONS?

There are many people who believe that people live numerous different lives, one after the other. For some it is a matter of religious faith, while others maintain that they can actually remember previous lives.

One of the bestselling books of 1956 was *The Search for Bridey Murphy*. It seemed to prove that some people had past lives. The book was written by amateur hypnotist Morey Bernstein, and described how a Colorado housewife he called "Ruth Simmons" (real name Virginia Tighe) had been led back in a trance-like state to a past life as an Irish woman of the early 19th century. Under hypnosis she spoke of herself as "Bridey Murphy" and described how she had

MASTER MESMERISER Morey Bernstein, a hypnotist, was at the center of the Bridey Murphy controversy that rocked the United States from 1956.

been born in Cork in 1798, daughter of a barrister, Duncan Murphy, and his wife Kathleen. She had lived in a wooden house outside Cork in an area called The Meadows, and recalled a book called *The Green Bay* being read to her. Bridey's story included an account of her marriage and her death, resulting from a fall in 1864, as well as a wealth of fascinating detail about 19th-century Irish life and the Irish coastline. The story was all the more remarkable in that Tighe had been born in 1923 and had never been to Ireland.

Doubts are raised

However, when reporters went to Ireland to try to verify the details of Bridey's story they discovered that places that she had mentioned did not seem to have existed. Local records contained no mention of Bridey's birth or death, there was no record of a wooden house fitting Bridey's description, and no known book of that time called *The Green Bay*. The housewife's narrative seemed to be a mixture of fact and pure fantasy. How had she obtained her memories?

Investigation revealed that Virginia Tighe had an aunt who had been born in Ireland. As a child in Chicago, Virginia had listened

TRANCE TRAVELER A magazine investigates the case. Did housewife Virginia Tighe have a past life in Ireland?

to her aunt's tales of her own childhood. Another Irish woman had lived across the street from the young Virginia. The woman's name was Bridie Murphy Corkell.

Skeptics are satisfied that there was no reincarnation. It seems that hypnosis had simply released in the adult Virginia Tighe remarkably detailed memories of conversations heard, or overheard, in her infancy.

The human memory is astonishing in its capabilities. People can retrieve fantastically precise information that they have absorbed casually and unconsciously, perhaps by flicking through a library book.

Those who claim to remember their past lives say that it is impossible to prove. If they provide names and dates from the past that are confirmed, critics will suggest that the subjects must have had access to the relevant information.

Believers in reincarnation, however, simply regard the Bridey Murphy case as unproven. The practice of "regression hypnosis" pioneered by Morey Bernstein is now widespread among those seeking to experience past lives of their own.

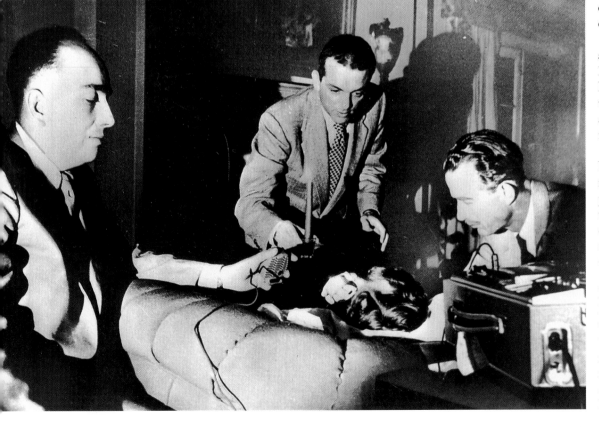

COULD THIS BE THE FACE OF JESUS CHRIST?

HOW SCIENTISTS INVESTIGATED THE HOLY MYSTERIES OF THE TURIN SHROUD

On April 21, 1988, under the gaze of delegates from selected laboratories, the Italian professor Giovanni Riggi carefully stripped a 3 inch sliver from a corner of the most famous relic in Christendom. With the approval of Church authorities, this fragment of the Turin Shroud was placed on a precision balance, then cut into portions that were put in specially coded and sealed canisters, and finally handed over to the heads of three laboratories in Arizona, Oxford and

MYSTERY FIGURE A 16th-century painting (above) shows the body being laid in the cloth. Right: the front view of the cloth.

Zürich. The purpose was to obtain three independent carbon-dates for this supremely controversial fabric. And the aim was to find out whether it really dated back to the time of Christ—and could, therefore, be the genuine Shroud of Jesus.

A baffling image

Turin Cathedral's extraordinary linen cloth bears the imprint of the body of a bearded man who seems to have been beaten, crowned with thorns and pierced with nails through the wrists and feet. The long rectangle of linen was apparently folded over his body, leaving images of both the front and back of the figure. Only faint outlines are visible to the naked eye, but photographic

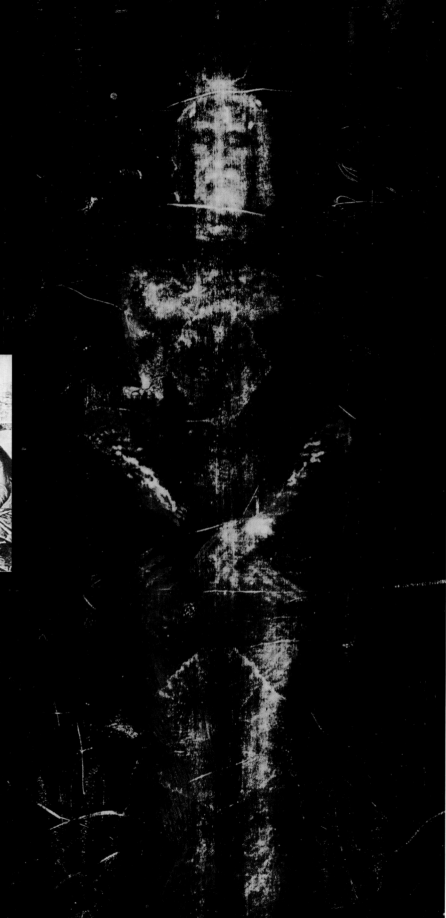

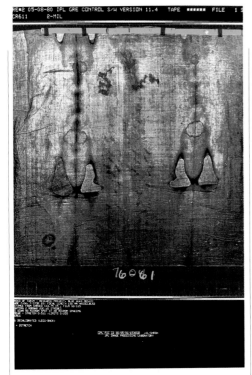

LABORATORY TESTS Computers enhance the colors (right). Magnified 18 times (above), a bloodstain on the small of the back is visible.

techniques reveal clearer detail: lash marks, for example, inflicted with a scourge—a type of flail—and the mark of a spear wound in the man's side. One scientist reportedly found traces of rare pollen in the cloth which suggested that it had once been in Palestine.

The Shroud is certainly hundreds of years old. In 1502 it was in the possession of the dukes of Savoy, and was kept in the chapel of their chateau at Chambéry. Despite being folded up in a silver casket, it was damaged when fire swept the chapel in 1532. It was moved to Turin Cathedral in 1578.

One of the biggest mysteries surrounding the Shroud is how the image was imprinted on the cloth. Most official investigators have denied the presence of paint or dye on the Shroud, as might be expected if it were the work of a forger. An exception was micro-analyst Walter McCrone, who did claim to find significant amounts of the pigment red ochre and of tempera paint. However, the official Shroud of Turin Research Project refused to endorse his report.

And how was the imprint absorbed? Did strong sunshine create a natural photograph? Was the cloth somehow stained by a vapor from secretions of sweat and body oils combined with ritual burial spices, aloe and myrrh? These are widespread speculations; but attempts to create Shroud-like images by

similar means have yielded disputed results. Besides, as critics have pointed out, corpses do not sweat and give off feverish vapors. The oddest claim made by investigators is that the image appears only on the surface of the material; it seems to have got onto the cloth without penetrating the fibres. According to one popular theory, the image was produced by some supernatural release of energy which scorched the linen. U.S. Air Force scientists have speculated that the figure was formed by a burst of intense radiation that lasted about a microsecond; a side-effect of the Resurrection, perhaps?

However, no satisfactory explanation has yet been found for how the image was formed.

The shocking results
The more that scientists investigated it, the more convincing the Shroud appeared. Then came the bombshell. The 1988 carbon-dating test results dated the cloth to between 1260 and 1390. The Turin Shroud was a medieval fake.

Not everyone accepted the radio-carbon findings. A French priest, Brother Bruno Bonet-Eymard, was among the first to claim

that it was the carbon-dating—not the Shroud—that had been faked. An astonishing theory subsequently proposed that the test results had been manipulated by the Church. In *The Jesus Conspiracy*, writers Holger Kersten and Elmer R. Gruber claimed that the real evidence proved that the Shroud was genuine, but implied that Christ had still been alive when laid in the tomb. To protect its central religious doctrine of the Resurrection, the Vatican had had the Shroud dismissed as a fake.

Even if the linen is medieval, many riddles remain. Fake relics were abundant in the 14th century, and manufacturing them was big business. But the figure on the Shroud is much more naturalistic than any of the medieval painters were capable of.

Also, medieval painters always showed the crucified Christ with nails passing through the palms of his hands. A contemporary forger would surely have done the same. In reality, to support the weight of a crucified body, the nails had to pass through the wrists. The figure on the Shroud has wounds at the wrists.

The Leonardo connection
It has been said that if the Shroud was the work of a forger he must have been a genius.

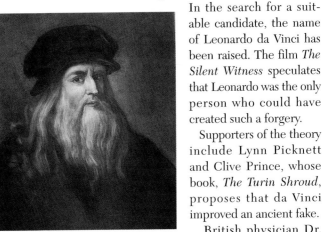

RENAISSANCE MAN Did Italian painter and inventor Leonardo da Vinci, who produced the first-ever design for an aircraft, also create the Shroud image?

In the search for a suitable candidate, the name of Leonardo da Vinci has been raised. The film *The Silent Witness* speculates that Leonardo was the only person who could have created such a forgery.

Supporters of the theory include Lynn Picknett and Clive Prince, whose book, *The Turin Shroud*, proposes that da Vinci improved an ancient fake.

British physician Dr. Straiton suggests that the Shroud wrapped the real-life body of a 14th-century crusader who was captured and crucified, in a parody of the death of Christ, by the Saracens.

For those who believe that the Shroud wrapped the body of Jesus, and those who think it is a fake, the question remains—how was the image of a crucified body formed on the Turin Shroud?

1950   2000

1978 Shroud displayed to the public for 42 days   1988 Radio-carbon results announced   1994 *The Turin Shroud* is published

THE THIRSTY STATUES

THE MONTH WHEN EFFIGIES OF HINDU DEITIES APPEARED TO DRINK MILK OFFERINGS WORLDWIDE

Traffic was disrupted across the whole of northern India, and roads were clogged by tens of thousands of people traveling to make offerings of milk to statues. "MILK-DRINKING DEITIES UNLEASH MASS HYSTERIA," reported *The Pioneer* newspaper, while the *Indian Express* said that the nation had gone berserk.

It was September 1995, and India's 800 million Hindus were gripped by a frenzy of devotion with reports that statues of the gods —chiefly Siva, his wife Parvati and their elephant-headed son Ganesh—were drinking milk offered to them by worshippers. The episode seems to have begun on Thursday, September 21, with a report that a statue of Ganesh in a New Delhi suburb had drunk half a cup of milk. Rumors spread that other statues of the Hindu gods in New Delhi were drinking milk. The city was reduced to chaos as crowds bearing milk rushed to watch the white liquid apparently vanishing before them.

Soon the phenomenon had spread across all of northern India. Crowds formed at statues, especially those of Ganesh, god of auspicious beginnings, the most popular of the Hindu pantheon. While milk stalls ran dry and prices soared, the temples of Ganesh were awash.

Mahani Srikant Ravi of the Hanuman temple in central Delhi told a reporter: "It is magic. The gods have come down to Earth to solve all our problems." The mahani added that his temple had been under siege since dawn. Over 2,500 people had visited by mid-morning, and the crowds had not been disappointed. Parmeesh Soti, an executive, was just one of the worshippers convinced. "It cannot be a hoax. Where would all that milk go? It just disappears in front of your eyes."

The gods athirst

One theory suggested that the whole phenomenon was a priestly deception wrought with statues containing suction devices rigged to bring crowds back to the temples. Others saw it as a stunt, worked by the hardline Hindu political parties in India, to whip up faith before a forthcoming election. But the craze soon spread beyond India to Hindu communities all around the world. Many crowds formed at temples in

SACRED SIPS Worshippers offer milk to idols of Nandi (above) and Ganesh (below) during the frenzied devotions of 1995.

Singapore, Indonesia and Bangkok. In Hong Kong an official claimed that a small silver statue of Ganesh had drunk 40 pints of milk. In Britain, a supermarket in West London sold out of 28,000 pints in one morning as throngs converged on a Hindu temple where a statue was said to be drinking milk at a phenomenal rate. The phenomenon quickly spread across the Atlantic as statues in the homes of Hindus in Long Island and New Jersey were also swallowing milk. For many in the U.S., the craze surrounding the incident was reminiscent of a "miracle" said to have occurred at St. Luke's Episcopalian Church, near Philadelphia. In 1975, thousands ran to the church to view a 28-inch-high plaster statue of Christ said to bleed from its hands on Fridays and Holy Days.

Scientists put the milk drinking phenomenon, and other liquid marvels like it, down to the way in which plaster and stone can act like blotting paper due to capillary action. Such effigies can be even "thirstier" if they have a hollow core filled with absorbent materials. However, capillary action cannot explain the many reports of metal Hindu statues "drinking" the milk.

The whole episode, which lasted a few days, left doubters as dubious as ever, but for believers it was a sign that the coming century would be Hindu in character.

MANLY DEITY A modern gouache of the four-armed god Siva. In the Hindu religion it is Siva who represents the male principle of generation.

MYSTERIES OF MODERN SCIENCE

FROM THE TITANIC FORCES THAT DRIVE THE DRIFTING CONTINENTS TO THE MICROSCOPIC MECHANISMS OF GENE-CARRYING CHROMOSOMES, MODERN SCIENCE HAS REVEALED MANY WONDERS IN THE WORLD AROUND US. YET OTHER REALITIES ARE POSSIBLE IN THEORY. T.H. HUXLEY, A PHILOSOPHER AND PIONEER OF SCIENTIFIC METHOD, ONCE CLAIMED: "I AM TOO MUCH A SKEPTIC TO DENY THE POSSIBILITY OF ANYTHING."

THE RIDDLE OF HYPNOSIS

TRANCE WITH A STRANGER: UNLOCKING THE SECRETS OF THE DEEPEST PART OF THE MIND

It has been said that one of the great medical questions of the 20th century—what happens under hypnosis—can be answered in three words: "We don't know."

Hypnosis is much easier to describe than to explain. People who have been hypnotized enter a sleep-like trance in which the mind remains fully alert yet passive and suggestible. At the hypnotist's command, the subject will carry out instructions; take fantastic suggestions for reality; reveal secrets from the subconscious; and become insensible to pain. Although it is generally held that people cannot be hypnotized into doing things against their will, the dangers inherent in the hypnotist's control are obvious.

An obsession with onions

Effects on memory are particularly eerie. If a stage hypnotist asks subjects to forget everything that has happened during the

HYPNOTIC VISIONARY Medical pioneer Franz Anton Mesmer (1734-1815) used his own theory, known as "animal magnetism," to cure patients in strange séance-like sessions.

trance they generally do. However, during the period of "post-hypnotic amnesia" they will respond to suggestions planted during the trance: barking like a dog, say, when the hypnotist gives the previously arranged signal. Casual hypnotism has other perils. In 1994 two drama students in York, England, were hypnotized by a friend who could not then get them out of their trances. Doctors had to call in a hypnotherapist to wake them up.

Hypnosis has been coopted for more sinister ends. During WWII, the Office of Strategic Services—the forerunner of the CIA—made plans to hypnotize a German prisoner to kill Hitler and then set him free to do the dirty deed.

Authorities have the powers to regulate or prohibit stage hypnosis because of its potential dangers. In November 1994 a woman won an out-of-court settlement of $30,600 after being hypnotized in a Scottish theater and then falling from the stage and breaking her leg. Dr. Prem Misra, a Glasgow specialist in the subject, has described various disorders resulting from sessions, including fits and persistence of hypnotic suggestions. One man became obsessed with eating onions after a stage hypnotist persuaded him during a show that they were Golden Delicious apples.

Medicine and crime

Although "borrowed" for the stage, the modern techniques of hypnotism were actually developed for healing purposes. The great pioneer was the 18th-century German physician Franz Anton Mesmer, who tried to cure illnesses by conducting séance-like sessions with his patients. Hypnotism (or "mesmerism") also interested the 19th-century French physiologist Jean-Martin Charcot, under whom Sigmund Freud studied. Freud used hypnosis to treat his patients in his early days. Working with another physician, Josef Breuer, he probed for emotionally charged repressed memories in his patients while they were in a hypnotic state.

Later, although Freud continued to probe for forgotten memories in his patients, he abandoned hypnosis as a form of treatment. He had deduced that to tell a patient with an

MEETING OF MINDS Patients gathered together for Mesmer's therapeutic sessions in hotels, which sometimes involved sitting round a vat of diluted sulphuric acid.

affliction such as a twitch to stop when under hypnosis was like trying to cure measles by painting out the spots. The important thing was to get to the underlying cause of the disorder, not to erase the symptoms. Besides, Freud had also discovered that not all patients are readily hypnotized.

Nonetheless, hypnosis is still used in medicine—as a technique for inducing relaxation and reducing reaction to pain, and in unlocking the deeper parts of the mind. It is sometimes employed as an alternative to anaesthetics. It can help burn victims feel less pain, and it has also achieved moderate success in treating phobias and addictions. In clinical hypnosis the subject usually remains mentally alert throughout the session.

Attempts to use hypnosis in crime detection have proved more controversial. "Eyewitness" accounts recovered through hypnosis would be too unreliable to be used as evidence in court, but the police have tried to use it to enhance witnesses' memories of details, such as the registration

1918 Hypnosis used to treat neuroses in soldiers after First World War

1945 During Second World War, hypnosis again used to treat soldiers with neuroses

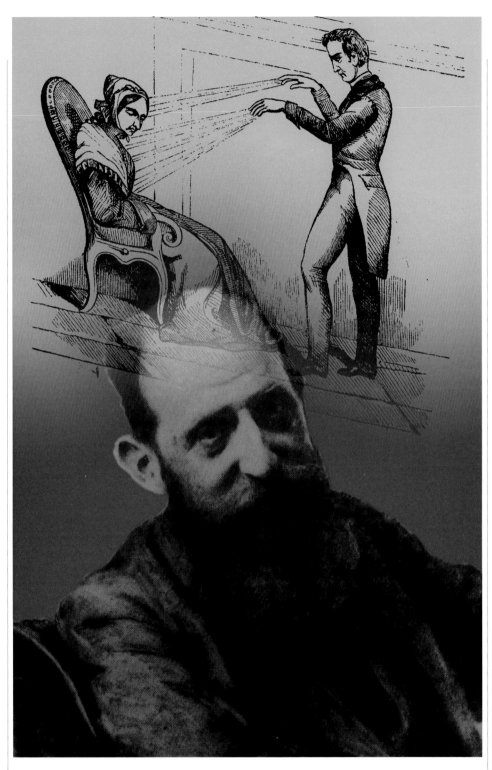

she relaxes; the pulse rate slows, and body temperature and blood pressure fall. Gradually he or she enters a condition akin to sleep or day-dreaming, and is ready to accept the hypnotist's influence.

Research suggests that some personalities are more easily hypnotized than others. Creative people make good subjects. Women are slightly easier to hypnotize than men, and children in the 8-12 age range are the best of all. Thereafter, it seems, suggestibility decreases with age.

A special brain state?

Among investigators a debate rages between two schools of thought. Some believe that subjects are basically play-acting—they have agreed to let the hypnotist "write the script" for them during hypnotism, and are experiencing a form of intense concentration. The alternative view holds that hypnotic trance is a brain state which is cut off, or dissociated, from normal waking consciousness.

The theory of the special brain state appears to have been confirmed by recent experiments. Students sat in front of a TV monitor that flashed lights that normally generate electrical discharges in the brain. Hypnotized students, however, had been told that a box was blocking out the lights. As a result, the researchers found that brainwaves in the visual parts of their brains were significantly reduced. Hypnotism, it seemed, had physically altered brainwave behavior—but still no one could explain why.

YOU ARE FEELING SLEEPY Mesmerism was a forerunner of psychotherapy, and was used by physicians such as Josef Breuer (above) in conjunction with Sigmund Freud.

number of a car seen at the scene of a crime. In a murder case in Britain, in the 1990s, the results were unfortunate for the police. A key witness was hypnotized, but the procedure confused him and led him to make statements damaging to their case.

In fiction, the glaring-eyed hypnotist may use hocus pocus, but in real life methods are not especially exotic. A hypnotist may, perhaps, ask a patient to focus on a fixed point and count backwards from 300. As the patient performs the monotonous task, he or

FREUDIAN SLIP The man himself (right) used hypnosis on patients in his early days, but later abandoned it as a form of treatment in favor of other techniques.

1994 British woman wins out-of-court settlement of $30,600 after breaking her leg during stage hypnosis.

SEARCHING FOR ANSWERS TO THE DIVINE QUESTION

EVEN TODAY, THE ANCIENT ART OF DOWSING STILL DEFIES RATIONAL EXPLANATION

Few sights are more curious or bewitching than that of a dowser at work. Clutching a two-pronged, usually hazel, twig, the dowser twitches and jerks towards an unseen quarry under the ground in almost a parody of a cartoon character drawn to a magnet—an image that is strangely at odds with the modern world.

Certainly, dowsing—the traditional method of looking for underground water using a divining rod—is an ancient art form. And when the ability to find water could mean life or death to a whole community, it is not surprising that the art was cherished. By the Middle Ages, dowsing or divining rods were being used in mining and treasure-

AN ANCIENT ART 16th-century dowsers used rods to find veins of metallic ores such as silver. From Georgius Agricola's *De Re Metallica*, Basle, Switzerland, 1556.

hunting to find subterranean minerals, much as metal detectors are today. Even at the end of the 20th century, with the multitude of hi-tech aids available, the services of professional dowsers are still being called upon by farmers, water authorities, oil companies and civil engineers.

These days, their equipment is not much more evolved than the old forked twig, although L-shaped metal rods are also employed. These are held like pistols in the hands, parallel and a few inches apart until they swing across one another. The pendulum is another common dowsing device; it is swung back and forth until the swing changes to a circular motion.

Earth magnetism, cosmic rays

Many researchers believe that dowsers have a special sensitivity to small changes in the Earth's magnetism. The dowser experiences a discernible muscular reaction when tuning in to the fluctuations caused by the presence of water or minerals underground. Perhaps all human beings—and other living things too—have a built-in magnetic detection system that is normally dormant but can be brought into play when necessary. This authentic inner "sixth sense"—a compass sense—almost certainly plays its part in animal migration.

Earth magnetism—the force that makes a compass needle point north – remains an ill-understood planetary phenomenon with many curious features. It is as if there were a giant bar magnet at the core of the Earth, whose pull, scientists have discovered, has

STILL WATERS "Nothing supernatural or magical about it," says Hugh Leftwich (left) of his divining talents.

fluctuated in strength at various times in the past. Astonishingly, the Earth's magnetic field has also reversed itself at intervals in history, so that north became south and vice versa. Scientists

OFF THE MAP Some diviners, such as Andrew Beastley, even claim to be able to make finds without actually visiting the site.

who first made this discovery in the 1950s could hardly believe the evidence of their own investigations, but it was undoubtedly true; studies of rock strata have demonstrated that repeatedly, and for varying periods throughout the Earth's history, the poles have flipped into reverse.

The Earth's magnetic field stretches some way into space and partially deflects incoming cosmic rays. Some recent research into dowsing suggests that attention should be directed toward those incoming cosmic rays rather than the Earth's magnetism. In 1994 Professor Vincent Reddish, a former Astronomer-Royal for Scotland, conducted a series of experiments into dowsing that led him to conclude that the force could not be electrical or electromagnetic.

His theory is that the cosmic radiation field reacts with water or minerals above or below ground to create the energy waves that dowsers detect. The professor found that, while most solid materials conducted the dowsing force, aluminum seemed to

INVESTIGATIVE POWERS Controversy always reigns when the police call in so-called psychic detectives, such as Gerard Croiset, to help locate missing persons.

block the charge. This indicated that the source of the mystery force was not electrical, as aluminum is a very good conductor of electricity. To test his belief, Professor Reddish asked six dowsers in different parts of Britain to try putting aluminum foil over their shoes and walking over water pipes that they already knew about. All reported that the foil eliminated the dowsing effect.

The psychic detectives

Whatever mystery still surrounds the mechanism of dowsing, few people doubt that it works on some basic level. If we are all sensitive to the Earth's magnetism, there is nothing particularly odd in supposing that professional dowsers—whose natural aptitude is enhanced by years of training—should develop highly sophisticated skills. In a different field, wine-tasters have developed the amazing ability to identify the vineyard a

HAND TO MOUTH Science still cannot explain the success of traditional dowsers such as S. J. Searles of Kent.

wine comes from by one sip in a blindfold test. Far more controversial are the claims of those dowsers who profess to make their discoveries at long distance—without visiting sites at all—and have extended their repertoires to include locating missing persons or even dead bodies.

The Dutch clairvoyant Gerard Croiset has gained a reputation for helping police in Europe to locate missing people. He has often offered information simply by dowsing aerial photographs or holding a pendulum over a map and interpreting the response.

Croiset first came to attention in 1959, when he reportedly helped in finding the whereabouts of a Kansas professor's missing daughter. In 1961 he was called in by an official of KLM, the Dutch airline, to help in the case of a missing four-year-old who was eventually found murdered in Brooklyn, New York. When the killer and the child's body were discovered, some circumstances supposedly matched information supplied by Croiset (although several details turned out to be wrong).

Skeptics remained unconvinced of his psychic powers. In 1978 he was brought in on the British case of the serial killer known as the "Yorkshire Ripper." A phoney tape-recorded message

had misled the police into believing that the culprit must come from the northeast, and Croiset focused attention on that area; in fact the killer came from elsewhere. Croiset was also consulted in the same year in the case of missing British schoolgirl Genette Tate. At the time, the police made many references to the help offered by psychics because—knowing the media fascination with all things paranormal—it helped to keep the case before the public eye. Croiset could offer no solution in either case.

Such failures do not, of course, invalidate psychic detection. Remarkable claims have been made for remote viewing by seers and mediums since the dawn of history. Believers point out that the universe is full of information that is beyond the range of our five normal senses. There are sounds too high for us to hear, and colors that are beyond the visible range of the spectrum. Why should we doubt that other information is being transmitted, to which suitably gifted individuals are able to tune in?

MAGNETISM AND MIGRATION

The pinpoint accuracy with which swallows return each spring to the same nest they used last year ... the salmon coming home to find the stream where they were born after journeying thousands of miles ... the skill with which green turtles from the Brazilian coast navigate 1,368 miles of ocean to find tiny Ascension Island, a mere pinprick on the vast map of the Atlantic ... These are just a few prodigies of animal migration. Butterflies, bats, lemmings and whales also travel long distances in accordance with seasonal climate changes or breeding cycles.

How do they find their way? Their means of navigation is still only partially understood, but it seems to involve a range of skills. Birds, which have been the subject of careful, extensive research, evidently take sightings of landmarks such as mountains, forests and estuaries. Scientists believe that they also steer by the sun and the stars. (Experiments in a planetarium during the 1950s showed that warblers recognize patterns of stars and use them for orientation.)

But recent theories also indicate that, like dowsers on land, birds are sensitive to the Earth's magnetism. Experiments with homing pigeons have shown that even when fitted with opaque contact lenses that prevent them from seeing more than a few yards ahead, they can still find their way home. However, when small magnets are attached to their heads, the pigeons get lost—presumably because the devices block out the Earth's fainter magnetic signals. Tiny particles of magnetic material have been found in the birds' skulls and neck muscles, which are thought to let them sense the magnetic map of the earth below.

JOURNEYS INTO THE FOURTH DIMENSION

DO BLACK HOLES PROVIDE THE MEANS FOR TRAVELING THROUGH TIME?

Until 1905, when the brilliant German-born physicist Albert Einstein first formulated his theory of relativity, there was one fundamental concept of time. Known as "linear time," it is the easily explainable belief that only the present exists. In other words, we cannot go back to the past and relive that time because it is gone. The future does not exist yet, because it has not started. We only live in the time which is happening now.

However, Einstein's work brought about a whole new theory to explain the concept of time. Using highly complex mathematics, he was able to show that the dimensions of time

TUNNELS FOR TIME TRAVEL So intense is the gravity within a black hole that it causes time to be "bent." It is usually depicted as a "gravitational well," as below.

and space are not fixed and separate from one another. They are variable and intimately connected. In this theory, believed by most scientists, both time and space are "bent"—for example, by the gravity that occurs near large bodies such as stars and planets.

According to Einstein, time would slow down for anyone traveling through space at the speed of light but it would carry on at the same pace back on Earth. A man taking a hypothetical journey lasting 14 years hurtling through space would find that 65 years had gone by on Earth. Effectively, he would have traveled forward into the future.

This concept underlies a wealth of fiction, from Ray Bradbury's stories, to the British "Dr. Who" television series, to Steven Spielberg's popular Back to the Future movies. Yet the discovery of black holes in space has prompted the idea that vehicles for time travel may already exist as natural features of the universe.

The Hamlet paradox

Scientists believe that a black hole can result when a celestial body such as a star dies. The star contracts dramatically, becoming denser, and eventually undergoes such a complete gravitational collapse that no light can escape from it.

Black holes cannot be seen directly, but their presence has been deduced from the movements of other stars that are under the influence of their gravitational fields. A black hole was first identified during the 1970s, and others have since been located at the core of supernova explosions and the centers of certain galaxies. In 1995 a black hole was identified at the center of our own galaxy, and is believed to be a million times heavier than the Sun.

Scientists theorize that a black hole's gravitational field may be so vast as to reverse the flow of time

and tunnel into another dimension. They have even hypothesized about the existence of a "worm hole": two black holes linked by a funnel, offering mind-bending possibilities. A person time-traveling might disappear into one end and emerge at the other in a

NEW TO THE FAITH Cosmologist and mathematician Stephen Hawking is a recent convert to the possibility of time travel.

different time, or even collide with himself coming the other way. The problem with this is what has been called the Hamlet paradox: a man might go back into the past and kill his own grandfather—and so fail to be born.

Scientists have proposed two ways round this apparent absurdity. The first is a Consistency principle, by which all acts must be consistent with past history (that is, one can go back in time and "look" but not "touch"). The second is the Multiverse principle, by which our own universe is one of an infinite number of parallel universes. A person might kill his own grandfather in one universe, and still be born in another.

Some scientists reject time travel as impossible, but there are new converts all the time. Mathematician and cosmologist Stephen Hawking was at one time a disbeliever, but in 1995 called for government funds to research into time travel. "If you combine Einstein's general theory of relativity with quantum mechanics," he says, "it does begin to seem a possibility."

RELATIVE THEORIES According to the Multiverse principle, Professor Albert Einstein (right) could be alive and well in another universe parallel to our own.

1900   1950

1905 Albert Einstein formulates his theory of relativity
1907 German astronomer Karl Schwarzschild
predicts the existence of black holes

1967 Professor John Wheeler coins
the term "black hole" in New York

1995 A black hole
is identified in the
Milky Way

THE HEALER ARIGO

WITH THE HELP OF THE SPIRITS, A BRAZILIAN COUNTRY BUMPKIN MADE MEDICAL HISTORY

At the height of his fame in the late 1950s, up to 200 people a day were treated by the Brazilian healer Arigo, who operated on patients while he was in a trance-like state, using no more than a pair of nail scissors or a rusty pocket-knife. The humble practitioner used neither antiseptics nor anesthetics, and had no formal training; the authorities were so alarmed by his nightmarish procedures that they had him arrested and twice sentenced to jail on the charge of practicing illegal medicine.

Yet none of the healer Arigo's patients ever brought a complaint against him, and many testified that he had cured them of serious illnesses. After his death in a car accident in January 1971, 20,000 people turned up to mourn at his funeral.

"He just picked up a paring knife"

Born to a farming family in 1918, José Pedro de Freitas was nicknamed Arigo ("country bumpkin") because of his rural background. In his youth he was often disturbed by strange dreams, headaches and hallucinations, and he came to believe that he was possessed by the spirit of a German physicist, Dr. Fritz, who had died during the First World War. Arigo thought that the doctor could only find peace by operating through him to relieve the sick and distressed. Witnesses noted that when he performed his "psychic surgery" Arigo would speak with a German accent and in a sharp, imperious tone very different from his amiable everyday manner.

Eyewitness accounts have survived of the cures he effected in his clinic at Congonhas do Campo, his hometown. An American investigator of psychic phenomena, Dr. Andrija Puharich, wrote: "These people step up—they're all sick. One had a big goiter. Arigo just picked up the paring knife, cut it open, popped the goiter out, slapped it in her hand, wiped the opening with a piece of dirty cotton and off she went. It hardly bled at all." Taking no precautions against infection, Arigo performed an eye operation in the same brusque fashion.

It was an extraordinary feature of all Arigo's reported operations that his incisions hardly bled, and that his patients experienced little or no pain. Puharich later went on to experience the healer's skills for himself, when he agreed to allow Arigo to remove a benign tumor from his arm. This was done with a penknife, and apparently caused no pain or discomfort to the patient.

Often, though, Arigo's treatment consisted only of scribbling rapid prescriptions which, on examination, turned out to be medical absurdities: obsolete medicines in weird combinations and sometimes dangerous doses. Yet his cures are alleged to have

DAMNING EVIDENCE   On trial in 1964, Arigo (left) went back to jail for a second time for refusing to stop practicing medicine. On his release he simply reopened his clinic.

extended from cysts and small benign tumors to virulent cancer. The healer's manner was notably brusque; he made no hypnotic passes over patients. And he claimed to know nothing about his miraculous powers, saying only that they were wrought by Jesus and the German doctor whose spirit worked through him. It is said that when, on one occasion, Arigo watched a film of himself performing operations, he fainted.

He treated rich and poor alike and is reported not to have accepted payment for his services; incredibly, he fitted his healing sessions in around a regular day job in a government welfare office. However, not everyone was convinced that Arigo should be allowed to continue with his medical career, and in 1956 the Minas Gerais Medical Association succeeded in having him prosecuted for "illegal practice of medicine." He was sentenced to 16 months in prison, but there was such an outcry this was reduced to eight months and a fine. Shortly before he was due to go to jail the Brazilian president, Juscelino Kubitschek, proclaimed a pardon.

In 1964 Arigo's persistent refusal to abandon his illegal practice earned him another jail sentence, which he served in two stretches —first of seven months and then of two.

However, the appeal judge, Filippe Immesi, was much impressed by Arigo. With a friend from the legal profession, he paid an unofficial visit to the healer's clinic and watched him operate with a pair of nail scissors on a woman half-blinded by cataracts. The judge declared himself speechless, amazed: "She was cured."

Arigo was examined by the Brazilian Medical Academy, who found that his snap diagnoses matched those of professional doctors in most cases. His ability was tested with X-ray, microscope, film camera and electrocardiogram. No evidence of fraud was ever uncovered. Was he a quack? If so, his deceptions were almost as miraculous as his cures. Arigo was perhaps the 20th century's most celebrated faith healer, and his case must remind all but the most hardened skeptics of how deeply mysterious are the capabilities of the human body and mind.

THE WOMAN WHO BURST INTO FLAMES

A CLASSIC CASE OF HUMAN COMBUSTION? THE UNACCOUNTABLE DEATH OF MRS. REESER

At 8 a.m. on July 2, 1951, a landlady took a telegram to the door of her tenant, Mrs. Mary Reeser, of St. Petersburg, Florida. When she put her hand on the doorknob, however, she noticed that it was hot to the touch and called for help. Two painters working nearby ran over, and on opening the door felt a blast of hot air. There was no great conflagration inside, however, just a little smoke and a small flame burning on the beam of a partition dividing the living room from the kitchenette. Mrs. Reeser's bed was empty; the 67-year-old widow was nowhere to be seen.

When the firemen arrived they needed only a handpump to put out the feeble flame. But when they tore away the burnt

STRANGE BUT TRUE Officials sift through the charred remains of Mrs. Mary Reeser (right), of St .Petersburg, Florida—apparently the victim of spontaneous combustion.

partition they found a blackened circle on the floor, little more than 3 feet in diameter, in which lay several coiled chair springs, a charred liver attached to a piece of spine, a skull shrunk to the size of an orange, a small heap of ashes and a human foot, burnt off at the ankle but still wearing a satin slipper.

Police, fire officials, insurance men and arson experts were baffled. There seemed to be nothing to explain the cause of the fire. Besides, there was no great damage except around the chair where the woman had died —and there the heat had been extraordinarily intense. The inquest heard that crematoria customarily generate temperatures of 2500°F for as much as four hours to incinerate a body. Even then they would have to use grinders to reduce the remains to the state of Mrs. Reeser's residue. The widow, an amply built 175 pounds in weight, had been incinerated into just $8\frac{1}{2}$ pounds of ash.

The slippered foot

Despite the phenomenal heat attained, the damage around the small blackened circle was minimal. A wall mirror had cracked and two pink wax candles

on a dressing table had become puddles, but the wall paint adjacent to the chair was only faintly browned, and the carpet where it had rested was not even burnt through. A pile of newspapers just outside the circle was wholly unharmed. The slippered foot also defied belief. It was known that Mrs. Reeser experienced some discomfort in her left leg and was in the habit of stretching it out. It looked as if the foot had survived because she had extended it just outside the circle of heat.

Dr. Wilton Krogman, a leading authority on deaths by fire, confessed himself mystified. "They say truth is often stranger than fiction and this case proves it," he said. And he drew attention to the curiously shrunken state of Mrs. Reeser's skull. When a body is burnt in intense heat the skull would normally expand and shatter explosively. Despite this the FBI released a statement suggesting that the victim had taken her usual sleeping pills and fallen asleep on the chair while smoking a cigarette— although neither her nightgown nor the chair was especially flammable.

Other possibilities were also examined. Death by lightning was dismissed by an expert in such fatalities. Murder and suicide were both rejected; in either case the body would have had to have been doused with gasoline or something similar, yet no trace of a chemical agent was found. Besides, the central paradox remained unexplained. How could a fire generate the temperature needed to reduce a body to ash while leaving nearby combustible materials untouched?

The death of Mrs. Reeser is often cited as a classic case of spontaneous human combustion—a phenomenon in which a human body appears to ignite and burn of its own accord. Reports of it date back to the 17th century and, although most scientists deny its possibility, many well-documented cases in modern times survive as testimony to a phenomenon that seems to defy analysis. As Dr. Krogman said during the Mrs. Reeser investigation: "I regard it as the most amazing thing I've ever seen. As I review it, the short hairs on my neck bristle with vague fear. Were I living in the Middle Ages, I'd mutter something about black magic."

July 1951 The charred remains of Mrs. Mary Reeser are discovered in her apartment in Florida

HUMAN ELECTRICITY

NATURAL FORCES THAT RESULT IN BIZARRE FORMS OF ENERGY

In 1920 a remarkable trend was observed by the chief physician at Clinton Prison in New York. It seemed that 34 convicts suffering from severe food poisoning had somehow become electrically charged. Paper stuck to their hands when they tried to throw it away, compass needles swung wildly in their vicinity, and metal objects were deflected from their grasp. Only when the illness started to ebb did the effects

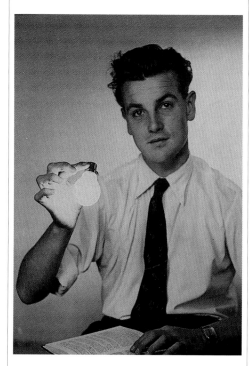

BIZARRE TALENTS Brian Williams of Wales was so full of electricity he could light up a lightbulb just by rubbing it with his hands.

diminish, in a peculiar condition that had also been recorded back in the 19th century. In 1877, in Ontario, Canada, a teenager named Caroline Clare, recovering from a wasting disease, began to give shocks to anyone who touched her. Pieces of iron stuck to her body and had to be pulled off by force.

Such cases of "human batteries" are often explained by science as static electricity—although why this should be exacerbated during illness remains unknown. In some cases, such as that of Brian Williams, it is present all the time. Williams had a bizarre talent for lighting lightbulbs simply by rubbing them with his hands. He had to put rubber grips on the handlebars of his bicycle to stop other people from getting shocks.

Freak disturbances

It is accepted that the human body possesses its own electromagnetic field, and that it is susceptible to interference. Franz Mesmer, the pioneer of hypnotism, was among the medical pioneers who tried to use magnets to effect healing. And electro-ailments have recently made headlines, with scientists establishing causal links between overhead power lines and certain cancers.

Freakish electromagnetic disturbances may account for some paranormal phenomena. Cases of poltergeist haunting often occur when a particular person is present—often the focus is female and under the age of 20. Psychic researchers have suggested that the intense anxiety that tends to come with

METAL MAGIC Does Uri Geller use poltergeist activity to bend all that cutlery, or is it simply trickery?

pubescence may find unconscious expression in electromagnetic turmoil around that person. Poltergeist activity is associated with frustrated male adolescents too. Colin Wilson, a prolific writer on the paranormal,

RELIGIOUS AURA A stained-glass depiction of Saint Michael, in the Basilique du Bois-Chenu, Domrémy, France.

has suggested that many supposed psychics, such as Matthew Manning and Uri Geller, employ controlled poltergeist activity.

Human glow-worms

Human electricity is sometimes associated with radiance, and there have been many curious cases of sick people giving off light. In May 1934, Italy's Luminous Woman of Pirano caused a worldwide press sensation. Signora Anna Monaro, an asthma patient, baffled doctors by emitting a blue glow from her breasts as she slept. Was this, though, an electrical phenomenon? Scientists theorized

---

THE LIGHT OF LIFE

Luminous beings are a fact of nature. Fireflies glow in the dark, as do various other insects, fungi and fish. Their radiance derives from the biochemical oxidation of the compound luciferin. Some scientists believe that occasional reports of sick people with glowing limbs may be prompted by luminous bacteria feeding off the nutrients in human sweat.

KIRLIAN PHOTOGRAPHY: REVEALING THE INVISIBLE TRUTH?

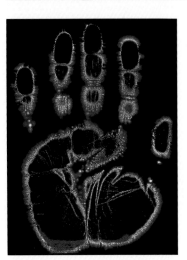

PALM READING A Kirlian photograph of a human hand shows the glow that surrounds living tissue.

Do human beings possess an aura invisible to the naked eye? Yes, according to believers in Kirlian photography, a technique which claims to reveal a strange, glowing corona around all living things. The process takes its name from the Russian Professor Semyan Kirlian who devised it in the Soviet Union in 1939. Using a high-frequency generator with two metal plates acting as electrodes, he placed a photographic film on one of the plates. Then he placed his hand between the plates and turned on the current. When the film was developed it revealed a remarkable luminous aura around his hand. A live leaf photographed between the plates also showed an aura, but a dead leaf did not. Amazingly, when a torn leaf was photographed the result appeared to show a phantom image of the piece that had been torn away.

When Kirlian's experiments became known to the West in the 1970s they provoked much excitement among students of the paranormal. Here, it seemed, was proof of spiritual reality; a luminous energy uncaged by the form of living things. On Kirlian photographs, psychic healers were said to produce flare-like effects from their fingertips when they were exerting their powers. People speculated that the Turin Shroud's image might have been created by some natural Kirlian process, but scientists were quick to dismiss the results. It was already known that a sudden spurt of voltage could create strange patterned effects on film as tiny particles in the air become ionized, or charged

with current. Moreover, when Kirlian apparatus was set up in the West, scientists discovered that they could create all kinds of effects by methods no more "spiritual" than altering the current. Kirlian photography still has its supporters, but there is no general agreement on precisely what it shows.

IN CLOSE UP The "corona" from a fingertip. The image results from interaction between the subject and an applied electric field.

that her weakened state had increased the amount of sulphides (a chemical compound) in her blood. Sulphides can be stimulated into luminescence by ultraviolet radiation, and, since human blood radiates in the ultraviolet range, perhaps this was responsible.

Images of luminosity are widely employed to denote the sacred and the superhuman. Christian saints were portrayed in halos of light, and Mohammed is seen in a golden flame. Are such reports merely symbolic? Or have the world's great spiritual leaders been charged with an inexplicable energy that expresses itself as bodily radiance?

SEEING IS BELIEVING British healer Matthew Manning treats a patient at a healing demonstration in Germany.

1952 Press attention focuses on Brian Williams's talent for lighting lightbulbs

GREAT BALLS OF FIRE

WITNESSED BY MANY, EXPLAINED BY NONE: THE PECULIAR PHENOMENON OF BALL LIGHTNING

Passengers on board Eastern Airlines Flight 539 flying from New York to Washington in 1963 were astonished when they were treated to an unexpected form of in-flight entertainment. Following a bright crack of lightning, a luminous orb about 8

exist—so it was something of an irony that an example should choose to make its presence felt at the Cavendish Laboratories in England, an establishment famed for nurturing Nobel prize-winning scientists. Many of the employees witnessed this phenomenon in August 1982, and eminent physicist Sir Brian Pippard sent off eyewitness accounts to the scientific journal *Nature*. "It was most remarkable," he said. "It went through a window as a secretary was closing it and passed by without singeing her hair."

CAUGHT ON FILM? Photograph taken in Yorkshire, in England, claiming to show the path and explosion of ball lightning.

inches in diameter emerged from the door leading to the pilot's cabin. It floated down the aisle to disappear in the direction of the bathroom at the back of the airliner.

What the amazed passengers experienced was ball lightning, the name given to spheres of bright light that hover, bob or bounce around indoors or out, and can pass through doors and windows without causing any damage. They come in varying colors—red, orange, yellow and blue have been reported—and rarely last longer than a few seconds before disappearing. According to orthodox science, ball lightning cannot

Researchers believe that ball lightning may account for many paranormal phenomena, from luminous apparitions to UFO sightings. The writer Francis Hitching has speculated that large manifestations could account for reports of spontaneous human combustion. Crashing into a human being, ball lightning "might affect the body in much the same way as a microwave oven would, cooking the tissue inside and leaving the outer covering untouched."

A faint hissing sound

The problem is that ball lightning is not much more acceptable to scientific thought than spontaneous combustion. Hampered by

the lack of solid physical evidence, scientists are at a loss to explain it. Some have put forward a nuclear radiation theory; others believe that it may be the result of some sort of atmospheric electrical discharge. Another view suggests that it may be due to stored chemical energy in the atmosphere. Eyewitnesses have reported that the floating orbs appear with a faint hissing sound, and a distinct chemical smell.

Another mystery of ball lightening is its apparent "unwillingness" to injure humans. In once case, described by the astronomer Camille Flammarion, an orb moved across a French farmyard, toward a stable where two children were hiding. The ball exploded when one of the children kicked it. They were left unharmed, but the explosion killed eleven less-fortunate cows. Ball lightning has also been observed to do substantial damage to property, while sparing human onlookers.

BLAST FROM THE SKY Lightning literally blew a Swedish girl out of her soccer shoes and shinpads during a game in July 1994.

CALLING SPACE: IS THERE ANYBODY OUT THERE?

SEARCHING THE CELESTIAL HEAVENS FOR EVIDENCE OF EXTRATERRESTRIAL LIFE

Skeptics scoff at some of the wilder UFO reports, but experts do not dismiss the idea of intelligent life in space. In 1993, when NASA launched a deep space project designed to seek out extraterrestrial intelligence, bookmakers in Britain cut the odds against its discovery from 500-1 to 33-1. Arnold Wolfendale, Britain's Astronomer-Royal, declared that it was not a crazy bet: "I feel that there is intelligent life of some sort out there." His views were echoed by veteran American astronaut Dr. Story Musgrove, one of the team involved in repairing the Hubble Space Telescope.

Sadly for believers, NASA withdrew funds from the Search for Extraterrestrial Intelligence (SETI) organization after criticism in Congress. The search was resumed in 1995 in a privately funded experiment in Australia, where 14 scientists scanned the heavens with a 210 foot telescope for a five-

IN SEARCH OF LIFE Storing Earth music and the American flag on Voyager 2 (right); and the Hubble Space Telescope (below).

THE FACE ON MARS

In recent years a growing number of enthusiasts have accused the American space agency, NASA, of covering up astonishing evidence of life on other planets. The Mars Mission is a group of scientists headed by former NASA consultant Richard Hoagland. Its members complain that the space agency is refusing to investigate what looks like a humanoid face carved on the surface of the planet. The "Face on Mars" was first identified by the Viking orbiters in 1976, and since then it has inspired a small industry of devotees who have written widely and attend conferences on the subject. NASA asserts that the image is no more than a trick of the light created by shadows playing across the planet's rock-scattered terrain.

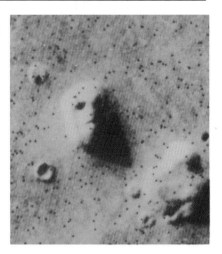

month period for signs of extraterrestrial life. They also transmitted radio and TV signals to Alpha Centauri which, at 4.25 light years from the Earth, is the star nearest to our own solar system. The messages were expected to reach Alpha Centauri at the turn of the century.

Greetings from Mozart

Since 1960 astronomers have been listening for alien radio messages. The American space probes Pioneer 10 and Pioneer 11 carried plaques designed for alien eyes,

which showed a map of the solar system, the location of our Sun, and representations of two human beings. Voyager 1 and Voyager 2, launched in 1977, carried recorded messages of greeting to any intelligent life form they might meet, with samples of music ranging from Mozart to Chuck Berry.

No acknowledgment from extraterrestrials has been received yet, but the more that scientists learn about space, the more plausible it seems that other life forms exist. During the 1990s experts studying data sent back from the Pioneer 12 spacecraft discovered evidence suggesting that shallow seas once covered the surface of Venus—the planet closest to the Earth and the one it most closely resembles. The seas are thought to have evaporated about 3 billion years ago, under the impact of a runaway greenhouse effect, but they existed long enough for life to have developed. And in 1996 examination of a meteorite from Mars suggested that some form of primitive life may have existed there.

There are about 100,000 million other stars in our galaxy alone, and many are likely to have their own orbiting planets. In fact, in April 1999, scientists confirmed the discovery of another solar system, with multiple planets, orbiting the nearby star Upsilon Andromedae, "just" 44 light years (259 trillion miles) away.

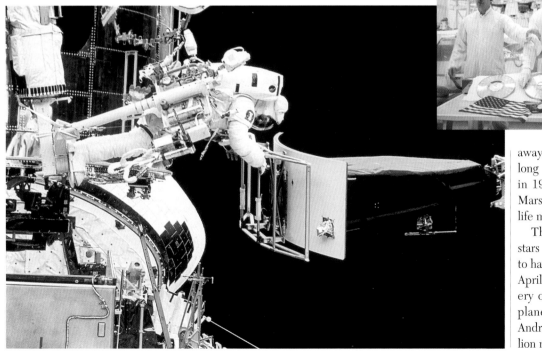

1900   2000

1960 Astronomers start to listen for alien radio messages   1977 Launch of Voyagers 1 and 2   1996 Meteorite from Mars is thought to contain evidence of life on Mars

THE VIRUS OF DEATH

IN THE SHADOW OF A HOLOCAUST: THE NEW DISEASE THAT MAKES AIDS LOOK LIKE A COLD

No one knows where it came from. No one knows where it will turn up next. All that scientists do know is that the mystery virus that first made its appearance on the

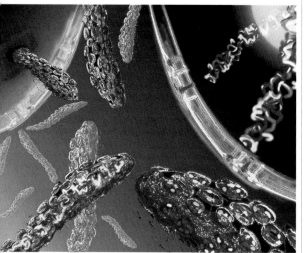

THE ENEMY WITHIN Once the Ebola virus enters a human cell, its ability to multiply is rapid, dramatic and nearly always fatal.

Zaire/Sudan border in 1976 is so lethal and infectious that it has the potential to become the Black Death of the modern world.

Ebola, as the virus is known, kills nine out of ten people whom it infects, wreaking devastation on the body of its victim. It starts with a headache and fever and swiftly moves on to uncontrollable internal bleeding. Within days, organs turn to a jelly-like pulp, which patients expel through every orifice— eventually dying in a massive pool of blood.

So far, the source of Ebola is unknown. Although it has been found in monkeys, the actual reservoirs may be insects, bats or other creatures of its inhospitable jungle home—thought to be somewhere in Africa. The major concern is that jet-age travel means that just one infected person or animal could trigger an epidemic anywhere. This was demonstrated in 1989, when a strain was discovered in monkeys imported

AWAITING THE HOLOCAUST Hospital staff bury the body of the fifth Italian nun to die of Ebola during the 1995 outbreak in Zaire.

from the Philippines for research in the U.S.—to a laboratory just 10 miles from the White House. Extreme measures had to be taken to control the risk of outbreak.

Being a virus, Ebola is extremely difficult to treat medically. Antibiotics are only effective against bacterial infections, and, because viruses actually take over the cells of their victims, it is hard to stop the virus without affecting the other healthy cells at the same time. The usual method is to develop a vaccine, which stimulates the body's own immune system to fight the infection. However, vaccines take time to develop, and the ability of viruses to mutate means that new strains can emerge and make any previous vaccinations ineffective. No vaccine exists for Ebola, but it has already proved cunning in its ability to mutate. It is ferocious, too. It does in ten days what it takes AIDS ten years to do—in scientific terms, a "biohazard level four," two levels above HIV.

Out of the "hot zone'"

Like AIDS, Ebola is thought to come from central Africa, and it is no coincidence that they have emerged from the same "hot zone." The World Health Organization (WHO) fears that settlement of jungle areas, combined with rapid population growth and increased mobility, may be creating ideal conditions for an explosion of new diseases. Dr. Ryder, infectious disease specialist at Yale University, says of Ebola: "It is almost as

if the virus is saying to man, 'I'll leave you alone if you leave me alone, but as soon as you step on my turf I'm going to get you.'"

A disaster averted

The most recent outbreak, in 1995, was centered on the Zairean city of Kikwit, and at first seemed likely to fulfil all the doomsters' prophecies. Terror spread so fast among the population of 400,000 that people avoided physical contact with each other, and the dead were left where they fell. However, WHO teams were quickly flown in with experts from the Center for Disease Control (CDC), who wore chemical warfare suits to protect themselves. By imposing quarantine regulations and strict sanitary measures, the experts were able to keep the death toll down. The fatalities strictly attributable to Ebola were given as 79 people.

Each was a horrific death, but the relatively low numbers came as a surprise. One reason is that the known strains of Ebola appear to spread through body fluids but not through the air. Another is connected with the speed of death. The incubation period can be 21 days, but averages about seven to ten and can be as little as two. Basically, Ebola can kill so quickly that the victim does not have time to spread the virus.

Once again, Ebola had vanished as quickly and mysteriously as it had arrived. Now only one question remains: how long will it be before it make its next appearance?

1976 First outbreaks reported in Sudan and Zaire

1995 Major outbreak in Kikwit, Zaire

SOARING BODIES AND SOARING MINDS

SUSPENDING BELIEF: THE STRANGE WORLD OF PHYSICAL AND MENTAL LEVITATION

The geneticist J.B.S. Haldane claimed: "The universe is not only weirder than we imagine, it is weirder than we can imagine." His observation was borne out in 1996 when scientists in Geneva announced that

INSIDE STORY A computer display shows the point of collision between matter and antimatter particles at a Swiss laboratory.

they had created the first antimatter atom—a substance that consists of antiparticles. These antiparticles are like a mirror image of the subatomic particles to which they correspond. They have the same mass, but the opposite electrical charge. Just as atoms of hydrogen exist, nuclear scientists had now created atoms of antihydrogen—making hypothesis reality. The substance was in existence for only a 30 millionth of a second, but its creation opened up new realms of scientific possibility. When particles meet antiparticles they annihilate each other, releasing a burst of energy with unpredictable results on physical forces. In future, antiparticles may be used as fuel, to make a bomb, or to create antigravity—so permitting levitation.

Can humans defy gravity?

Gravitational force is a phenomenon still not wholly understood by science, and oddities have often been reported over the centuries, notably in accounts of human levitation. Some of the most convincing pictures of a

levitation published this century were taken in southern India by English tea planter P.T. Plunkett and appeared in *The Illustrated London News* of June 6, 1936. He recorded a performance by a fakir called Subbayah Pullavar, who lay horizontally about 3 feet in the air with his hand resting on a cloth-draped stick. Apparently, he remained there, motionless, for fully four minutes, while photographs were taken from every angle. Plunkett passed a long stick over and under and around the fakir's body, which he reported to be stiff—as if in rigor mortis.

The photographs of Subbayah Pullavar have often been reproduced and sometimes used as proof that humans are capable of levitation. However, evidence published in a subsequent edition of *The Illustrated London News* indicated that it had all been an elaborate—albeit successful—fake.

Out-of-body experiences

Stage magic aside, in most religious traditions physical levitation is a secondary effect of spiritual detachment—the mystic's indifference to the material world. And reports of psychic soaring are much more common than those of physical levitation. At the point of death, many ordinary people have reported a convincing sensation of leaving the body and observing themselves from above (or from a distance). In his book *Life After Life* (1975), physician and psychologist Raymond A. Moody discovered that this was common to all 150 accounts of near-death experience that he analyzed, including the now clichéd sensation of entering a long, dark tunnel.

Out-of-body experiences have been reported throughout time—in Ancient Egyptian tomb paintings the *ba*, or soul, is shown hovering bird-like about the body after death. One modern survey found that over a quarter of Americans have experienced OBE's. This experience is especially common among writers and artists. Ernest Hemingway, Virginia Woolf, D.H. Lawrence and Arthur Koestler are just some of the 20th-century authors who have

FAKE OR FAKIR? Images of Subbayah Pullavar taken in southern India, 1936, have been used as proof of levitation.

LEVITATION IN THE LUNCHBREAK

In her book *The Decline and Fall of Science*, psychical researcher Celia Green quotes antigravity operating in a manner which is all the more extraordinary because of its mundane setting:

"My only experience of levitation occurred during a lunchtime break at school when I was 17 ... Each girl took her turn lying on a long wooden table at the front of the classroom, with the others gathered tightly around her, so that there were no gaps ... As one lay there, the girls chanted a rhyme—the actual words of which I have forgotten, but which referred to the person on the table looking white, ill and then dead. It was spoken quite slowly and in unison so that its drone-like tone had great depth and was very penetrating.

"Several girls took part before me without much success. Some ... were quite disillusioned. Others, however, did admit to feeling a strange sensation ... and it was this plus the declaration of a friend that she had experienced slight levitation that encouraged me to try it.

"I have absolutely no explanation why I was able to rise approximately 3 feet from the table surface. I was perfectly conscious that I was rising and might even have uttered an exclamation of surprise ... The rapidity of the rise and indeed the fact that I had risen at all caused me to jerk my body out of the lying position, and with much commotion the girls cushioned my fall."

reported the phenomenon. But does the mind merely compensate for impending death by creating an illusion of detachment, or does the soul really soar?

1936 *The Illustrated London News* publishes apparent evidence of levitation in Southern India

1996 Antimatter is created by scientists in Switzerland

INDEX

ACKNOWLEDGMENTS

Abbreviations:
T = Top; M = Middle; B = Bottom; R = Right; L = Left

AP = Associated Press/Wide World Photos
CB = Corbis-Bettmann
FPL = Fortean Picture Library
HG = Hulton Getty
MEPL = Mary Evans Picture Library
MSI = Mirror Syndication International
SPL = Science Photo Library
SSPL = Science & Society Picture Library
TPP = Topham Picturepoint
UB = Ullstein Bilderdienst

3 HG, L; Russian State Library, Moscow, LM; Rex Features, RM; FPL, R. 6 Popperfoto, BR; Magnum/Inge Morath, B. 7 CB, TL; Rex Features/Brian Wolfe, TR, BL; Camera Press, MR. 8 SPL/Peter Menzel, TL; SPL/A. Barrington Brown, ML; SPL/Hale Observatories, BR. 9 SPL/Wellcome Dept of Cognitive Neurology, TM; SPL/Philippe Plailly, ML; HG, BR. 10 Times Newspapers Ltd/Martin Beddall, TL; Rex Features Ltd, BR. 11 FPL, MM; Fortean/Llewellyan Publications, MR. 12 FPL/Stephen Pratt, TL; Images Colour Library, TR; TPP, BR. 13 Graphics/Bradbury & Williams; HG, L; Magnum/Eve Arnold, LM; TPP, RM; Sygma/T. Orbau, R. 14 Graphics/Bradbury & Williams, TL; CB, BL, BR. 15 CB, T, BL, BM. 16 CB, TR, BL, BM. 17 CB, TL, TM, TR, BL. 18 Popperfoto, TR; TPP, ML; CB, B. 19 HG, TL; Peter Newark's Western Americana, TM, TR; Popperfoto, MR; CB, BL, BM. 20 TPP, background, TR; CB, foreground, TR; photo montage/Laurence Bradbury, TR; TPP, BL. 21 CB, TL, TR, BR; John Frost Historical Newspaper Service, ML. 22 Image Library, State Library of New South Wales, TM, TR, BL, MM. 23 TPP, TR; Nina Drury/from White Mischief by James Fox, published by the Penguin Group, 1984. 24 TPP, TR, BL. 25 TPP, MM; Hugh Dickinson/from White Mischief by James Fox, published by the Penguin Group, 1984, BL. 26 HG, ML; CB, TM, BR. 27 CB, TL, TR, BR; AP/Wide World Photos, ML; HG, MR; TPP, BL. 28 Graphics/Bradbury & Williams, BL; AP/Wide World Photos, TR. 29 Popperfoto, TL; CB, BL. 30 HG, ML, BR; Popperfoto, TR. 31 Magnum/Eve Arnold, T; Popperfoto, BR. 32-33 Magnum/Eve Arnold. 33 Magnum/Philippe Halsman, TM; Magnum/Cornell Capa, TR, MR. 34 CB, TL, BR; Cecil Stoughton, Life Magazine

© Time Warner Inc/Katz Pictures, TR; TPP, BL. 35 CB, TR, MR; Popperfoto, BL. 36 CB, BL; John Frost Historical Newspaper Service, TR. 36-37 Illustration Graham White. 37 CB, ML; TPP, MM; HG, BM. 38 TPP, background, BL; CB, foreground, BL; photo montage/Laurence Bradbury, BL; Illustration Graham White, TR. 39 TPP, TL; CB, ML, BM; Popperfoto, MR. 40 Popperfoto, TL; TR; TPP, TM. 41 Magnum/W. Eugene Smith, TR; Magnum/P. Jones Griffiths, MR; MEPL, BL, BM. 42 AP, TR, MM, BL. 43 AP, TL; TRW, MR. 44 DRK Photo/Peter Vert, TR; National Geographic Society Image Collection/Robert M. Campbell, BL. 45 DRK Photo, TL; Sygma/ W. Campbell, TR; National Geographic Society Image Collection/Robert M. Campbell, BL. 46 CB, TM; CB, TR; CB, BL. 47 CB, TR, BL. 48 Express Newspapers, TR; TPP, MR; Sygma/Frederic De Lafosse, BL. 49 Universal Pictorial Press & Agency Ltd, background, TL; Daily Mirror, background, MM; Camera Press/Martin Parr, background, MR; HG, foreground; photo montage/Laurence Bradbury. 50 Gamma/FSP/Esaias Baitel, TR; Gamma/FSP, BL; Daily Mirror, BR. 51 Brown Brothers, background; HG, L; Russian State Library, Moscow, LM; TPP, CB, BR; Dennis R. Kromm, R. 52 From The Fire Came By by John Baxter & Thomas Atkins, published by Macdonald Jane's, 1976/TBA, TM, BR; TPP, ML. 53 Camera Press/James Pickerell, TR, BL. 54 Dalkeith Publishing Co. Ltd, TR; Illustration Graham White, MM. 54-55 TPP, B. 55 HG, TL; Illustration Graham White, TR; Gamma/FSP, BR. 56 CB, ML; HG, BR. 57 HG, TL; Popperfoto, MM; TBA, BL. 58 Sotheby's/Sygma, TR; Popperfoto, BL. 59 L'Illustration/Sygma, TL; TPP, MM; Camera Press, CB. 60 TPP, TR; Wide World Photos, BL, BM. 61 CB, TL, TR, BR. 62 Dennis R. Kromm, TM, BL; Popperfoto, BR. 62-63 CB. 63 TPP, TR, BR; The Mansell Collection, MR. 64 CB, TR; Wide World Photos, BL, BR. 65 David King Collection, T; Gamma/FSP, B. 66 John Frost Historical Newspaper Service, background; TPP, foreground; photo montage/Laurence Bradbury. 67 HG, TL; CB, ML. 67-68 From The Death of Hitler by Ada Petrova & Peter Watson, published by Richard Cohen Books, 1995/courtesy Ada Petrova & Peter Watson. 68 Illustration by Graham White, BM. 69 Popperfoto, TL, BL; TPP, TR. 70 David King

Collection. 71 HG, TL, TM, B; Our Army and Our Country are Strengthened with the Spirit of Stalin!, 1939 poster, V. Deni & N. Dolgorukor, Russian State Library, Moscow, TR. 72 Popperfoto, ML; John Frost Historical Newspaper Service, MR; TPP, BL. 73 TPP, TR, BR; Camera Press/Stern, BL. 74 John Frost Historical Newspaper Service, TR; CB, ML, BR. 75 Abraham Zapruder/Colorific. 76 CB, TL, B; TPP, TR; John Frost Historical Newspaper Service, MR. 77 Illustration Graham White, T; CB, BL. 78 TPP, BL, BM, BR. 79 TPP, TL; HG, BR. 80 CB, TR; ML. 81 CB; MM; CB, BR. 82 John Frost Historical Newspaper Service, TR, BR; Magnum/J.A.F. Collection, ML. 83 John Frost Historical Newspaper Service, TL; Popperfoto, BR. 84 John Frost Historical Newspaper Service, TM; Camera Press, BL; TPP, BR. 85 Illustration Graham White, T; Camera Press, ML, BR. 86 Associated Press, TL; Sygma/T. Franck, BM. 86-87 Sygma/T. Franck. 87 Rex Features Ltd, TR, MR. 88 Sygma/Perscal le Segretain, TR; Marc Deville/Gamma/FSP, ML; Camera Press/Benoit Gysembergh, BR. 89 Laurence Bradbury; L, CB, LM; HG, RM; CB, R. 90 Camera Press/Bassano, TR; HG, B. 91 CB, TL; National Center for Missing & Exploited Children, BR. 92 The Mansell Collection, background, TR; AP/Wide World Photos, foreground, TR; photo montage/Laurence Bradbury. 93 Associated Press, TR; CB, ML, MR, BL. 94 CB, TR; TPP, ML, B. 95 Illustration Graham White, TR; AP/Wide World, TL; HG, MR; TPP, BM. 96 Chattanooga Choo Choo, TBA, background, TR; CB, background, TR; TPP, foreground, TR; photo montage/Laurence Bradbury. 97 Sygma/Keystone, TR; Popperfoto, ML; HG, MR; Camera Press, BL. 98 HG, TR; Popperfoto, BL; TPP, BM; TBA, BR. 99 Sygma/David Gamble, TR; Popperfoto, ML; TPP, BM. 100 Camera Press, TR; AP/Wide World Photos, ML; TPP, B. 101 Magnum/ Peter Marlow, T; Cadres Decide Everything, 1988, poster, Alexander Konduvov, from The Posters of Glasnost and Perestroika, published by Sovietsky Khndozhnik Publishers, Moscow, 1989, MR; Novosti (London), BL. 102 HG, ML; TPP, BR. 103 TPP, B. 104 TPP, TR; HG, BL; John Frost Historical Newspaper Service, BM. 105 AP/Wide World Photos, TR, BL. 106 AP/ Wide World Photos, ML; Gamma/FSP/R. Neven, MM. 107 TPP, TL, B. 108 CB, TL,

MM, MR, BL. 109 BC, TL, TM, TR, MR. 110 CB, TR, BL.. 111 CB, TL, MM, BR. 112 Allsport/Steve Powell, MR; Allsport, BL. 113 SPL; Rex Features Ltd, L; MEPL, LM; Jürgen Liepe, RM, FPL, R. 114 Images Colour Library Ltd, TR, BL. 115 TPP, TR; FPL, ML; CB, BM. 116 Popperfoto, background, R; HG, foreground, R; photo montage/Laurence Bradbury; Popperfoto, BL. 117 MEPL, TM, TR; CB, BL. 118 TPP, BM. 118-19 From The Wolf Children, Charles Maclean, Allen Lane, Penguin Books Ltd/Mrs P.L. Jana, ML. 120 Rex Features/Leo Dickinson, TR; Popperfoto, BL; TPP, BM. 121 MSI, TM; FPL/René Dahinden, TL; Filmworks/From Arthur C. Clarke's A-Z of Mysteries: From Atlantis to Zombies by Simon Welfare & John Fairley, HarperCollins, BR. 122 Jürgen Liepe, TR; MSI, BL; HG, MR. 123 Highclere Castle, TM; CB, BL; BPK/Egyptian Museum Berlin/Jürgen Liepe, BR. 124 MEPL, ML, BR. 125 Ann Ronan Picture Library/Image Select; MEPL, ML; TPP, BM. 126 CB, TR, MM, BL.. 127 CB, TL. 128 MEPL, ML; Popperfoto, B. 129 FPL, TR, MM; MSI/ Academy of Applied Science, Boston. 130 AP/Wide World Photos, BL; TPP, BR. 131 AP/ Wide World Photos, TM, TR; Illustration Graham White. 132 Images Colour Library Ltd, TR, B; MEPL, ML. 133 FPL, TR; SPL, BL. 134 FPL, TR; Images Colour Library Ltd, ML; TPP, BL. 135 FPL, TL, BR; Popperfoto, BL. 136 SPL/David Parker, T, B. 137 FPL/Llewellyn Publications, TR; Popperfoto, BL. 138 TPP, ML; Popperfoto, R. 139 TPP, TL, TM; MEPL, BR. 140 Popperfoto, TR; Rex Features Ltd, MR; Images Colour Library Ltd, BL. 141 SPL, background, L, RM; TPP, LM; MSI, R. 142 MEPL, TR; Images Colour Library, BL. 143 TPP background, TL; CB, foreground, TL; Photo montage/Laurence Bradbury; MEPL, BR. 144 Popperfoto, TM; TPP, MR; Images Colour Library, BL. 145 TPP, TM, BL. 146 MSI, TR; SPL, BL. 147 SPL, background; TPP, foreground; Photo montage/Laurence Bradbury. 148 TPP. 149 FPL, MR, BL. 150 MSI, ML, BR. 151 Images Colour Library, ML; SPL, TM, MR; FPL, BM. 152 FLPA, TL; Popperfoto, BR. 153 SPL, TR, MM, BL. 154 SPL, TL; Popperfoto, BR. 155 SPL, TL; MEPL, BR.

Front Cover: SPL, T; Laurence Bradbury, B; Jürgen Liepe, L; HG, LM; Dennis R. Kromm, RM; Press Association, R.

Back Cover: SPL, T; Laurence Bradbury, B; David King Collection, TL; Camera Press, TR; SPL background, BL; TPP foreground, BL; CB background BR; AP/Wide World Photos, foreground, BR.

Endpapers: John Frost Historical News Archives

The editors are grateful to the following publishers for their kind permission to quote passages from the books below:

Bantam Press, A Conspiracy of Crowns, Alfred de Marigny, 1990
Bloomsbury, Kiss the Boys Goodbye, Monika Jensen Stevenson and William Stevenson, 1980
Jonathan Cape, No Other Choice, George Blake, 1990
Faber and Faber Inc., Tom Slick and the Search for the Yeti, Loren Coleman, 1989
Facts on File, The Guinness Encyclopedia of Ghosts and Spirits, Rosemary Ellen Guiley, 1992
HarperCollins, Arthur C. Clarke's Mysterious World, Simon Welfare and John Fairly, 1980
HarperCollins, Mysteries, Colin Wilson, 1979
Inverness Courier, May 2, 1933
McGraw-Hill, The Kennedy Conspiracy, Anthony Summers, 1980
John Miles, The Story of the Secret Service, Richard Rowan,1938
Penguin, Hitler – A Study in Tyranny, Alan Bullock, 1962
Piatkus, Strange but True?, Jenny Randles and Peter Hough, 1994
Thames & Hudson, Phenomena – a Book of Wonders, John Michell and Robert J.M. Rickard, 1977
Yale University Press, Fall of the Romanovs, Mark D. Steinberg and Vladimir M. Khrustalëv, 1995.